THAILAND
History, Politics and the Rule of Law

JAMES WISE

Marshall Cavendish
Editions

Published by Marshall Cavendish Editions
An imprint of Marshall Cavendish International

A member of the
Times Publishing Group

Other Marshall Cavendish Offices: Marshall Cavendish Corporation. 99 White
Plains Road, Tarrytown NY 10591-9001, USA • Marshall Cavendish International
(Thailand) Co Ltd. 253 Asoke, 12th Flr, Sukhumvit 21 Road, Klongtoey Nua,
Wattana, Bangkok 10110, Thailand • Marshall Cavendish (Malaysia) Sdn Bhd,
Times Subang, Lot 46, Subang Hi-Tech Industrial Park, Batu Tiga, 40000 Shah
Alam, Selangor Darul Ehsan, Malaysia

Marshall Cavendish is a registered trademark of Times Publishing Limited

National Library Board, Singapore Cataloguing-in-Publication Data

Name(s): Wise, James, 1954-
Title: Thailand : history, politics and the rule of law / James Wise.
Description: Singapore : Marshall Cavendish Editions, [2019] | Includes
bibliographical references and index.
Identifier(s): OCN 1086365850 | ISBN 978-981-48-4154-2 (paperback)
Subject(s): LCSH: Thailand--History. | Thailand--Politics and government.
| Law--Thailand.
Classification: DDC 959.3--dc23

Printed in Singapore

To Teresa, Matthew and Anita

CONTENTS

Thailand Map

PREFACE

"This is Thailand."

The great letters in English and Siamese seemed to stare down insolently from the blatant, newly erected sign that, edging out from the jungle wall, encroached a foot or two onto the highway with the very evident intention that none should mistake its implied warning.[1]

Thais often tell foreigners—or, more specifically, Westerners or *farang*[2]—that we don't, won't or can't understand Thailand, especially Thai politics, particularly when Thailand is experiencing political instability, a coup or the aftermath of a coup.

Sometimes, Thais make this claim simply to mask their own difficulty in explaining Thailand's complex and confusing politics.

On other occasions, Thais prefer to say to a foreigner, "You'll never understand," and move on to a simpler topic. I feel the same when Thais ask me to explain the game of cricket. I can explain it, and I enjoy the game, but with a foreigner I'd rather talk about something that is more familiar and less intricate.

Other Thais want to avoid talking to *farang* about Thailand's politics because it embarrasses them. Thai politics, like politics everywhere, has villains and scandals. Thais, like most people, don't like to air their dirty laundry in public. As an Australian I feel embarrassed when foreigners ask me about our less appealing politicians and their more shameful policies and practices. Sometimes I don't want to talk about them. In the same way, some Thais don't want to talk about Thai politics.

---

1   H.G. Quaritch Wales, *Years of Blindness* (New York: Cromwell, 1943), 1.
2   *Farang* is the Thai word for a person of European origin or a white person. *Farang* can also be used to describe the West generally.

Also, as a rule, Thais believe it is impolite to disagree. Rather than risk discord, Thais will lightly dismiss our attempts to discuss Thai politics with a seemingly casual, "You don't understand," or, "You won't understand," or, "You'll never understand." This is another way of saying *"mai pen rai"*, the Thai phrase that means "it doesn't matter", which Thais use habitually to minimise or avoid disagreement or conflict.

Some Thais, though, truly believe we don't understand their politics. They aren't avoiding a conversation because they find it hard to explain Thai politics. They aren't embarrassed by disarray in Thai politics. Nor are they trying to avoid a disagreement. They genuinely believe that we fail to comprehend. I hope that, having read this book, they will agree that any continuing failure on my part to comprehend is not for want of trying.

Perhaps because I was a government official for over 30 years, I am more interested in the practice of government and politics than the theory. I have some sympathy for the choices faced by leaders and officials, whether they are kings, ministers, judges, generals or bureaucrats. Each day, they have to deal with what is urgent as well as what is important; and in the face of everyday pressures it is not always easy to detect the difference. All will make mistakes and, because governing a nation is not easy, the longer they are in office the more mistakes they will accumulate.

When I have made judgments about the decisions of Thailand's political leaders—elected and unelected—I have tried to assess whether, given the challenges and choices they faced at the time, those decisions were reasonable, not whether they illuminated a political theory.

I have written for the general reader. In particular, I have in mind the diplomat, journalist, businessperson or NGO employee whose new posting is Thailand, as well as the student who is new to Thai history, politics and law. Often they have little or no prior experience of Thailand and, unnervingly for them, very soon their employer, clients or professor will expect an explanation of modern Thai politics from them. At least initially, these readers may not have the time or appetite to grapple with the theory development and testing that is usually critical to academic writing, or at least provides a framework for it.

My conclusions about Thailand have also been influenced by my experiences elsewhere as a diplomat, especially my postings to Papua New Guinea (1983–85), the Soviet Union (1987–91) and Malaysia (2003–07). Unlike Papua New Guinea, Thailand is not a new nation. It does not face the nation-building challenges, especially linguistic diversity, forbidding geography and socio-economic indicators that Papua New Guinea faces. The authoritarian strain in Thai politics is not comparable with the authoritarianism of the Soviet Union. Some commentators on authoritarianism in Thailand tend to demonise what is not truly demonic. I am not excusing authoritarianism in Thailand. Nor am I excusing human rights abuses that occur in Thailand. But I wonder what vocabulary these commentators would use if Thailand ever drifted towards Soviet-style authoritarianism, which is highly unlikely. The eminent Thai historian, Nidhi Eoseewong, has written: "If Hitler and Stalin are taken as the standard of dictators, Thai dictators of every era are only clowns."[3] At the core of Malaysia's politics are race and religion. For all their complexity and seeming intractability, the problems at the core of Thailand's politics are not as difficult to overcome as Malaysia's problems—which is not to minimise the significance of race and religion in the politics of Thailand, especially in the southern border provinces.

My broadly positive view of Thailand's achievements and my sympathy for government officials may prompt some readers to question my reliability—and perhaps my sanity. I hope they will

---

3   Nidhi Eoseewong, "The Thai Cultural Constitution," *Kyoto Review of Southeast Asia*, Issue 3, March 2003 (translated by Chris Baker; originally published in Thai in 1991)—https://kyotoreview.org/issue-3-nations-and-stories/the-thai-cultural-constitution/

be more forgiving of the value I have placed on history. History helps us to understand the present. I have therefore tried to explain contemporary political developments and issues in Thailand within an historical context.

Because I am not concerned with theory development, and because I am not an activist-scholar who sympathises with either the existing regime or the resistance to it, this book seldom considers what might have happened or what should happen. It tries to be a book about what has happened and why.

I owe a debt, first of all, to Thais who have discussed Thai politics with me. Many of them did so when I was a diplomat. They spoke in confidence and I will not mention them by name. Some of them also shared with me their fears and hopes as well as their thoughts and ideas, which stimulated me to try to understand their story and the story of Thailand.

I should add here that this book does not reflect the views of the Australian Government, to which I am thankful for the opportunity to work in Bangkok for over seven years. The views in this book are entirely my own.

Those views are clearer in my mind and articulated more clearly thanks to the kindness of Stephen Henningham, Craig Keating, Joel Akins, David Armstrong, Paul Stephens, Anita Wise, Gwen Robinson, Greg Raymond, Mark Warnock and Kyle Wilson, who read the entire manuscript or parts of it, made valuable comments, and encouraged me to continue.

I am grateful to Kirida Bhaopichitr and Punpreecha Bhuthong of the Thailand Development Research Institute for their assistance with the graphs; to Brendan Whyte for drawing the maps; and to Watcharapat Kongkhaow for the cover photograph of a wooden panel of a temple pediment, which was included in the "Revolutionary Things" exhibition in 2018 at the Cartel Art Space, curated by Chatri Prakitnonthakan and Kittima Chareeprasit. The panel shows an angel carrying the 1932 Constitution on a traditional Thai tray—an example of the government's use of Buddhist imagery and rituals in the 1930s to persuade Thais of the significance of their first constitution, and a wonderful illustration of a principal theme of this book—the co-existence of traditional and modern political legitimacies in Thailand.

Conducting research was easier than it might have been thanks to the resources and efficient staff of the Siam Society in Bangkok and the National Library of Australia in Canberra.

From the very start of my relationship with Marshall Cavendish International (Asia), Anita Teo has been an understanding as well as a proficient editor. A first-time author could not have wished for more. Michael Spilling was a thoroughly professional copy editor. Thanks to Benson Tan for his work on the design of the book.

Finally, my thanks to Teresa, Matthew and Anita for supporting me in this endeavour, and in so much more.

ABBREVIATIONS

CEO   Chief Executive Officer

IMF   International Monetary Fund

ISOC   Internal Security Operations Command

NACC   National Anti-Corruption Commission

NGO   Non-Governmental Organization

PAD   People's Alliance Of Democracy

PDRC   People's Democratic Reform Committee

THB   Thai Baht

UDD   United Front For Democracy Against Dictatorship

INTRODUCTION

A billionaire tycoon is praised as the champion of the poor. A scandal–tainted politician leads a mass movement against corruption. Protesters declare that they need to block elections to save democracy.[1]

Chronic instability is an abiding feature of Thai politics. In the last century, Thailand has been a world leader in its number of coups, attempted coups, constitutions and ministerial reshuffles. Millions of Thais have protested against governments they don't like, most notably in 1973, 1976, 1992, 2005, 2008, 2010 and 2014. They have seized control of parts of the national capital, sometimes for several months. In 2008, yellow-shirted dissenters forced the closure of the international airport. In 2009, red-shirted dissenters forced the government to abandon a meeting of regional heads of government. Just as readily, governments have ordered security forces to shoot protesters. Or security forces and paramilitaries have shot them anyway—with impunity.

Over the same period, few countries have pulled such a high proportion of their population out of poverty and few can match Thailand's achievements in areas like child mortality, life expectancy, universal health care, universal education, maternal health, and gender equality in certain sectors. Thailand usually scores well in the World Bank's ease-of-doing-business survey and the World Economic Forum's report on economic competitiveness. Few peoples have the cultural stability and composure of the Thais, or the resilience and community spirit that Thais exhibit when disasters strike, like the

---

1   Thomas Fuller, "Taking on Thailand's Crisis with a Bit of Western Bite," *New York Times*, 8 February 2014.

tsunami in 2004, massive floods in 2011, or the plight of 13 young Thais trapped in a cave for more than two weeks in 2018. And which Southeast Asian nation has accommodated millions of Chinese and other migrants as well as Thailand has?

Without doubt, Thailand is hard to understand. At the height of the demonstrations in Bangkok in February 2014, Thomas Fuller wrote the three sentences in the epigram at the head of this chapter, which capture neatly how confusing Thai politics can be. The billionaire tycoon is Thaksin Shinawatra. The scandal-tainted politician is Suthep Thaugsuban. Fuller might have added that most of the protesters claiming that they were saving democracy by blocking an election would have been supporters of a party called the Democrat Party.

Some Foreign Viewpoints

When we try to understand the politics of other countries, we bring certain preconceptions to the task. Commonly, we try to understand an unfamiliar political culture and an unfamiliar political system by comparing them with the political culture and system of places with which we are familiar.

In the first instance, this is likely to be our own country. For *farang*, the political culture and system of our own country fit within the broader Western liberal democratic tradition. We have three independent branches of government—legislature, executive and judiciary—and a range of other institutions, conventions and practices, like elections and the rule of law, that are rooted in the ideas of equality and individual rights. These are so familiar to us that we almost take them for granted.

Our second point of reference is likely to be other non-Western countries that we have experienced directly or indirectly. This experience could be in Southeast Asia, Asia more broadly, or elsewhere in the non-West. We may have lived or worked there, or we may have become acquainted with one or more of these countries through reading and study.

To bring these broad observations back to Thailand, and to run the risk of over-simplification: we tend to think of our first reference point—our Western homeland—as "not like Thailand". And although we are usually not blind to the obvious differences between Thailand and other non-Western countries, we tend to think of our second reference point—our non-Western experience—as "like Thailand" or "more like Thailand" than our Western homeland is.

Colonial Heritages

More likely than not, the non-Western countries that we already know were colonized. In colonized societies, in the place of traditional political authority, the colonial powers substituted themselves (as viceroys, governors-general, political residents and the like) as well as certain Western-style institutions (like centralised bureaucracies, disciplined police and military forces, law courts and, over time, consultative or quasi-consultative bodies). And, by both design and accident, and to a greater or lesser extent in different places, they introduced Western ideas like equality, individual rights, elections and the rule of law, which gradually infiltrated local political culture.

After the colonial powers were dislodged, the leaders of the newly independent nations relied to a certain extent on these imported institutions and ideas to govern. They had little choice. Traditional political authority was a dim memory or debilitated. Above all, it had lost much, if not all, of its legitimacy.

By the time of independence, the leaders of the new nations were informed about, and even steeped in, Western-style institutions and Western ways of thinking—because these institutions and ideas were clothed in a legitimacy previously worn by traditional political authority. The new leaders assumed the governing role of their colonizers and, naturally, relied on the institutions the colonizers had established—and, more or less, the ideas that underpinned them. Over time, they customised their inherited colonial institutions, conventions and practices to fit their post-colonial environment. Significantly, though, they didn't try to revive or re-establish pre-colonial political authority.

Thailand's Historical Context

Some non-Western countries are indeed more like Thailand than Western countries are. But Thailand differs from almost all other non-Western countries because Thailand wasn't directly colonized. Scholars debate whether Thailand was "indirectly colonized", or "crypto-colonized", or "semi-colonized", or colonized in some other partial manner. But they cannot deny that traditional political authority retained its legitimacy, and even thrived, during the period when traditional authorities in Thailand's neighbours ceded political control to Britain, France, the Netherlands, Spain and the United States. Because Thailand wasn't directly colonized, the threads connecting its pre-modern and modern political history are straighter and stronger. Understanding how and why these threads remained straighter and stronger helps to explain some of the distinctive features of Thai politics.

Although Western powers had fewer opportunities to directly transplant their institutions, conventions and practices into Thai soil, Siam—as Thailand was then called—was influenced by them.[2] Starting with Britain in 1855, through treaties of extraterritoriality (or "unequal treaties"), they dictated the tax rates that Siam could apply to its exports and imports. The same treaties also compelled Siam to replicate Western legal codes and processes. In addition, Thais found Western ideas both alluring and threatening. So traditional political

---

2   Before 1939 Thailand was known as Siam, and it was again from 1946–48. I have used "Siam" and "Siamese" when referring to the pre-1939 period and "Thailand" and "Thai" for the period since, except in cases covering both the pre- and post-1939 period, when it normally made more sense to use "Thailand" and "Thai".

authority in Thailand has been challenged and re-shaped in all sorts of ways by external forces. But Thais could control the nature and the pace of this influence in ways that directly colonized peoples couldn't.

To the extent that foreign institutions were introduced into Thailand, they were grafted on to a traditional political system. They were not substitutes for a traditional political system. Western ideas influenced Thai political culture, but they never crushed established ways of thinking. Thailand's traditional political system and traditional political culture, like native plants, continued to grow; they sprouted new shoots and were occasionally pruned into a different shape, but their roots and trunk remained the same. It is this hybrid nature of political authority in Thailand that makes its politics distinctive, even idiosyncratic—and harder to understand.

Western Political Heritage

If our experience of non-Western countries sometimes gets in the way of our understanding of the distinctiveness of Thailand's politics, our experience of our Western homelands can be an even bigger impediment.

First of all, our Western political culture and political systems differ from Thailand's culture and systems even more than those of non-Western countries. Our Western homeland is "not like Thailand". The organizing principles of our Western liberal democratic system are equality, individual rights, elections and the rule of law. Many Thais are not opposed to these ideas, which continue to influence political debate in Thailand. But these principles have not replaced the foundations of traditional political authority in Thailand, especially hierarchy, patron-client relationships and the dominance of personal connections. Nor have they been as appealing as nationalism.

There is another reason why a Western-centric perspective is problematic. When comparing one culture or political system with another, we may imply that one is superior to the other, even if we try hard not to. Both the *farang* and Thai observer can easily fall into that trap. But we *farang* are more likely to do so. The values and interests of the West have shaped the modern world powerfully. For several centuries, the West and modernity have been synonymous. Sometimes willingly and sometimes unwillingly, the non-West has sought to emulate the West in many fields, including politics and governance. Western ideas have held sway in many Western minds (unsurprisingly) and non-Western minds, including the idea that people and societies would be better off if they adopted democratic institutions and the rule of law.

I am not arguing against either democratic institutions or the rule of law. But assumptions that Western values provide some of the answers to Thailand's political challenges can make the foreign observer lazy and conceited. Presuming the superiority of our values, we *farang* can sometimes become judgmental and prescriptive. *Farang* commentators on Thai politics occasionally say things like: "To become a mature democracy Thailand needs to entrench the rule of law." Or "Thais will not be truly democratic until they narrow the gap between the rich and the poor." Or "Thailand will not be stable while Thais are subjects rather than citizens."

These sorts of conclusions about Thailand can help us to see more quickly how Thailand's political culture and political system are different. But they do not help us to understand why Thailand does not yet have the rule of law as we understand it; or why income disparities in Thailand may not be as problematic as many foreigners expect; or why many Thais believe they can happily be subjects, or believe that they can be subjects and citizens simultaneously. In other words, this approach does not help us to make sense of Thailand on its own terms.

Political Instability: Causes and Cures

Understandably, many studies of modern Thai politics have concentrated on the causes of the disputes that fuel Thailand's chronic instability. Analysts tend to point to one of, or a combination of, class conflict, regional loyalties, urban-rural tensions, disparities in incomes and the allocation of state resources, and an overbearing military protecting the interests of the elite. Or they have assessed why electoral democracy has struggled to take firm root in Thailand.

This study touches on the causes of Thailand's political instability, and on the uncertain course of electoral democracy. But it focuses more on the absence in Thailand of an agreed understanding on where political disputes should be mediated and arbitrated, and on the absence of an agreed understanding on how political conflicts should be arbitrated and, where necessary, adjudicated. The reasons Thailand has not yet reached a consensus on how to mediate, arbitrate and adjudicate political disputes and conflicts also explain the persistence of chronic political instability, as well as the fitfulness of electoral democracy.

In Western-influenced political systems, major disputes over policy and power are usually mediated and settled in the legislature. Failing that, they become key issues in the next election. Or disputes may be taken to the courts, where independent judges make rulings based on the law. Put simplistically, there are three referees: the legislature, the electorate, and the judiciary.

In some circumstances, these three avenues for dispute settlement have been available in Thailand, but not regularly and not consistently. Because traditional political authority has retained legitimacy in Thailand, the monarchy and the military continue, at times, to play a refereeing role in politics, regardless of the views of the legislature, electorate or judiciary, and regardless of the law. Again, put simplistically, in Thailand there are five referees: the monarchy, the military, the legislature, the electorate and the judiciary.

The survey of the course of modern Thai history in Part I of this book focuses more on the continuities than the discontinuities between the pre-1932 and post-1932 periods. This approach helps to explain both the durability of the political role of the monarchy and the military as well as the comparative powerlessness of the legislature, electorate and judiciary, and the comparative unimportance of constitutions and laws. In addition to offering an institutional approach to Thai politics, Part I shows how socio-economic conditions have affected the political temperature in Thailand.

Part II explores some features of the Thai political landscape through lenses which are more familiar to Thais: hierarchy, protection, patron-client relations, personal connections, identity and nationalism. These are so familiar to Thais that they almost take them for granted. On most days, they are as invisible as the air they breathe. An appreciation of Thailand's hierarchical political culture helps us to understand why Thailand does not have independent agencies to mediate and arbitrate political disputes. An appreciation of Thais' sense of identity and nationalism helps us to better understand the continuities between the pre-1932 and post-1932 periods, and to appreciate why open discussions in Thailand about politics and governance are hard.

Part III discusses the role of the law in Thai politics, because so often *farang* and Thais alike express frustration at what they see as the weak application of the rule of law, or even the absence of the rule of law; and because in countries where the rule of law applies there is a trusted adjudicator of political disputes and conflicts: an independent judiciary.

Jointly, the three parts of the book introduce the reader to the politics and the rule of law in Thailand in an historical context. At the same time, each part is more-or-less a stand-alone essay on modern political history, elements of Thai political culture, and the rule of law.

There are two important addenda. The following chapters fall short of being a comprehensive history or assessment of Thai politics and society over the period since 1932, and they hardly touch on economic or religious developments. The interested reader will find an annotated guide to further reading as well as a conventional bibliography at the end of the book.[3]

Secondly, as this book is about the impact of history on mainstream Thai politics, it focuses on the traditional political authority of the Chakri dynasty centred in Bangkok. Bangkok's traditional political authority often thrived at the expense of the authority of traditional rulers and traditional systems of government on the periphery of the territory now called Thailand. The literature on the perspective of the "periphery" on Bangkok's political expansion and consolidation has grown over the last 25 years, especially since the publication of Thongchai Winichakul's ground-breaking *Siam Mapped: A History of the Geobody of a Nation.*[4]

---

3   The best general histories are Pasuk Phongpaichit and Chris Baker, *Thailand: Economy and Politics* (New York: Oxford University Press, 2002, revised edition); Chris Baker and Pasuk Phongpaichit, *A History of Thailand* (Cambridge: Cambridge University Press, 2014, third edition); B.J. Terwiel, *Thailand's Political History: From the 13th Century to Recent Times* (Bangkok: River Books, 2011, revised edition); David K. Wyatt, *Thailand: A Short History* (Chiang Mai: Silkworm Books, 2003, second edition); and Charles F. Keyes, *Thailand: Buddhist Kingdom as Modern Nation State* (Bangkok: Editions Duang Kamol, 1989).
4   Full publication details are: Thongchai Winichakul, *Siam Mapped: A History of the Geobody of a Nation* (Honolulu: University of Hawaii Press, 1994).

PART I

BRANCHES OF GOVERNMENT: HISTORICAL INTRODUCTION

Chapter One

FROM ABSOLUTE MONARCHY TO ONE-FIFTH MONARCHY

If we analysed Thai constitutionalism in terms of the separation or balancing of powers in actual practice rather than in the written text, ... we can see that there are not three branches of the State (Executive, Legislature and Judiciary) but five, if we regard both the monarchy and the military as having powers of their own.[1]

Two scholars of Thailand's constitutional system have observed that, in practical terms, the state in Thailand has five branches, not just the three branches that are a feature of the western democratic system: legislature, executive and judiciary.[2] In Thailand, the monarchy and the military exercise authority in their own right, often without reference to the more familiar legislature, executive and judiciary.

In Western systems, and many Western-influenced systems, the monarch has either become a figurehead—a constitutional monarch with no political authority—or been replaced by a president who, depending on the country, can be a figurehead (for example, in Ireland) or the head of the executive (for example, in the United States). And in Western systems the military is under the control of the civilian government; it rarely plays a domestic political role. So, because monarchs and generals aren't major players in politics in

---

1   Andrew Harding and Peter Leyland, *The Constitutional System of Thailand: A Contextual Analysis* (Oxford and Portland, Oregon: Hart Publishing, 2011), 30.
2   *Ibid.*

the West, Westerners don't consider the monarchy and military as branches of government.

People who have been brought up in a Western democracy also have a sense of the separate roles the three branches of government fulfil. We understand that the parliament, the government and the courts, separately but jointly, form an institutional skeleton for our politics. We also understand that political disputes are mediated and arbitrated in the parliament and, if necessary, disputes can be adjudicated in the courts or by the electorate.

Part I of this book sketches the evolution of the five branches of the Thai government since the late 19th century. In addition to providing an essential overview of Thailand's modern political history, this institutional approach was prompted by the broadly accepted view that strong institutions, especially a representative and sovereign legislature and independent judiciary, promote the development of more democratic forms of government, better protection of human rights, and lower levels of corruption.

An institutional approach to Thai politics has limitations. Unavoidably, it overlooks or covers incompletely all sorts of motivations for political action: economic, class, factional, ideological, personal ambition, foreign policy and so on. It also focuses narrowly on the political role of each of these institutions and pays little attention to their important, often critical, non-political roles. Above all, this approach may lead us to conclude that Thais think about their politics in these institutional terms. They don't. Thais tend not to see the five branches of their government, separately or jointly, as a skeleton for politics. In other words, an institutional approach to Thai politics does not help us understand Thai politics in the way most Thais do; and it does not help us make sense of Thailand on its own terms (we try to do that in later chapters). Still, an analysis of the political role of the five branches of the Thai government does help Westerners understand important features of Thai politics and how

Thailand's political system differs from ours—and why the monarchy and military continue to adjudicate Thai politics.

Pre-1932 Monarchy

King Chulalongkorn (the fifth king of the Chakri dynasty, often referred to as Rama V) provided the following sharp definition of Siam's absolute monarchy:

> The king rules absolutely in his own royal desire. There is nothing greater than this. The king has absolute power as 1) ruler over the realm and refuge for the people; 2) the source of justice; 3) the source of rank and status; 4) commander of the armed forces who relieves the people's suffering by waging war or conducting friendly relations with other countries. The king does no wrong. There is no power that can judge or punish him.[3]

Chulalongkorn was accurately describing the system of government he fashioned for Siam from the mid-1880s. He was also describing an idealised view of Siamese political authority, which was based theoretically on cosmological principles that elevated the king to a sacred and all-powerful position. Yet it would be a mistake to assume that, before Chulalongkorn, Siam had an absolute monarchy. In reality, theoretically absolute monarchs before Chulalongkorn, and Chulalongkorn himself during the first half of his own reign, were

> sharply circumscribed by the limited capacity of the central administration and the difficulty of communications, by the factionalism of court cliques, and by the view that the role of the king was not to initiate but rather to maintain the social and political order as handed down by his predecessors.

---

3   Quoted in Baker and Pasuk, *A History of Thailand*, 70.

Thus, the actual authority of the king tended to decrease as a function of distance from the capital, and even in the court was limited, and new departures in policy were justified in terms of traditional precedence.[4]

Paradoxically, from the late 19th century, Chulalongkorn simultaneously created an absolute monarchy and inadvertently built a platform for the emergence of a five-branch form of government—by overhauling the governance of Siam. His radical reforms were inspired by, first, his domestic vulnerability to princely and aristocratic rivals; secondly, the military and technological threat posed by Britain and France, who had imposed their authority on all his neighbours; and, thirdly, a civilizational challenge from the West, which was setting new norms and goals for the rest of the world.

Pre-1932 Executive

Chulalongkorn's two immediate predecessors had consolidated the monarch's financial and territorial authority. Chulalongkorn went much further. He replaced the traditional administrative system (or the executive arm of government), which was subject to competing demands from the monarchy and nobility, with a cabinet of ministers supported by centrally appointed officials who were answerable to Bangkok. He was influenced by the administrative system the British and Dutch used to control their colonies. Over time, unlike previous kings, Chulalongkorn replaced nobles with his close relatives, mostly uncles and brothers, in senior ministerial and administrative positions. Until 1932, these kindred cabinet ministers were more advisers than executives. Chulalongkorn and his successors, Vajiravudh (Rama VI) and Prajadhipok (Rama VII), did not delegate significant decision-making responsibility to them.

---

4   Benjamin A. Batson, *The End of the Absolute Monarchy in Siam* (Singapore: Oxford University Press, 1984), 9.

All major decisions were still decisions of the absolute monarch. And all officials—civilian and military—who worked under the ministers were "servants of the crown" (*kharatchakan*).[5]

Under Siam's version of the British banner "God, King and Country", Siamese absolute monarchs accumulated more domestic political power than British kings and queens had wielded in Britain for centuries. When rivals, rebels, bandits, immigrants or workers questioned Bangkok's authority, the king of Siam could deploy his army and police to deal with them, without worrying whether a legislature, judiciary or public opinion would question his motives or judgment.

Bangkok's growing control of both territory and finances, as well as the growing complexity of government, saw the number of salaried officials multiply—from 12,000 in 1890 to 80,000 in 1919. This growth could be sustained only by recruiting more and more commoners into the increasingly pervasive, but also increasingly frustrated, bureaucracy. Efforts by commoner officials (especially those who had been educated abroad) to institute a merit-based approach to appointments, promotions and salaries were rebuffed; one's birth, connections and loyalty to the throne remained paramount.[6] The commoner officials wanted a better deal for themselves and a better deal for Siam. By 1932, they were ready for change.

Pre-1932 Judiciary

Judicial reform was a natural part of Chulalongkorn's administrative overhaul. Chulalongkorn and his most trusted adviser (and brother), Prince Damrong, "considered the judiciary to be an arm of the absolutist state, existing in order to serve state interests". They overruled the Justice Minister, Prince Ratburi, who wanted "to establish the judiciary as an autonomous body independent from

---

5   *kharatchakan* remains the Thai term for civil or public servant.
6   Baker and Pasuk, *A History of Thailand*, 110; Pasuk and Baker, *Thailand: Economy and Politics*, 251–4.

the executive".[7] In this regard, the king was also following colonial practice, which combined the judiciary with the bureaucracy, thereby giving the executive greater control and denying the judiciary full independence. Chulalongkorn also favoured the centralised civil law system, rather than the more decentralised common law. "The king was able to control this newly centralised system at all levels both through his Special Commissioners, who acted as observers, teachers, and magistrates, and through his Minister of Justice, who appointed judges in all courts."[8]

The implications of judicial reform were far-reaching. First, the new judicial system increased substantially the power of the king, who was now better able to control his subjects and territory.

Secondly, the new judicial system ultimately led to the end of extraterritoriality and the affirmation of Siamese sovereignty.[9] Since 1855 (when Chulalongkorn's father Mongkut—or Rama IV—signed the Bowring Treaty with Britain) Siam had entered into "unequal treaties" with 15 foreign powers.[10] These foreign powers had insisted that their subjects (including Asian subjects from colonized Asia) be tried under their laws, not Siamese laws (which were considered "uncivilized"), until Siam reformed its laws and courts. The treaties also forced Siam to agree to low tariffs and taxes on foreign trade.

Thirdly, Chulalongkorn and his successors realised that Siam would be able to engage more effectively in international commerce if it had a legal system that recognised property rights and enforced contracts.

Fourthly, Chulalongkorn believed that his subjects were poorly served by the existing system, which included almost 30 different uncoordinated and poorly supervised courts. He complained "he was overburdened with the day-to-day details of the judicial function to

---

7   Kullada Kesboonchoo Mead, *The Rise and Decline of Thai Absolutism* (London: Routledge/Curzon, 2004), 112.
8   David M. Engel, *Law and Kingship in Thailand during the Reign of King Chulalongkorn* (Ann Arbor, Center for South and Southeast Asian Studies, University of Michigan, 1975), 78.
9   We will look at extraterritoriality in more detail in later chapters.
10   The 15 foreign powers were Austria-Hungary, Belgium, Denmark, France, Germany, Italy, Japan, Netherlands, Norway, Portugal, Russia, Spain, Sweden, United Kingdom and United States.

the extent that he was unable to perform his other duties as king". He compared the judiciary with "a merchant ship which was fully loaded but rotten and decayed. Until the present time, each hole had been plugged as it became apparent, but the decay had continued and the cargo was increasingly damaged. It was time, he concluded, to build a new vessel out of stronger planks."[11]

Pre-1932 Military

Before Chulalongkorn's reforms, armies in Siam were formed whenever a need arose, then disbanded. Chulalongkorn's main reason for establishing a standing army in the 1880s was to protect himself from princely and aristocratic rivals who could muster armed forces against him. In 1875 he had almost lost his throne to a well-armed rival. Domestically, he also reasoned that a standing army could subjugate the semi-autonomous regional nobles within the territory that had not yet been occupied by the Europeans. The greater the political and administrative control he could demonstrate over this territory, the lesser the risk that the Europeans would seek to take it. The standing army also quashed rebels. In addition, the army helped the government to overpower rural "bandits", who operated in the overlapping realms of village protection and criminal extortion.

The modern standing Siamese army also had a strategic purpose. Chulalongkorn was alarmed by British and French military successes in the neighbourhood, but when he established his new armed forces he could not reasonably expect them to match these Western adversaries. The existence of Siamese armed forces might, however, give Western powers cause to pause before they intruded on Siamese territory—because the cost of aggression would be higher. So Chulalongkorn was distressed in 1893, after he had naively challenged France militarily, to find French gunboats menacingly moored on the Chao Phraya River in front of his Grand Palace in Bangkok. His distress deepened

---

11   Engel, *Law and Kingship*, 66.

when France exacted territory and reparations from Siam, which also lost lives, dignity and a measure of autonomy. Fearful of total annexation, Chulalongkorn conceded. He immediately boosted the military budget and introduced conscription, quickly expanding the size of the armed forces. In the mid-19th century Siam had about 2,000 full-time soldiers. In 1910 the army included 20,000 active personnel and 30,000–40,000 reserves, while the navy was 5,000-strong, with 20,000 reserves.[12]

To develop more professional armed forces, Chulalongkorn sent princes and talented commoners to European military academies. The next king, Vajiravudh or Rama VI (reigned 1910–25), graduated from Sandhurst and his successor, Prajadhipok or Rama VII (reigned 1925–35), from Woolwich Royal Military Academy (both leading British military schools). The prime minister from 1933 to 1938, Phahon Phonphayuhasena, attended military academies in Germany and Denmark. His successor, Phibun Songkhram, who was prime minister for 15 of the next 19 years, graduated from Fontainebleu in France.[13]

Many of the commoners returned from their overseas military studies with a deeper understanding of meritocracy, democracy and nationalism. Until 1932 they found their career paths blocked because senior positions were reserved for princes and nobles. Vajiravudh made their predicament worse by establishing a paramilitary organization, Wild Tiger Corps, which began to rival the army in both size and prestige. Already, as crown prince, Vajiravudh had offended the army when he ordered the public caning of two junior officers who had scuffled with his pages. Brewing military frustration with the absolute monarchy was evident in the detection of coup plots in 1912 and 1917. Prajadhipok, who succeeded Vajiravudh in 1925, was uninterested in paramilitary bodies like Wild Tiger Corps, but

---

12 Pasuk and Baker, *Thailand: Economy and Politics*, 229, 230.
13 Born Plaek Khitasangkha, but normally referred to in English as Phibun or Phibun Songkhram, which are shortened forms of his official title "Luang Phibunsongkhram".

he responded to the global recession of the early 1930s by cutting the defence budget, retrenching staff and raising taxes, including on the income of soldiers and other salaried people (while barely touching the conspicuous wealth of either the extended royal family or Chinese merchants). By 1932, the military had accumulated a battery of grievances against the monarchy.

Pre-1932 Legislature

Of all the branches of the Thai government, the legislature had to struggle hardest to establish itself. Each of the three kings who ruled Siam immediately before 1932 rejected proposals to introduce a parliamentary system of government. In the 1880s, Chulalongkorn argued that his efforts to ward off the colonial powers through domestic reform would be hampered and corrupted by a parliament.[14] He also claimed: "It would be impossible for the king to govern the country following a European system because it is hard to find able persons to be members of parliament. Besides, the people would never be pleased with Western institutions. They have more faith in the king than in any member of parliament, because they believe that the king practises justice and loves the people more than anybody else."[15] Almost 20 years later, he again dismissed Western political ideas: "We cannot cultivate rice in Siam using European agricultural text books about wheat."[16] Shortly before he died in 1910, Chulalongkorn's position softened. He told his ministers: "I entrust onto my son Vajiravudh a gift for the people and that upon his accession to the throne he will give to them a parliament and constitution."[17]

Vajiravudh found his father's earlier views more appealing, calling proponents of Western ideas "believers in the cult of imitation" who

---

14   Eiji Murashima, "The Origins of Modern Official State Ideology in Thailand," *Journal of Southeast Asian Studies*, 19, 1 (March 1988), 85.
15   Quoted in *ibid*, 86.
16   Quoted in *ibid*, 88.
17   Quoted in Scot Barmé, *Luang Wichit Wathakan and the Creation of a Thai Identity* (Singapore, ISEAS, 1993), 21.

should instead "imitate our glorious ancestors who were able to integrate and preserve our nation for the last 200 years".[18] He believed Thais "were not well educated enough to know how to elect their representatives to a legislative assembly".[19] Vajiravudh also penned an article depicting an imagined Siamese parliament as "an utterly useless body of absurdity and confusion. The members spent long hours in tedious debate and meaningless speech-making. The left and right wings were locked in continuous and ridiculous conflict, and many MPs were Chinese and could not speak Thai properly."[20]

On assuming the throne in 1925, Prajadhipok realised that his predecessor had damaged the monarchy's image and public support, so he quickly established a Supreme Council of State because he wanted "to do something at once to gain the confidence of the people."[21] But by appointing only senior royals to the Council, Prajadhipok failed to impress "the people". His misgivings about democracy were confirmed in 1926 when he asked one of his foreign advisers, Francis Sayre from the United States, whether Siam was ready for representative government—adding, "my personal opinion is an emphatic NO." Sayre, who was also the son-in-law of President Woodrow Wilson, replied: "A workable parliament is absolutely dependent upon an intelligent electorate... Until the rank and file of people in Siam have generally received a higher degree of education than at present it would seem therefore to be exceedingly dangerous to try to set up a popularly controlled parliamentary body."[22] The influential Prince Damrong gave the same advice: parliamentary government should be delayed until "the people are sufficiently educated to understand their responsibility in the election".[23] A year later, Prajadhipok echoed Vajiravudh's concerns about Chinese immigrants, writing that a

---

18   Quoted in *ibid*, 95.
19   Chula Chakrabongse, *Lords of Life* (London: Alvin Redman, 1960), 290.
20   Murashima, "The Origins of Modern Official State Ideology in Thailand," 91
21   Benjamin Batson, ed., *Siam's Political Future: Documents from the End of the Absolute Monarchy* (New York: Cornell University Southeast Asia Program, 1974), 17.
22   Batson, *Siam's Political Future*, 15, 27.
23   *Ibid*, 41.

"parliament would be dominated by the Chinese Party".[24] Although unenthusiastic about parliamentary government, Prajadhipok was attracted to the idea of greater self-government at the municipal level, but he lost power before any steps were taken.[25]

---

24   *Ibid*, 48.
25   Terwiel, *Thailand's Political History*, 254.

Chapter Two

BETWEEN REFORMATIONS: 1932 TO 1997

In the Indies there is no state that is more monarchical than Siam.[1]

The Thai love the military more than all other officials, because they don't see the military as rulers, but rather as elder brothers who help to protect them from the rulers. But this love lasts only as long as the military have only influence and not power, that is, they do not themselves become the rulers.[2]

Like Chulalongkorn's reforms from the 1890s, the events of 1932 were an attempt to recast Siam's governance. What happened in that watershed year? Contrary to Chulalongkorn's claim that no one could judge or punish the king, on 24 June his son, King Prajadhipok, was judged and punished—by overseas-educated Thais who, under the banner of the People's Party, rebelled against royal absolutism. About 120 ambitious and young civilian officials and military officers, concerned about the incompetence of the monarchical regime and influenced by foreign ideas of constitutional government, used the armed forces to assume the political power of the monarchy.

Military officers were able to overthrow the absolute monarchy and muster sufficient troops to keep their regime in power. But leaders

1   Nicolas Gervaise, 1688, quoted in Chris Baker and Pasuk Phongpaichit, *A History of Ayutthaya: Siam in the Early Modern World* (Cambridge: Cambridge University Press, 2017), 148.

2   Nidhi, "The Thai Cultural Constitution."

of the new government did not overestimate their achievement. All participants in the events of 1932, military and non-military alike, "understood full well that the success of their seizure of power was superficial, since it was merely due to their tactics which had caused bewilderment among their opponents while drawing only token cooperation from some opportunistic elements".[3] They were anxious about royalist opposition, which remained strong. The risk of foreign intervention played on their minds. They faced an international financial crisis. Importantly, they could not rely on public support if royalists made a comeback. Their campaign against absolute monarchy, though inspired by democratic ideals, was not motivated by grassroots or even middle-class demands for a say in government. So it lacked the general sense of grievance and the depth of passion that motivated nationalists as well as communists in South and Southeast Asia. The Thai reformers, influenced by Western political ideas, national pride and an increasingly potent nationalist ideology, thought Thailand would be better governed and better respected internationally if they assumed the king's power. So they did. The king didn't—or couldn't—resist too much.

At a personal level, Prajadhipok was judged and punished more for the failings of his brother Vajiravudh than his own. Vajiravudh's critics pointed to "his public image as a swindler of state revenue, his close association with unsuitable company, his circle's open pursuit of pleasures unfitting to the role of a monarch, and the unpopularity of the Wild Tiger Corps".[4] He spent more than 10 per cent of the government budget on royal expenses (while monarchs in selected other nations spent between 0.13 and 0.33 per cent), which was four times more than the amount spent on education and five times more than expenditure on roads.[5] After Vajiravudh's death, his

---

3   Thawatt Mokarapong, *History of the Thai Revolution: A Study in Political Behaviour* (Bangkok: Chalermnit, 1972), 103.
4   Kullada, *The Rise and Decline of Thai Absolutism*, 176.
5   Batson, *The End of the Absolute Monarchy*, 17–18.

highly regarded uncle, Prince Damrong, wrote: "The authority of the sovereign had fallen much in respect and confidence, the treasury was on the verge of bankruptcy, and the government was corrupted."[6] In a jibe against his brother, Prajadhipok said that the absolute monarchy was viable "as long as we have a good king".[7]

Yet the events of 1932, while radical to the extent that they led to the overthrow of royal absolutism, did not overthrow the monarchy. The People's Party did not want a republic. The only whiff of republicanism was in a handbill issued on 24 June and broadcast repeatedly over the radio, which threatened to impose "a republican form of government" if Prajadhipok did not agree to become a constitutional monarch. This handbill, which also upbraided the king and his predecessors for gross misgovernment, was a tactical ploy by anxious coup-makers who wanted to place maximum pressure on the king. The content and tone of their separate formal message to Prajadhipok, who was in Hua Hin (a seaside town 200 km south of Bangkok), were quite different: they paid him the customary courtesies, said they would replace him with another member of the royal family if he did not accept their demands, and concluded: "Whether the matter will be proper or not, in whatever respect, ultimately will be up to royal kind consideration."[8]

Monarchy: Absolute Legitimiser

The People's Party needed the monarchy to legitimise their actions. From the outset, the new government decided that "King Prajadhipok … was to be left untouched: the plotters did not wish to arouse the indignation of the nation by humiliating the King".[9] On the first possible occasion, just two days after their coup, they apologised to

---

6   Quoted in Batson, *The End of the Absolute Monarchy*, 26.
7   Benjamin Batson, ed., *Siam's Political Future*, 15.
8   Sombat Chantornvong, "To Address the Dust of the Dust Under the Soles of the Royal Feet: A Reflection on the Political Dimension of Thai Court Language," *Asian Review*, 6, (1992), 147. Sombat notes that even the author (Pridi) of the handbill, which was disrespectful to the monarchy, "could not free himself immediately from the tradition of the honorific language system normally required of any reference by a commoner to a royal person." 145.
9   Thawatt, *History of the Thai Revolution*, 24.

Prajadhipok for the handbill. They repeated the apology publicly six months later. "In politics the people cared only about the king, and as the king had given his approval to the new order it was therefore acceptable to the people."[10]

For his part, Prajadhipok was a willing legitimiser. He wanted to preserve a role for the monarchy, and perhaps he hoped to regain the support of the army and re-establish monarchical rule. In response to the People's Party's 24 June demand that he submit to a constitution, Prajadhipok replied: "I have received the letter in which you invite me to return to Bangkok as a constitutional monarch. For the sake of peace; and in order to save useless bloodshed; to avoid confusion and loss to the country; and, more, because I have already considered making this change myself, I am willing to co-operate in the establishment of a constitution under which I am willing to serve."[11] On 26 June, just two days after the coup, at the implicit request of the coup leaders, Prajadhipok pardoned them for their "unlawful act" and approved a temporary constitution.

Prajadhipok couldn't reclaim the monarch's day-to-day political and administrative power, but he could remind the new government of the enduring authority of the monarchy. The would-be revolutionaries gained control, but struggled to establish an internationally recognised and domestically acceptable government without the blessing of the very king whose political powers they assumed.

By 1935, Prajadhipok realised that he could not undo the events of 1932, especially after royalist elements in the army, led by his former minister for war, Prince Boworadej, failed to overthrow the new government in 1933. He abdicated. Yet the People's Party government, which was now more firmly established, did not see Prajadhipok's abdication or his failure to nominate a successor as opportunities to rid Siam of the monarchy. Instead, the cabinet chose one of Prajadhipok's

---

10   Batson, *The End of the Absolute Monarchy*, 239.
11   Quoted in Chula, *Lords of Life*, 313.

nephews, Ananda, as the new king. Because Ananda (Rama VIII) was a minor, the cabinet appointed a regency council to perform the king's functions until he attained his majority. Still conscious of its legitimacy deficit, the government pressed for Ananda, who was living in Switzerland, to return home for his coronation. On arrival in late November 1938, Ananda was greeted by thousands of Thais, as well as senior government officials. During his two-month stay, "at every step, Ananda was treated as a holy, righteous dhammaraja".[12] The monarchy—the key traditional political institution—may no longer have been absolutist, but it continued to matter. It retained enough authority to resume a mediating and arbitrating role in the future.

In relying on the monarchy for legitimacy and, at the same time, not nurturing a system that made the government accountable to the legislature, judiciary and, ultimately, the electorate, the 1932 leaders and their successors left room either for an unaccountable government or for the monarchy to re-emerge to judge the government, not just legitimise it.

Legislature: Passion meets Power

The People's Party needed the monarchy to legitimise its grab for power because it could not count on popular support which, in institutional terms, might have been expressed through an elected legislature. Respected scholars agree that the events of 1932 were not an uprising or a revolution of the people. Thawatt Mokarapong has described the party as a movement that "did not touch the masses".[13] Fred Riggs observed: "The revolution did not emerge, as constitutional movements did in most Western countries, from a revolt of the middle classes, of industrial workers, of mass-based political parties, or of other widely supported organizations outside the government. Rather, the leaders

---

12 Paul M. Handley, *The King Never Smiles: A Biography of Thailand's Bhumibol Adulyadej* (New Haven and London: Yale University Press, 2006), 59. A *dhammaraja* is a king who rules according to Buddhist *dhamma* (*tham* is the normal Thai transcription) or law.
13 Thawatt, *History of the Thai Revolution*, 42.

of the revolution were themselves members—actual, would-be, or recently laid off—of the military and civil bureaucracy."[14] Benjamin Batson has written that the events of 1932 were met with "general incomprehension or indifference in the provinces".[15]

The incomprehension and indifference are perhaps partly explained by the comparatively benign living conditions of most Siamese villagers, which owed something to Siam's avoidance of direct colonization. Chulalongkorn and his successors, fearful of the sort of land reforms that had put prime agricultural land into the hands of the wealthy subjects of foreign powers in Siam's colonized neighbours, obstructed the development of modern property rights in Siam. That obstruction continued after fear of foreign domination was joined by fear that Chinese moneylenders might exploit Siamese peasants.[16] As a result:

> When the effects of the Great Depression began to be felt (i.e.
> during the period when Siam was moving from an absolute
> to a constitutional monarch), Siamese peasants, unlike those
> in many more developed neighbouring areas, enjoyed an
> enviable standard of living, in important respects, as well as
> the security of knowing that large areas of good agricultural
> land remained free for the taking. As a consequence, Siamese
> peasants in the Chaophraya Delta were further from a
> subsistence crisis than were their counterparts in the two
> neighbouring Southeast Asian rice baskets, the Irrawaddy and
> Mekong deltas, where commercialization had proceeded at
> break-neck speed over the previous few decades, unimpeded
> by sovereignty and security concerns.[17]

---

14   Fred W. Riggs, *Thailand: The Modernization of a Bureaucratic Polity* (Honolulu: East-West Center, 1966), 149.
15   Batson, *The End of the Absolute Monarchy*, 237.
16   Tomas Larsson, *Land and Loyalty: Security and the Development of Property Rights in Thailand* (Singapore: NUS Press, 2013), especially chapters 3 and 4.
17   Tomas Larsson, *Land and Loyalty*, 94. See also Porphant Ouyyanont, *A Regional Economic History of Thailand* (Singapore: ISEAS Yusof Ishak Institute, 2017), 73–4.

A survey in 1934–35 concluded that Siamese villagers "grow their own food, make what little clothing they require, and construct their own houses with materials which can be obtained at little if any cost". It "found that none of the general suffering and misery which have become commonplace in most other countries the world over".[18] In these circumstances, the People's Party might have been disappointed if it had looked to the masses for support and legitimacy.

Actually, the People's Party doubted the masses. Its first legislature was fully appointed. Under the "permanent" 1932 Constitution, which Prajadhipok approved in December, the single-chamber parliament—or National Assembly—had an equal number (78) of elected and appointed members. So, from the outset, the capacity of the legislature to hold the executive to account and to play a role in mediating and settling political disputes was constrained because the executive appointed half of the legislators.

Reflecting widespread misgivings about the maturity of the electorate, the constitution also said that the parliament was to be fully elected only after half the population had completed primary education or within 10 years, whichever was earlier. At the time, even the most liberal of the new leaders, Pridi Banomyong, shared the reservations of Siam's three most recent kings about the readiness of the Thai population for democracy:

> As for all the high sounding rhetoric about the people and their rights, Pridi clearly envisaged them in much the same way as did the monarchy. They were a concept to be invoked rather than individuals who could be expected to play any role in decision-making. Indeed, in advocating a lengthy period of political tutelage, Pridi was unwittingly echoing the views of royal advisors who had stated that the people

---

18   Larsson, *Land and Loyalty*, 95. At this time more than 80 per cent of Thais still lived in rural areas, engaged in farming. See Porphant, *A Regional Economic History*, 42.

were insufficiently educated or mature to cope with a more participatory form of government.[19]

This elite distrust of common people continued for decades, and still influences political thinking in Thailand. In the late 1970s, Interior Ministry researchers concluded that "the Thai people were not ready for democracy because of poor upbringing, an innate lack of ethics or seriousness, or simply a 'disposition to be under the command of others'".[20] During the demonstrations against the Yingluck government in 2013–14, some speakers advocated that the votes of Bangkokians should have greater value than votes of people who supported Yingluck, and only 30 per cent of the anti-Yingluck demonstrators disagreed with the statement that "Thais are not ready for equal voting rights".[21]

In 1932, the new government naturally gave the establishment of a legislature a higher priority than the monarchy had, but it was not under pressure to move quickly, and it did not want a fully-fledged deliberative and consultative body to which it should be accountable. The new government's main objectives were to overthrow absolutism and to withstand the royalist counter-attack and possible foreign intervention. It was also swept up in the daily but unfamiliar responsibilities of leading a nation facing significant challenges. Establishing a legislature mattered, but not as much as survival. This survival instinct prompted the People's Party to bar the emergence of opposition political parties, its greatest fear being the establishment of a formal royalist party. The People's Party wanted to avoid disputes, not establish a legislative forum that might either foster disputes or help to avert, mediate or settle them.

---

19   Judith Stowe, *Siam Becomes Thailand: A Story of Intrigue* (Honolulu: University of Hawaii Press, 1991), 26.
20   Baker and Pasuk, *A History of Thailand*, 236.
21   Asia Foundation, *Profile of the "Bangkok Shutdown" Protestors: A Survey of Anti-Government PDRC Demonstrators in Bangkok* (Bangkok: Asia Foundation, January 2014), 18.

Yet from the very first parliament, elected MPs refused to be docile. "Although the Assembly had little effective power given to it, it could be a serious annoyance to the government."[22] Elected MPs were not daunted by the dominance of the executive arm of government. As early as 1934 they forced the cabinet to resign over a policy difference, in relation to Siam's participation in an international scheme to stabilize the price of rubber. From the outset, the elected MPs, especially from Isaan, the northeastern region of Thailand, criticised the government's heavy expenditure on the military, under-expenditure on education and public works, appointment of military officers to purportedly civilian positions, inefficiency and corruption. In 1938, they again forced the cabinet to resign, after demanding fuller details of the government budget.

This early defiance was the start of a pattern in modern Thai politics of elected MPs, sometimes courageously, reminding authoritarian governments of the legitimacy that flows from elections and of the role the legislature can play in developing policy and averting and mediating disputes. In an observation that also helps to explain another feature of current Thai politics, an eminent scholar, Charles Keyes, has suggested that Isaan MPs "had much to gain by the greater democratization of the system. Their political strength did not lie with whom they knew in Bangkok, at least not initially, but with the rural people who had elected them. To enhance their positions they needed to espouse, dramatically if possible, programs and policies that would both increase their popularity in the countryside and bring them to the attention of the national leadership."[23]

Although history shows that, since the 1930s, elected MPs have

---

22   Charnvit Kasetsiri, "The First Phibun Government and Its Involvement in World War II," in Charnvit Kasetsiri, *Studies in Thai and Southeast Asian Histories* (Bangkok: The Foundation for the Promotion of Social Science and Humanities Textbooks Project and Toyota Thailand Foundation, 2015), 282.

23   Charles F. Keyes, *Finding Their Voice: Northeastern Villagers and the Thai State* (Chiang Mai: Silkworm Books, 2014), 66. Other historians, drawing on cultural practices and mural paintings, have also noted a more democratic world-view in Isaan. See Katherine A. Bowie, *Of Beggars and Buddhas: The Politics of Humor in the Vessantara Jataka in Thailand* (Madison: University of Wisconsin Press, 2017), 101–2, and Bonnie Pacala Brereton and Somroay Yencheuy, *Buddhist Murals of Northeast Thailand: Reflections of the Isan Heartland* (Chiang Mai, Mekong Press, 2010), 47.

tried to hold Thai governments to account, history also shows that elected MPs have rarely been able to outlast a military leader determined to have his way—in other words, a military leader who by implied or actual use of force settles disputes on his own terms. Just after becoming prime minister in 1938, General Phibun warned that, if the legislature persisted in disrupting the government, he would delay the phasing out of nominated members.[24] Undeterred, elected MPs questioned the government again, this time over its attempt to set up special courts under the Ministry of Defence. Equally undeterred, in 1940 Phibun amended the constitution to extend the practice of a half-appointed legislature to 20 years.

The military faction within the post-1932 civilian-military government, led by Phibun, gained political ascendancy because it could argue, on one hand, that the new government faced an existential threat; and, on the other hand, that ultranationalism was the most compelling state ideology for Siam in the 1930s. In an environment where survival instincts were paramount, the civilian wing of the People's Party, led by Pridi, was unable or unwilling to develop an independent power base, which might have found a natural home in the legislature. Instead, Pridi expressed his commitment to a more democratic form of government, mostly through his promotion of education that would lead to a more democracy-ready electorate, advocacy of a constitution, and socio-economic policies that favoured the common people. These were more important to him than support for a fully elected parliament or efforts to mobilize more Thais to participate in politics, including by voting in elections, or advocacy of a serious mediating or arbitrating role for the legislature. Pridi's commitment to democracy was qualified in other ways, too; he did not oppose the ban on other political parties, curbs on media freedom, or a law that imprisoned people who questioned the constitution. And,

---

24   Judith Stowe, *Siam Becomes Thailand*, 113. Under the 1932 Constitution, the Parliament was to be fully elected only after half the electorate had completed elementary education or no later than 10 years.

at an ideological level, in the nationalism-ridden 1930s, Pridi's plan in 1933 to socialise agriculture and bureaucratise the economy could not compete with the military faction's yearnings for Siamese glory under a strong leader.

The Ascendancy of Phibun and the Military

In 1932, Phibun was the most dynamic uniformed coup plotter. He soon emerged as the strongest leader in the military. In particular, in 1933, he won support from the younger generation of army officers by leading the successful military response to the royalist Boworadej rebellion. Phibun retained their support by increasing the military's personnel and budget, creating a precedent that has normally seen an increase in military spending after coups or when military personnel dominate cabinets.[25] He also appointed a large number of military officers to senior civilian positions in the government and allowed senior military officers to enrich themselves by sitting on company boards. In addition, he eliminated his political opponents, who had also tried to eliminate him (by 1938, he had survived one shooting and two further assassination attempts). Furthermore, Phibun held tight personal control: in addition to being prime minister, at various stages he was simultaneously defence minister, interior minister, foreign minister and army commander. For good measure, in 1941 he promoted himself from major general to field marshal, skipping the two ranks in between.

Phibun portrayed himself as a "father", to the people as well as a "strongman-saviour" or *phunam*, "the guardian of the national will and whose decisions were to be unquestionably followed".[26] In his own words, "I allowed the campaign depicting me as the Phunam/Leader because I wished others to believe that we, the people of the

---

25   Gregory Vincent Raymond, *Thai Military Power: A Culture of Strategic Accommodation,* (Copenhagen, NIAS Press, 2018), 223.
26   Thak Chaloemtiarana, *Thailand: The Politics of Despotic Paternalism* (Chiang Mai, Silkworm Books, 2007 [originally published in 1979]), 8, 66.

whole nation, can put our trust in one man, namely, the Phunam, who must be followed because of the good deeds he has performed."[27] The *phunam's* authority was "grounded in the traditional absolutism of the Thai monarchs legitimized by historical and cosmological sources", and "its fundamental essence approximated, but yet was alien to, traditional Thai political values".[28]

Yet despite his reliance on traditional absolutism, Phibun, more than any other leader, distrusted the monarchy and its royalist supporters. He arrested royalists who hadn't already fled Siam or kept their heads down at home, and executed or imprisoned them. Others were dismissed from government positions. The Ministry of the Royal Household was downgraded, the Ministry of Finance took control of royal assets, Prajadhipok was denied immunity from prosecution and sued for transferring assets overseas. Phibun abolished the practice of royal titles and royal language *(rajasap)*, and he either abolished palace ceremonies or converted them into state rituals. In steps laden with symbolism, he built Democracy Monument in the middle of Bangkok's main thoroughfare leading towards the Grand Palace, and treated Constitution Day as a bigger holiday than the king's birthday. He had the government assume control of the *sangha*[29] and build new temples, previously a royal prerogative. He rubbed salt into royal wounds by having his own portrait, rather than the customary portrait of the king, hung in government offices.

More than any other leader, Phibun also grasped the potency of nationalism, and harnessed it to the armed forces.[30] Domestically, ethnic nationalism was directed against the Chinese, who controlled important parts of the Thai economy. Externally, grievance-laden nationalism was directed against France and Britain, which since

---

27   Quoted in Kobkua Suwannathat-Pian, *Thailand's Durable Premier: Phibun through Three Decades, 1932–1957* (Kuala Lumpur, Oxford University Press, 1995), 82.
28   Thak, *The Politics of Despotic Paternalism*, 8. We explore the values underpinning Thai kingship later in this chapter. The importance of personalism in Thai politics is considered in Chapter Five.
29   The *sangha* is the monastic community of ordained Buddhist monks.
30   Phibun's ultranationalist ideology is covered in more detail in Chapter Six.

the 19th century had usurped political power from Cambodian, Lao, Malay and Burmese kingdoms and fiefdoms, some of which had previously recognised Thai suzerainty. In keeping with an international proclivity at the time for reclaiming "lost territories", and taking advantage of Japanese strength and French and British impotence, in the early years of World War II the Thai armed forces restored Thai control over parts of French Cambodia and Laos and British Malaya and Burma—a hugely popular achievement, which also boosted the self-esteem of the military.

Military Retreats, Legislature Muddles

The fortunes of Phibun and his military government suffered as Japan began to lose the war, the Thai economy began to collapse under the weight of Japanese occupation and Allied bombing, and as the cost of some ill-conceived domestic policies became more apparent. These grandiose policies included a new national capital in Phetchabun (300 km from Bangkok) and a "Buddhist city" in Saraburi (100 km). In July 1944, the National Assembly defeated Phibun's bills to construct both of them. Phibun resigned as prime minister, but expected to be reappointed. He wasn't. Because circumstances no longer favoured the military, the legislature could again express itself. Elected and appointed MPs alike, influenced by Pridi, who enjoyed growing support because he led the underground anti-Japanese resistance (called *Seri Thai* or Free Thai), chose Khuang Aphaiwong as the new prime minister. They considered that Khuang would have the skills and temperament to out-wit the still-present occupying Japanese and appease the soon-present occupying allies.

When the war ended, the authority of the military shrank even further. Soldiers were demobilized, the military budget was cut, and Phibun-aligned generals were purged. France and Britain also reclaimed their previously colonized territory in the region.

After playing a critical role in ousting Phibun in 1944, for the next three years the legislature became the main forum for political debate and reform. Under the 1946 Constitution, for the first time, Thailand adopted a bicameral system of government. For the first time, the entire lower house was directly elected, for a four-year term. The 176 members of the lower house then elected 80 senators, who were to serve for six years. For the first time, civil servants and military officers were barred from holding seats in the parliament—in an attempt to reduce the authority of the executive, especially the military, vis-à-vis the legislature. Also for the first time, members of the royal family were allowed to hold seats—as a concession to royalists, who had mostly supported *Seri Thai* and who deeply distrusted Phibun. And for the first time, political parties were permitted.[31]

Thailand appeared to have become a parliamentary democracy. An elected government faced an elected opposition and the political struggle between them occurred on the floor of parliament and was reported in the media. Provincial politicians, especially from the northeast and the north where regional loyalties were strong, were able "to give vent to their regional grievances".[32] Political parties formed around the liberal-leaning Pridi, who was *de facto* head of the elected government, and around Khuang and Seni Pramoj, who were the dominant figures in the royalist-conservative opposition.

But these nascent political parties were largely vocal groupings of like-minded MPs with personal attachments to a particular leader. Parties lacked the coherence that comes with ideology, organizational machinery and internal discipline. The key leaders—Pridi, Seni and Khuang—were plagued by personal as well as political differences. Pridi wanted to continue to modernise the political and economic system, as well as restore the country's international credibility, which had been battered by its alignment with Japan. Seni and Khuang, who founded

---

31   Although the People's Party had overthrown absolutism in 1932 and its leaders continued to identify themselves with it, the People's Party was a grouping of like-minded, ambitious individuals. It never developed the organizational structure of a political party; nor did it have a mass following.
32   David A. Wilson, *Politics in Thailand* (New York: Cornell University Press, 1962), 215.

the Democrat Party, favoured a more gradual approach to reform and baulked at any measure that might further weaken the authority of the monarchy and remaining privileges of the extended royal family.

If we assess the immediate post-War developments in terms of the legislature's evolution as a branch of government, we see that the leaders of these political parties did not recognise that they might share a common purpose in promoting the idea that the legislature, and ultimately the electorate, might play a bigger political role. Nor did they recognise that they might share a common purpose in protecting the institution of parliament from extra-parliamentary assault. They did not think in institutional terms. This attitude would persist for the next 70 years.

Ultimately, Thailand's post-war parliamentary democracy was besieged by the accumulated burdens of Japanese and then British occupation, unresolved questions about the role of the monarchy, and anti-communist rhetoric. Thailand's forced "loans" to Japan and reparations to Britain boosted inflation, disrupted trade and created shortages, including shortages of rice in one of the world's major rice-producing countries. Corruption, black markets, smuggling and other criminality grew, including armed clashes because many demobilized Thai and *Seri Thai* soldiers had not surrendered their weapons. Demonstrations and strikes in Bangkok became more common. The looming Cold War influenced ideological debates and political tactics. If all this wasn't tumultuous enough, in June 1946, barely six months after returning to Bangkok from Switzerland where he had been studying, 20-year-old King Ananda was shot dead in circumstances that remain a mystery. His unexplained death weighed heavily on the country's politics and mood.

The Military: A New Dawn

The military, which had been fretting over the political influence of Pridi (whom they saw as a leftist), staged a coup in November 1947.

The coup-makers offered the prime ministership to Khuang, the leader of the pro-monarchy Democrat Party. His acceptance of the offer foretold of a willingness for the next 70 years of elected Thai politicians to strike bargains with the military.

By April 1948, military officers concluded that they had done enough to appease royalists, who had distrusted the anti-monarchy Phibun, and the West, which hadn't forgotten Phibun's role during the Japanese occupation. So they replaced Khuang with Phibun.

The beleaguered Khuang's reaction when the military intimated that it wanted him to resign tells us a lot about the ultimate political weakness of the legislature as an institution. Khuang did not turn to his parliamentary colleagues for support; as far as we know, the thought did not cross his mind. Instead, he checked whether the leaders of the army, navy or air force would back him rather than Phibun. None of them would, so he knew he had to go. Again, when the military was steady in its conviction, it did not have to worry too much about the legislature which, notwithstanding the activism and defiance of some individual MPs, lacked institutional resolve.

Still, because Phibun was so easily able to persuade the legislature to endorse his return to power, he was not tempted to disband it. Moreover, parliament was becoming an inescapable feature in the political landscape and MPs were now included in the new, more broadly-based Thai elite. The legislature could be bullied, but not ignored. As Phibun had discovered in 1944 when it sacked him, and in 1948 when it sanctioned his reinstatement, the legislature could play a meaningful role when the incumbent executive seemed to have lost its way.

From 1948, Phibun remained prime minister for almost 10 years, but he ruled with less authority than in his first prime ministership. Increasingly, he had to share power with Generals Sarit Thanarat and Phao Siyanon, who dominated the army and police respectively (the police assumed a bigger political role during this period because of massive Cold War funding from the United States as well as Phao's strong, often brutal, leadership). Phibun tried to play a balancing role between Sarit and Phao; in doing so, he further entrenched the dominance of the security forces in Thai politics.

Struggling to compete with Sarit and Phao, and lacking a strong domestic power base, Phibun pursued anti-communist policies, thereby attracting US assistance to modernise and expand the army. The military's coercive powers were further buttressed by state-of-emergency and anti-communism laws. Phibun also adopted ultranationalism. Phibun's anti-communism and ultranationalism helped him to remain in office, but not at the expense of Sarit or Phao, who also profited politically (and personally) from American largesse, and by repressing the local population under the guise of fighting communism.

Phibun tried to counter them by flirting with democracy, which in institutional terms meant trying to breathe life back into the legislature. In 1955, he re-legalised political parties and announced he would be a candidate in the 1957 elections. Phibun also gambled against his own horse, the army, by saying publicly that soldiers should not be involved in politics or commerce, and that coups were old-fashioned. He relaxed censorship, legalised unions and encouraged political debate and rallies. Phibun's scheme backfired when the wily Phao encouraged public criticism of Phibun himself. Phibun quickly banned public meetings and gave fewer press conferences. Although the military's political party, with Phibun at the head, won the February 1957 elections, Phibun secured his own seat only by tampering with the votes. The public outcry eventually created an opening for Sarit to oust Phibun (and Phao) in a coup in September 1957.

Judiciary: In the Shadows
Having outlined how three of the five branches of government—the monarchy, military and legislature—evolved until the overthrow

of Phibun in 1957, let's look at the role of the judiciary, starting with how its role was depicted in constitutions. Constitutions in Thailand have rarely been considered the supreme law. But Thailand's myriad constitutions have been, and remain, useful in outlining the relative importance of prevailing political forces in the country, or the relative importance the constitution-drafters aspire for them.

In 1932, it seemed that the judiciary hardly mattered. The judiciary barely rated a mention in Thailand's first constitution, the "provisional" constitution of June 1932, which said sovereignty belonged to the people. This short-lived constitution, largely written by Pridi, was divided into five sections. The first section (two clauses) dealt with general matters, followed by sections on the monarchy (five clauses), parliament (20 clauses), executive (11 clauses) and, taking up last place, the judiciary—under the heading of "Courts"—which had a solitary clause: "The revocation of a judgment shall proceed according to the law in current use."[33] The sections on both the legislature and executive set out the "powers and duties" of each; the powers and duties of the judiciary were not defined.

The "permanent" constitution of December 1932, which said the people's sovereignty would be exercised by the king, was only slightly more expansive. There was no chapter on the judiciary, while the chapters on the legislature and executive had 30 and 23 sections respectively. One of the nine sections in the chapter on the monarchy said that: "The King exercises judicial power through the Courts duly established by law" (Section 8). The chapter on the rights and duties of the Thai people stated that all people were equal before the law (Section 12); all people enjoyed full liberties of "person, property, speech, writing, publication, education, public meeting, association and profession" (Section 14); and all people had a duty to respect the law (Section 15).[34]

The 1946 Constitution was the first constitution to have a

---

33 The effect of this clause was to decree that existing laws would continue to apply under the new government. *Pridi by Pridi: Selected Writing on Life, Politics, and Economy.* Edited by Chris Baker and Pasuk Phongpaichit (Chiang Mai, Silkworm Books, 2000), 79.

34 Thak, *Thai Politics: Extracts and Documents 1932–1957* (Bangkok: The Social Science Association of Thailand, 1978), 98–9.

separate chapter on the judiciary. The chapter contained provisions on the exercise of judicial power, the establishment of courts, the independence of judges and the method of judicial appointment.[35]

The comparatively low priority of the judiciary in the minds of the leaders of the new government was illustrated as early as 1934, when Phibun claimed that Siam possessed four basic political institutions—monarchy, parliament, bureaucracy and military—of which only the military was "abiding and permanent".[36] The judiciary, seemingly, did not count at all as a separate institution. Presumably, Phibun saw it as part of the bureaucracy.

Ironically, 12 years later the judiciary came to Phibun's rescue. He was in prison, awaiting trial for alleged war crimes because he had facilitated Japanese occupation. In 1946 the Supreme Court ruled that the War Criminals Act 1945 under which Phibun had been charged was unconstitutional because it imposed *ex-post facto* penalties; in other words, Phibun's alleged war crimes were not crimes under Thai law when they were committed. Phibun was released and two years later he was again prime minister—thanks to this political intervention in the judicial process. "Although portrayed as a purely legal decision, the evidence suggests that it was part of a behind-the-scenes effort to mend the rift between the civilian and military factions of the People's Party. The military members of the National Assembly had become a critical swing bloc"[37]—so the *de facto* leader of the government, Pridi, had political reasons to release the still popular Phibun from prison.[38] Perhaps, he had some personal reasons, too. Pridi may have arranged for Phibun's release, "out of loyalty to an old comrade and because of an oath shared by members of the Promoters Group [People's Party] which pledged each member never to allow harm to come to another member. Indeed, Phibun's widow ... wrote

35   *Ibid*, 519.
36   Stowe, *Siam Becomes Thailand*, 84.
37   E. Bruce Reynolds, *Thailand's Secret War: The Free Thai, OSS, and SOE during World War II* (Cambridge, Cambridge University Press, 2005), 425.
38   Wyatt, *History of Thailand*, 237.

in her memoirs that Pridi Banomyong had no desire 'to see Phibun hanged' and so arranged for his release."[39] For these political, and perhaps personal, reasons, Pridi persuaded the judiciary to employ some creative jurisprudence to help. Creativity was essential because the Thai constitution at the time did not provide for judicial review of the constitutionality of laws.

In addition to demonstrating the scope for political and, possibly, personal interference in the judiciary, this judgment revealed the potential political power of the judiciary. It disturbed MPs deeply. They criticised it "for shaking the very foundations of democracy" and they made sure the new constitution prohibited the court from exercising judicial review over an Act of Parliament.[40] Unlike the 1932 Constitution, which was silent on the question of judicial review, the 1946 Constitution stated explicitly that "Parliament is vested with the absolute right to interpret this Constitution" (Section 86).[41] It also decreed that Parliament would appoint a Judicial Committee of the Constitution to determine whether any law conflicted with the constitution. Quite deliberately, the judiciary had no authority to review the constitutionality of legislation.

In summary, from 1932 until 1946 the judiciary appears to have been almost an afterthought in the minds of the builders of Thailand's new political system. In 1946 the nation-builders glimpsed the potential political power of the judiciary and the political risks of a judiciary that was independent. It worried them, so they pushed the judiciary back into the shadows. For the next 50 years, every constitution purposely denied the judiciary the right to review the constitutionality of legislation. The legislature, which was usually dominated by the executive—which in turn was dominated by the military—had sole authority to determine whether its legislation was constitutional.

---

39   Joseph Wright, *The Balancing Act: A History of Modern Thailand* (Bangkok: Asia Books, 1991), 173.
40   James R. Klein, *The Constitution of the Kingdom of Thailand: A Blueprint for Participatory Democracy* (Bangkok: Asia Foundation, 1998), 17.
41   Thak, *Thai Politics: Extracts and Documents 1932–1957*, 520.

For 50 years, these formal constitutional arrangements for judicial review, and the limited role they afforded the judiciary, were uncontroversial. Constitutionalism—the idea that the power of government is both determined by law and limited by law—had no influential champions in Thailand. Royalists argued that the universal truths underpinning the monarchy were superior to constitutions based on foreign ideas. For ultranationalists like Phibun, devotion to the nation trumped the rule of law. And Sarit—the paternalistic military strongman who replaced him—organized the state around the trilogy of Nation, Religion and King, and opposed the "sudden transplantation of alien institutions onto our soil without careful preparation".[42]

Even the judiciary itself did not champion constitutionalism. Perhaps nothing gives a clearer idea of the judiciary's view of its own role, including as a potential mediator and arbitrator of political disputes, than its submissive response in the 1950s when asked to rule on the constitutionality of military coups. It concluded that a government was "an individual or group of individuals who exercise administrative power over the country and can maintain the peace and happiness of the country and whose authority is uncontested". A government becomes legitimate, the Supreme Court said, once "people come to accept and respect it".[43] One assumes that the judiciary, at least implicitly, has therefore relied on such governments for its own legitimacy, and not found its legitimacy in the supremacy of the law.

Since the 1950s, the judiciary has not cared about the way a government comes to power, even when the military has overthrown a constitution or an elected government, or both. No senior Thai judge seems to have ever spoken out against a military coup. In the early 1970s

---

42   Sarit's international spokesman, Thanat Khoman, quoted in Thak, *The Politics of Despotic Paternalism*, 100.

43   Quoted in David Streckfuss, *Truth on Trial in Thailand: Defamation, Treason and Lèse Majesté* (New York and London, Routledge, 2011), 119.

the judiciary went so far as to imprison three MPs who had the temerity to bring a charge of rebellion against generals who had staged a coup.[44]

In this benign environment, it is hardly surprising that until 2006 no Thai coup leader ever felt the need to dismiss or arrest a judge of the Supreme Court or Constitutional Court, or to dissolve a court (that year the military government replaced the pro-Thaksin Constitutional Court with its own hand-picked Constitutional Tribunal). In contrast, in 1962 the military regime in Burma, worried about its uncertain legal status, arrested the chief justice and locked him up for six years, and in 1998 the military junta there sacked five supreme court judges.[45]

Thai judges were, however, prepared to defend the independence of the judiciary in some circumstances. In 1972, after the military government put the Minister of Justice in charge of the Judicial Commission that controlled the appointment of judges, judges objected strongly.[46] Following all-night protests by university students, supported by the Lawyers Association and the media, the government rescinded the decree.

Because post-1932 governments continued, like Chulalongkorn, to see the judiciary as an extension of the bureaucracy, at times, unsurprisingly, the judiciary has been affected by the factionalism, favouritism and corruption that has dogged the bureaucracy. Yet Thai judges have enjoyed a public reputation and status that bureaucrats never secured. In 1991, one of Thailand's leading historians, Nidhi Eoseewong, wrote that, "in the Thai ideal, the power of the judiciary is the power which is purest, that is, free of any concealed influence at all. In the view of the Thai, judges are clean and pure people, the only ones in the whole judicial process".[47]

---

44   *Ibid*, 129–34.
45   David Cheesman, *Opposing the Rule of Law: How Myanmar's Courts Make Law and Order* (Cambridge: Cambridge University Press, 2015), 78, 104 fn 30.
46   For background on the efforts to subvert the independence of the judiciary which culminated in Decree 299, see William J. Klausner, "Reflections on the Independence of the Thai Judiciary: Past, Present and Future," in *Thai Institutions and National Security: Danger and Opportunity*, ISIS Paper 3 (Bangkok: Institute of Security and International Studies (ISIS), 1999), 55–79.
47   Nidhi, "The Thai Cultural Constitution."

This reputation owes something to the judiciary's historical ties with the monarchy. While Siam's courts were reformed and placed under the Minister of Justice in the 1890s, the Supreme Court remained directly responsible to the king until 1909. Judges and some other judicial officers are the only state officials who pledge a personal oath of loyalty to the king; they are then royally appointed by the king. All court judgments are rendered in the king's name. The king's portrait hangs above and behind judges in all courtrooms. And in his speeches King Bhumibol (Rama IX) tended to accord greater prestige to judges and the judiciary than to others. So criticism of a judge risked being interpreted as criticism of the monarch.

Even after its growing and sometimes controversial involvement in politics since 1997,[48] the judiciary has retained the respect of a majority of Thais. In a nationwide poll in 2010, 59 per cent of respondents rated the integrity of the courts as "high" or "very high", down marginally from 64 per cent in 2009, but still well ahead of the military (34 and 44 per cent) and parliament/MPs (11 and 10 per cent). The 2010 poll showed that 63 per cent of respondents thought the judiciary was politically unbiased, compared with 64 per cent a year earlier. The result for the military was 38 and 37 per cent.[49]

Sarit Thanarat and Despotic Paternalism

After gaining power in 1957, Sarit soon lost patience with Phibunesque constitutional democracy and the freer parliament and press it encouraged. In Sarit's view, parliamentary democracy in Thailand was "an obstacle to national development and the root cause of dangerous

---

48 We will consider this in the next chapter and in Chapter Eight.
49 The Asia Foundation, *2010 National Survey of the Thai Electorate: Exploring National Consensus and Color Polarization* (Bangkok, The Asia Foundation, 2011), 67–73; and The Asia Foundation, *Constitutional Reform and Democracy in Thailand: A National Survey of the Thai People* (Bangkok, The Asia Foundation, 2009), 107–10.

divisive tendencies".[50] For him, politicians were "opportunists whose loyalty was to the ballot box and not to the state and nation".[51] Sarit sought legitimacy not from the legislature but from the monarchy, and from what he called a Thai tradition of paternalism, with the prime minister being the "father of the largest family".[52]

Sarit and his contemporaries, unlike Phibun's generation, had not had the opportunity to study abroad. "Liberalism and democracy were thus largely alien principles to the new military leaders, whose only frame of reference was Thailand. Furthermore, their observation of politics had always been from a commanding vantage point, and they became uneasy when politicians exerted pressures from below with which they were supposed to comply under the rules of the post-1932 political system."[53] So, in October 1958, Sarit staged another coup, which he called a revolution, and "tried to overthrow a whole political system inherited from 1932, and to create one that could be called more 'Thai' in nature".[54]

Sarit's political system has been aptly called "despotic paternalism".[55] Despotic in the sense that Sarit ruled with neither a constitution nor a parliament and bullied, arrested and sometimes executed extra-judicially political dissenters, journalists and intellectuals, as well as criminals. Paternalistic because Sarit modelled himself on the father-children concept of the Sukhothai kings,[56] who, according to popular belief, ruled in the manner of a father looking after his children. As a good "father", Sarit wanted to improve the economic and social welfare of his "children". So he made economic development, especially in rural areas, a priority of his administration. Relying on technocrats for advice, he and successor military governments encouraged the

---

50   Thak, *The Politics of Despotic Paternalism*, 226.
51   *Ibid*, 148.
52   Quoted in *ibid*, 147.
53   *Ibid*, 99.
54   *Ibid*, 92.
55   *Ibid*, especially 133–9.
56   The Sukhothai kingdom (1239–1438) in north-central Siam has traditionally been considered the founding kingdom of the Thais.

deployment of private capital, private property (especially through the formalization of land titles for villagers),[57] and foreign aid in the struggle against communism.

Sarit broadened and deepened the reach of the military in the Thai polity. Military officers could no longer confine themselves to their barracks, parade grounds and boardrooms. Sarit forced them to play a larger role in national administration. He expected them "to understand the social, economic and political issues that had earlier been mainly the field of civil bureaucrats and politicians".[58] Sarit also "tried to socialize top bureaucrats into recognising the importance of national security for efficient development administration, and to harmonize their outlook with that of responsible military officers".[59] At the same time, through this socialization Sarit aimed "to convince civilian bureaucrats of the legitimacy of military supremacy in government".[60]

In addition, under Sarit the military began to embed itself in society, especially through its direct involvement in development projects, and through community mobilization programs designed to counter the threat of communism. In 1965, with US encouragement, a military organization called the Communist Suppression Operation Command (CSOC) assumed formal responsibility for these efforts. CSOC, and its successor (from 1975), the Internal Security Operations Command (ISOC), became "the Thai Army's political, intelligence and psychological arm, using both violence and propaganda techniques during the counter-insurgency period against student, peasant and worker movements".[61] Sarit had ample resources to fund this politically motivated economic development and to unify

57 Tomas Larsson, *Land and Loyalty*, especially Chapter 5. Sarit also removed a 50-rai limit on landholdings. See Benedict Anderson, *The Spectre of Comparisons: Nationalisms, Southeast Asia and the World* (London and New York: Verso, 1998), 147.
58 Thak, *The Politics of Despotic Paternalism*, 198.
59 *Ibid*, 181.
60 *Ibid*, 188.
61 Puangthong R. Pawakapan, *The Central Role of Thailand's Internal Security Operations Command in the Post-Counter-Insurgency Period* (Singapore: ISEAS Yusof Ishak Institute, 2017), 3.

the armed forces. The United States, eager to secure Thailand's support in its regional war against communism, funded Thailand's counter-insurgency, including rural development projects aimed at winning the hearts and minds of existing and would-be communist sympathisers. It poured money into projects as diverse as roads, bridges, sanitation, health, water supplies, air force bases, army camps and other military facilities. Even today, ISOC continues to allow "the military extensive power over various state agencies and citizens. On the one hand, this power allows the conservative elite to undermine and control electoral democracy; while on the other, it permits the military to consolidate its own political power."[62]

Monarchy Rejuvenated

Under Sarit, the monarchy made a comeback. From his assumption of power in 1957, Sarit, unlike Phibun, sought legitimacy from the king. In the six years after he had returned to Thailand in 1951, King Bhumibol, still in his twenties, listened to advisers in the palace who helped him to make the most of the natural advantages of his exalted position in a steeply hierarchical, Buddhist society. Over time, simply by being in the country and publicly doing the things only a king can do, he had demonstrated to the younger generation—and recalled for the older generations—the traditional socio-religious status and aura of the monarchy. With wide media coverage, he conducted court and religious rituals; he visited Buddhist shrines; he granted royal decorations and titles; he swore in privy councillors and judges; he opened parliaments; he presented degrees; he received prominent international visitors and granted audiences to senior Thai visitors, and the latter prostrated themselves before him in the traditional manner (by placing their body in a prone position on the ground in the presence of the king). He made donations to good causes, including temples, and to Thais affected by natural disasters. In

---

62   *Ibid.*

1952, his popular queen, Sirikit, gave birth to a son, Vajiralongkorn, prompting nationwide celebrations.

With the exception of Phibun, members of the military government had not been troubled by Bhumibol's growing prestige, not least because he naturally backed their war against communism. Phibun, though, remained suspicious of the monarchy. For several years, he prevented Bhumibol from undertaking provincial tours, preferring to boost his own image by travelling widely and frequently, and by donating money to temples and presenting Buddha images—merit-making actions that traditionally were more the prerogative of the king. In 1957, Phibun appropriated (or, in the eyes of many Thais, misappropriated) for himself the leading role in celebrating the 2500th anniversary of the Buddhist era; tellingly, Bhumibol found a last-minute reason not to attend the event. Phibun also spearheaded legislation to limit landholdings in Thailand, a major source of wealth for the royal family and aristocracy.

Phibun recognised the potential political threat posed by a popular and revered monarch. Phibun's political instincts were sound. When, in 1955, he eventually allowed Bhumibol to travel upcountry, the public response to the sight of their monarch was overwhelming:

> At each stop the king was feted by local civil servants. He sat at length while offerings were made and the governor delivered a tedious statistical report on the state of the province. These meetings were held openly, and the people could see in the seating arrangements and behaviour of officials that the king commanded all, even the most holy monks and fearsome generals. After the presentation the king would receive gifts and walk among the people, slowing for their prostrations, touching their holy icons, and handing out coins. Sometimes he would sheepishly pat the tops of their heads, the holy blessings of a Buddha-to-be. It was enough to convince all that

here was good and omnipotent power above the oppressive
and corrupt police, bureaucrats, and merchants.[63]

In contrast to Phibun, Sarit boosted the monarchy's prestige and
basked in it. He sought the king's endorsement of his 1957 coup,
and the king responded with a decree naming him "Defender of the
Capital". Thereafter, Sarit spoke of the "army of the king" as well as the
"government of the king". The monarchy's symbolic authority was
no longer questioned; on the contrary, it grew. Bhumibol's birthday
became the national day, replacing the anniversary of the 1932 coup;
Queen Sirikit's birthday was also formally celebrated; elaborate
royal ceremonies and rituals resumed; allegiance ceremonies took
on a deeper meaning; the palace received a bigger budget and
greater control of the royal guards; the king's contributions to
charities grew; royal decorations were restored; regular provincial
tours reinforced Bhumibol's image as the father of the nation and
protector of his people; state visits to foreign capitals enhanced the
king's international and domestic status; and the application of the
lèse majesté law was strengthened.

Rajasap was revived. *Rajasap* is the complicated Thai court
language that is used when speaking to royalty or when describing
the world around royalty. One author put it this way: "To use English
approximations, whereas the people 'walked, ate, bathed and slept',
the Lord of Life [King] 'perambulated, partook of ambrosia, laved his
precious person and deigned to recline'."[64] Another author wrote: "A
subject called himself 'the servant of excellent enlightenment', and
addressed the King from 'under the dust of the sole of your august
feet'. When the King ascended the throne, he commenced to 'partake
of the royal treasure'; and when he passed an edict, the people were

---

63   Handley, *The King Never Smiles*, 128.
64   John Blofield, *King Maha Mongkut of Siam* (Bangkok: Siam Society, 1987), 4.

informed that 'These are His Majesty's words promulgated as Royal Order like the roaring of a Lion.'"[65]

In return for recalling and revering the traditional authority of the monarchy, Sarit's military government gained a legitimacy that its raw, and often arbitrarily exercised, power could not have delivered.

Magic of Monarchy

In addition to the abiding vitality of the monarchy in the popular mind, at the intellectual level a modern ideology for the Thai monarchy was developed. In 1946, Prince Dhani Nivat, senior adviser in the palace, instructed both Ananda and Bhumibol on kingship, including at a public lecture which both attended. His lecture was published the following year. Dhani's main ideas have underpinned subsequent efforts to provide an intellectual basis for a strong monarchy in the new era.

Tellingly, Dhani set the scene for his lecture with a quote from the celebrated anthropologist, Bronislaw Malinowski: "A society which makes its tradition sacred has gained by it inestimable advantage of power and permanence. Such beliefs and practices, therefore, which put a halo of sanctity round tradition, will have a 'survival value' for the type of civilization in which they have been evolved ... They were bought at an extravagant price, and are to be maintained at any cost."[66] In other words, Dhani wanted the new king to understand and perpetuate the magic of the monarchy.

Dhani then proceeded to write that, according to Thai tradition, "the monarch was of course the people's leader in battle; but he was also in peace-time their father whose advice was sought and expected in all matters and whose judgment was accepted by all. He was moreover accessible to his people."[67]

---

65   Tej Bunnag, *The Provincial Administration of Siam, 1892–1915: The Ministry of Interior under Prince Damrong Rajanubhab* (Oxford, OUP, 1977), 5. See also Sombat, "To Address the Dust of the Dust", 145–63.
66   Quoted in Prince Dhani Nivat, "The Old Siamese Conception of the Monarchy," *Journal of the Siam Society*, 36, 2 (1947), 91.
67   Prince Dhani Nivat, "The Old Siamese Conception of the Monarchy," 93.

This patriarchal kingship, he said, was formalised under "the Constitution of the *Thammasat*" (the cosmic law, including the teachings of the Buddha).[68] "The *Thammasat* describes its ideal of a monarch as a King of Righteousness, elected by the people[69]... According to the *Thammasat*, the ideal monarch abides steadfast in the 10 kingly virtues,[70] constantly upholding the five common precepts[71] and on holy days the set of eight precepts,[72] living in kindness and goodwill to all beings."[73]

Dhani said that the ten kingly virtues were usually coupled with "another curious quartette of the lines of conduct proper for an ideal monarch. These are... knowledge of food organization, ... knowledge of men, ... means of winning the people's heart, [and] ... gentle words".[74] "Thus fortified by the rules of right conduct," Dhani said, "the ideal monarch justifies himself as the King of Righteousness."[75]

On one hand, Dhani was simply reiterating the main concepts of traditional Siamese kingship, reminding his audience of the king's role in upholding sacred laws and morality and protecting his people. Additionally, in an environment where challengers to the monarchy wanted the king's role determined by a Western-style constitution, he was arguing that the king was bound by something bigger: the <u>constitution</u> of the *Thammasat*. He went on to say the constitution

---

68 *Thammasat* is the Thai language expression of the Sanskrit *dharmasastra*, the treatise on dharma (*tham* in Thai).

69 Patrick Jory has recently explained how the idea that the king was elected by the people, or 'elected kingship', is anchored in what he calls the 'great lineage' tradition, which was marginalised by King Mongkut and his successors in favour of an emphasis on the Chakri dynasty or bloodline. *Thailand's Theory of Monarchy: The Vessantara Jātaka and the Idea of the Perfect Man* (New York: SUNY Press, 2016), especially Chapters 3 and 4.

70 These 10 virtues are: charity; high moral character; renunciation; wisdom; strength; patience; truthfulness; resolution; kindness; and equanimity.

71 The five common Buddhist precepts are: to abstain from harming living beings; stealing; sexual misconduct; lying; and intoxication.

72 The additional three precepts observed on holy days are: to abstain from eating at the wrong time (i.e. eat only between sunrise and noon); to abstain from dancing, music, visiting shows and wearing make-up, flowers or decorative accessories; and abstaining from sitting or sleeping in a luxurious place, and from sleeping too much.

73 Prince Dhani Nivat, "The Old Siamese Conception of the Monarchy," 94.

74 *Ibid*, 95.

75 *Ibid*.

of the *Thammasat* was an "'Inspired Lore' which was the work supposedly of a superior agency, a Constitution in fact which was not to be tampered with even by the highest in the land."[76]

Put another way, Dhani was saying to the monarchy's challengers that, because the *Thammasat* constitution represented universal truths and was inviolable, this constitution was better than their new-fangled imported model. He reinforced the point by claiming that traditionally even the king's own ordinances and decisions (*rajasat*, or what Dhani called "King's Lore") did not have the "lasting form and authority" of *Thammasat*, which was imposed by (he repeated) a "superior agency".[77]

After cloaking the new monarchy with the spiritual-moral aura and protective paternalism that had been features of traditional monarchy, Dhani tried to show that the Thai monarchy had already successfully adapted to the modern age. He wrote that from the time of King Mongkut:

> in the bi-annual ceremonies of swearing allegiance to the king on the part of officials and the Court, the King initiated the custom of himself giving the sovereign's pledge to be loyal to His people thereby making it a bi-partite instead of the former one-sided oath of allegiance. His son Chulalongkorn followed up in the same policy by his abolition of slavery and his renunciation of the Treasury to form the nucleus of State property which he had just organized, and to which he transferred all the revenues from taxes and dues hitherto paid to the King. King Rama VI [Vajiravudh], grandson of the pioneer in reform, made further considerable sacrifices and thereby modified again the old conception of kingship. All these changes came from the sovereign's own initiative.[78]

---

76   *Ibid*, 98.
77   Recent scholarship has questioned Prince Dhani's interpretation of the role of the *Thammasat* in law-making in Siam. See Chris Baker and Pasuk Phongpaichit, tr. and ed. *The Palace Law of Ayutthaya and the Thammasat: Law and Kingship in Siam* (Ithaca: Cornell University Press, 2016), 29–31.
78   Prince Dhani Nivat, "The Old Siamese Conception of the Monarchy," 103.

Dhani also reminded his audience that the old conception of the monarchy was "kept before the public eye in literature, in sermons and in any other channel of publicity".[79]

In brief, Dhani created a modern ideology of kingship that rooted the living Thai king in a rich and even wondrous tradition that, he claimed, outshone the ideology and trappings of democracy, like constitutions. At the same time, his ideology gave the monarchy a license to adapt to the modern age, including by promoting itself through whatever media became available. In the struggle between traditionalists and reformers for public and political support, and ultimately for legitimacy, Dhani put some arrows into the quiver of Bhumibol and the advocates of a strong monarchy.

Yet it is worth digressing for a moment to consider whether the magic of the Thai monarchy could coexist with the secular magic of democracy. According to Theravada[80] Buddhist principles, the king sat at the top of a moral hierarchy because he had accumulated the most *karma*, or the merit an individual accumulated through generosity, virtue and mental discipline in previous lives and, possibly, earlier in this life.[81] On the basis of his accumulated merit the king was a *bodhisatta*, or future Buddha, and everyone else in the kingdom had a place beneath the king that was determined by their relative, and lesser, *karma*. Reconciling democratic theory with these Buddhist principles is difficult:

> In such a moral hierarchy liberal conceptions of democracy were naturally anathema, since in a democracy commoners were equal to *bodhisatta*-kings—in fact, they could be superior if they were able to organize themselves into

---

79   *Ibid.*
80   Theravada (or the 'Way of the Elders') Buddhism, which emerged between 500 and 300 BCE, is common in Thailand, Myanmar, Cambodia and Laos. The other main school of Buddhism, the Mahayana (or the 'Great Vehicle'), is more common in China, Japan, Korea, Tibet and Vietnam.
81   According to Buddhist theory, a person's body ends at death but consciousness continues and is re-born in some other realms of existence. The realm is determined by the merit one has accumulated (or not accumulated) at the time of each death.

political parties and win power. This was a revolutionary idea from the point of view of Theravada political theory, since it implied that those who were lowest on the scale of merit, hence morally inferior beings, had a more legitimate claim to power than the morally perfect being, the *bodhisatta*. It would mean literally the triumph of evil (those of low merit) over good (those of higher merit). Democratic theory imposed a morality that directly contradicted the pre-existing Buddhist one: the "people" were morally pure while the absolute monarch was "despotic". Democratic politics thus posed a mortal threat to the theory of the state under the *bodhisatta*-king.[82]

Three years after Dhani instructed both Ananda and Bhumibol on kingship, Thaksin Shinawatra was born in Chiang Mai. Over half a century later, some Thais interpreted Thaksin's unprecedented electoral support as a mortal threat to the magic of the monarchy.

Symbiosis between Military and Monarchy

The political system that Sarit Thanarat built continued for several years after his death in 1963, and US financial support continued to underwrite it. "Dollars consolidated Thailand's militarized state"[83] and in that state "the military officer elite became somewhat like a ruling caste, distinguished by its unique dress and rituals, vaunting its own purity, and claiming extensive privileges. Generals took over executive posts in state enterprises, and honorary posts in sports and social organizations. By their own machismo and corruption, they re-legitimized old-fashioned male privileges and habits of exploiting political power for personal gain."[84]

---

82   Jory, *Thailand's Theory of Monarchy*, 184.
83   Baker and Pasuk, *A History of Thailand*, 148.
84   *Ibid*, 169.

At the same time, a "symbiotic relationship" emerged between the military and the monarchy:

> Each needed the other for continued pursuit of its own objectives. Neither fully trusted the other, but each had by necessity found ways to accommodate the other's fundamental requirements. Most directly, the military's continued control over the political process—as exemplified in its periodic seizures of power—could not succeed without explicit or implicit support from the palace. At the same time, the palace has depended increasingly on the military as the guardian of national security and the continuity of the throne itself. Military leaders adeptly turned any opposition to the regime into opposition to the royal institution.[85]

This symbiotic relationship between the monarchy and the military has continued, practically unbroken, since Sarit's 1957 coup. Subsequent military leaders either sought or claimed the king's endorsement when they took over. Bhumibol either sanctioned their actions or responded ambiguously; he never denied them.[86] Early signs are that King Vajiralongkorn (Rama X), who trained as a military officer, takes his commander-in-chief responsibilities seriously. He has assumed direct control of soldiers responsible for his security. He has expressed views on how military personnel should dress, salute and cut their hair. He is reported to take a close interest in senior military appointments. He has also continued his father's practice of

---

85   David Morell and Chai-anan Samudavanija, *Political Conflict in Thailand: Reform, Reaction, Revolution* (Cambridge (Mass): Oelgeschlager, Gunn and Hain, 1982), 64.

86   In 1966, Fred W. Riggs wrote that all governments since 1932 had sought the King's endorsement: "In all the subsequent crises, coups and power shifts among the Thai elite, no matter by what means power has been seized, the new rulers have never failed to seek and obtain the king's sanction, and hence to legitimize their rule in the eyes of the masses, for whom the only true order is that which stems from the royal house." *Thailand: The Modernization of a Bureaucratic Polity*, 107. This is equally true of all crises, coups and power shifts since 1966.

having a large number of retired generals on the Privy Council, the king's main personal advisory body.

A Confident King Exercises Authority

The 1960s and 1970s were troubled times. Thais were confronted with wars in their neighbourhood, a communist insurgency at home, inflows of massive US aid, thousands of US troops based on their soil or visiting for "rest and recuperation", a boom in the sex and tourism industries, rapid economic growth, unprecedented urbanization and social change, and highly visible corruption at all levels of government. In this troubled and naughty world, the steadfast and family-oriented Bhumibol seemed to offer assurance and decency.

By emerging as a symbol of stability and virtue in a period of insecurity and venality, Bhumibol accumulated authority that was unrelated to his ties with the military. From the late 1960s, already 20 years on the throne, he started to engage more directly in political issues. He raised questions publicly about army violence and other heavy-handed government actions, student rebelliousness, the plight of hill-tribes, the suitability of imported ideas and practices, land speculation and corruption. Eventually, aware of international and domestic criticism of both the decade-long absence of constitutional government and the excesses of the military rulers, the king began to advocate for a constitution and elections. And, eventually, a reluctant military obliged—with a semi-democratic constitution in 1968 and an election in 1969.

Elected MPs, like their predecessors since the 1930s, began to question the authority of the military (including the authority of the appointed Senate, which was dominated by generals). Worse still, from the military's point of view, elected MPs blocked the military budget. In 1971, the frustrated prime minister, General Thanom Kittikhachon, revoked the constitution and dissolved parliament. By October 1973, public sentiment within Thailand's growing middle class swelled into a massive demonstration in Bangkok and a standoff between the military and demonstrators. The demonstrators moved towards the palace and asked Bhumibol to intervene. He granted them an audience, after gaining a lukewarm commitment from the military to draft a new constitution. The next day, though, clashes between demonstrators and security forces led to over 70 deaths. Critically, with the tacit support of the king, the army chief General Krit Sivara, whose army faction had been alienated by the Thanom faction, refused to send troops to suppress student demonstrators. The military was split and Thanom was suddenly powerless. Bhumibol pressed Thanom and other senior generals to go into exile. He then nominated his own prime minister as well as a body to help draft a new constitution. Bhumibol was exercising dispute settlement powers that had not been seen since the absolute monarchy.

Political Instability and Military Consolidation

As in the 1946–47 period, from 1974 to 1976 Thailand had an elected civilian government. In the legislature, neither the lower house (House of Representatives) nor the Senate had serving military officers or civilian officials, and the prime ministers were elected. The absence of serving military officers and civilian officials meant that this parliament focused more on issues affecting the rural electorate than previous parliaments had done.[87] Notwithstanding these signs of greater democratization, the elected legislature did not emerge as a forum through which student, peasant and labour organizations could express their grievances. They continued to favour protests on the streets and in the countryside. That was partly because it took well over a year to draft the new constitution and elect the new parliament; partly because the new and fragmented parliament (containing 22 political parties) led to

---

87   Morell and Chai-anan, *Political Conflict in Thailand*, 121–2.

three unstable coalition governments in 20 months; and partly because the implementation of well-meaning reforms was in the hands of a resentful bureaucracy that was feeling, uncharacteristically, side-lined.[88] In addition, the army-controlled media "condemned parliament as another route to communist victory".[89]

The military had other weapons that secured it a major political role. Behind the scenes, it continued to penetrate rural areas through the government's and the king's development projects.[90] The 1974 Constitution formally legitimised this role as well as the military's role in internal security, stating that, in addition to the conventional role of the military to engage in war, the Thai military's duties included protection of the monarchy, suppression of rebellions and riots, protection of state security and national development. These additional missions "paved the way for the military's role in other socio-political-economic affairs".[91] Subsequent constitutions, including constitutions promulgated by civilian governments, have contained similar clauses. Also, since 1975, national economic and social development plans, including plans approved by civilian governments, have included national security as an integral part of socio-economic development.[92] In brief, the higher political profile of the legislature, albeit temporary, did not signal the eclipse of the military's political power.

Monarchy: Magic and Might Merge

Nor did the higher political profile of the legislature signify a more passive monarchy. Whether Bhumibol deliberately sought to play such a direct role in resolving the 1973 political crisis, or whether circumstances thrust the role upon him, his actions entrenched the monarchy as a traditional institution that could intercede in the modern period. The events of 1973 showed that he could withdraw

---

88 *Ibid*, 131–2.
89 Baker and Pasuk, *A History of Thailand*, 193.
90 Puangthong, *The Central Role of Thailand's Internal Security Operations Command*, 9–12.
91 *Ibid*, 14.
92 *Ibid*, 15–22.

legitimacy from an incumbent government, choose his own prime minister, and set Thailand on a new course.

Over the next three years, Bhumibol would intercede again. Some would argue that he had a responsibility to intercede because the survival of Thailand was threatened by an accumulation of dangers: communist insurgency; student protests; labour and peasant unrest; a global economic crisis; severe unemployment; corruption; abuse of power; political violence; crime; the unpopular presence of US troops; US-China rapprochement; and regional instability, which included, worryingly for the Thai monarchy, the abolition of the monarchy in Laos. In tumultuous times, they would argue, the king had no choice.

Others would argue that, though the times were indeed tumultuous, Bhumibol could have chosen differently, that he could have encouraged advocates of a representative democracy a little more, and encouraged the military and their backers a lot less.

Among the choices the king (and, increasingly, the queen) made was to foster the emergence of three radical movements—Nawaphon, Red Gaurs and Village Scouts—to counter the mobilization of students, labour and farmers. Previously, the monarchy drew active support from the old elite (extended royal family, court officials, senior bureaucrats) and the emerging new elite (military officers, business-people), and it could rely on the spontaneous respect and affection of the broader population. In contrast, Nawaphon, Red Gaur and Village Scouts were well-organized movements with a broad social base and strong political and financial backing from security officials, especially ISOC, and the expanding business community. All three movements were also intensely ideological, dedicated to defending—violently, if necessary—the monarchy, nation and Buddhism. For the first time, the monarchy had its own vigilantes.

On 6 October 1976, these vigilantes were part of a brutal police-led assault on student activists at Thammasat University. Official records say that 46 students were killed; other estimates are much higher. At the university and elsewhere, several thousand people were arrested. Several thousand more, mostly students, fled Bangkok and joined the communist movement. On the evening of 6 October, the military staged another coup. The elected government, constitution, parliament and all political parties were abolished. Martial law was imposed. Political gatherings were banned and the press was censored. The coup leaders said: "The takeover of power ... is aimed at safeguarding the institution of the monarchy. The king and the royal family are being protected... They are all safe."[93] Two months later the king said, "the Thai military has the most important role in defence of our country at all times, ready always to carry out its duty to protect the country".[94]

Lèse Majesté

A trigger for the violence was a claim that, on 5 October, one of the actors participating in a mock hanging at Thammasat University had been made up to resemble Crown Prince Vajiralongkorn (the mock hanging was part of a protest against the earlier murder of two students in the nearby province of Nakhon Pathom).[95] This provoked accusations of *lèse majesté,* which many Thais consider an offence against the sacred qualities of the monarchy, as well as a crime. The spectre of *lèse majesté* would partly explain the absence of public protests after the appalling violence of 6 October; another disincentive was the risk of brutal counterattacks by the police and vigilantes.

This element of the 6 October tragedy showed how the *lèse majesté* law—another legacy of Thailand's history of uninterrupted traditional political authority—was a further arrow in the quiver of advocates

---

93 Quoted in Handley, *The King Never Smiles,* 237.
94 Quoted in Thongchai, *Siam Mapped,* 167.
95 Whether the resemblance to the Crown Prince was deliberate or accidental has not been established; and the photograph of the actor may have been doctored before it was published in newspapers. Additionally, the actors involved had already surrendered themselves to the Prime Minister before the attacks on the students began.

of a strong monarchy. The *lèse majesté* provisions (Section 112) of the Criminal Code outlaw whomever "defames, insults or threatens the King, the Queen, the Heir-apparent or the Regent". And the Thai constitution says: "The King shall be enthroned in a position of revered worship and shall not be violated. No person shall expose the King to any sort of accusation or action."

The law was used by Sarit's government to interpret anti-government protests as an attack against the monarchy. In addition, as a result of the mock hanging, the penalty for *lèse majesté* was lifted to imprisonment from a minimum of three years and a maximum of 15 years, instead of the previous maximum penalty of no more than three years (and no minimum term). This penalty remains in place. At times, including recently, the risk of being charged with *lèse majesté* has deterred open debate about political reform in Thailand.[96]

Premocracy

From 1976 to 1988, Thailand had several military governments or military-dominated but semi-elected governments. From 1980, these governments were led by General Prem Tinsulanond, who enjoyed the king's open support as well as the support of a broad but unstable parliamentary coalition which was unable to agree on a civilian prime minister, leaving the leadership of the government in the hands of the general. Elected MPs, like their predecessors in earlier elected legislatures, questioned the military's share of the budget, lucrative privileges enjoyed by the military, and the lack of transparency around arms purchases. Initially, though, Prem was threatened more by power struggles within the army than by anti-military sentiment in either the parliament or society. For eight years he balanced, on one hand, the interests of the military and the monarchy in preserving their authority with, on the other hand,

---

96   *Lèse majesté* is discussed in more detail in Chapter Six.

the interests of the legislature in securing a greater share of national resources for its constituents. Increasingly, those constituents had been drawn into a flourishing cash economy and, increasingly, the MPs were linked to the business community.

During Prem's period in office, domestic and international pressure gradually mounted for a more accountable military and a more democratic government. The military also became less allergic to some ideals of democracy, partly because the promise of greater democratization had helped to deflate the communist insurgency. At the same time, the monarchy assumed an even larger place in the national ideology. Previously, the "king" had shared equal billing with the "nation" and "religion". In the wake of the events of October 1976, the government

> concluded that the new touchstone would be "nation, religion, monarchy, and democracy with the King as head of state". In practice, this differed from the old formula in two ways. First, the monarchy would assume a much more prominent role as the focus for national loyalties in comparison with the other two components of the old trinity. Second, democracy was added in recognition that the 1973–76 era had revealed aspirations for liberty, participation, and self-expression which were too powerful to suppress.[97]

Another Elected Government Falls

Eventually, these aspirations for liberty, participation, and self-expression forced Prem to stand aside for an elected prime minister. After the 1988 elections the leader of the Chart Thai Party, Chatichai Choonhavan, became prime minister of a coalition government. Because the economy was booming and the perceived threats from

---

97 Baker and Pasuk, *A History of Thailand*, 236.

communists, students, peasants and workers had subsided, in 1988 the legislature had its best chance yet to establish itself as a central, sovereign institution in Thailand's political system, which could help to mediate and arbitrate political disputes. But in early 1991, after only two and a half years in office, Chatichai's government, like previous elected governments, was felled by the military.

Why was another elected government—and the legislature that gave birth to it—discarded so easily? First, generals and senior officials begrudged Chatichai's decision to appoint his fellow parliamentarians to ministerial jobs and other loyal nominees to key positions in state-owned enterprises, often robbing serving and retired military officers and civilian officials of their sinecures. Chatichai also relied on his own think-tank (called *Baan Phitsanulok*) to rival the previously influential National Economic and Social Development Board, and he tried to make the bureaucracy in general more accountable to the elected government.

Secondly, the military chafed at Chatichai's cuts to its budget and efforts to make arms purchases more transparent ("commissions" for arms deals were a common source of revenue for senior officers). And Chatichai's Indochina policy of "turning battlefields into marketplaces" reduced the military's role in foreign policy-making, as well as its profits from lucrative commerce in the border regions.

Thirdly, Bangkok-based businesses (and their political patrons) felt disadvantaged vis-à-vis provincial businesses (and their political patrons) because Chatichai spent public funds on infrastructure and development projects in the provinces, reflecting the growing power in the legislature of provincial MPs.

Fourthly, Chatichai's government was brazenly corrupt. A traditional Thai expression for corruption is to "eat the country". Chatichai's government was known as the "buffet cabinet" where ministers were offered "all you can eat" as they distributed some of the public funds designated for infrastructure and development projects to themselves and their associates. After the coup, Chatichai and some other ministers were charged with being "unusually wealthy"—a Thai euphemism for corrupt.

Fighting Like Dogs

The performance of the Chatichai government reinforced the low estimation in which some Thais had held elected politicians for decades. As early as 1949, villagers in Bang Chan on the outskirts of Bangkok are reported to have said of politicians:

> Why do they fight each other? They must be really fighting for their own pockets. It's not X versus Y; it's one gangster fighting against another gangster.

> Another said: "The whole thing is just the result of rivalries among politicians. They fight like dogs."

> A third commented more vehemently: "Curse those evil men of politics who use their position to collect wealth, and those who speak of democracy by mouth but who do not act in democratic ways."

> And a priest said: "It is painful to see bloodshed among the Thai people. We condemn the Chinese because they fight each other, but this time history will record that we Thai did not live in peace."[98]

About three decades later, Thai views on politics and politicians had not changed:

---

98   Quoted in Riggs, *Thailand: The Modernization of a Bureaucratic Polity*, 243–4.

The image of politics in Thailand is of an activity that is dirty, immoral, manipulative, corrupt, and chaotic. Politicians are seen as power-hungry, abusive, self-seeking, quarrelsome, good-for-nothing, inefficient, only-talk-but-nothing-is-done types of people. The often-cited reason for every coup in Thailand is that politicians have caused confusion and trouble, obstructing smooth administration of the government. Newspapers, government officials, and a few intellectuals have branded some elected politicians "political prostitutes" who sell themselves and their votes in the House of Representatives.[99]

Elections, and the hurly-burly surrounding them, did not find a home easily in Thailand. In 1991, the historian Nidhi Eoseewong wrote: "The time taken for an election nowadays, beginning from the time they start throwing mud at one another and shooting election agents in the head, is much longer than the time taken fighting over the throne in olden times."[100]

Public disenchantment with politicians and electoral politics generally was reflected in the low turn-out at elections. After the 1975 elections, when only 47 per cent of the voting age population voted, a survey showed that people chose not to vote because: "(1) the voters felt that candidates were primarily concerned with their own self-interest rather than with national concerns (84 per cent); (2) people were cynical because most candidates in previous elections had failed to fulfil their promises once elected (78 per cent); and (3) the respondents felt that there were too many political parties (69 per cent)."[101] The same sentiments would have affected voting behaviour in the 1988 election that brought Chatichai to office—when only 54 per cent of the voting-age population voted.

---

99 Morell and Chai-anan, *Political Conflict in Thailand*, 25.
100 Nidhi, "The Thai Cultural Constitution."
101 Morell and Chai-anan, *Political Conflict in Thailand*, 114.

Military Missteps and Monarchy Triumphs

In 1991, rather than have the military take on the responsibility of government itself, the leader of the anti-Chatichai coup, General Suchinda Kraprayun, appointed a respected civilian, Anand Panyarachun, as prime minister—perhaps to gain favour with the palace, which held Anand in high regard. Anand appointed respected technocrats as his ministers, who gained a reputation for governing cleanly and efficiently. They were untroubled by a parliament, which the military had sacked. After an election in March 1992, however, Suchinda took on the prime ministership himself, reneging on an earlier undertaking not to do so. Protests, and ultimately violence, erupted on the streets of Bangkok. Between 40 and 60 people were killed. On the evening of 19 May, national television showed Suchinda and the leader of the protesters, Chamlong Srimuang, prostrating before the king, who asked them to

> sit down and face the facts together in a conciliatory manner, and not in a confrontational manner, to find a way to solve the problem, because our country does not belong to any one or two persons, but belongs to everyone ... What is the point of anyone feeling proud of being the winner, when standing on a pile of ruins and rubble? ... You will feel much better, knowing that you have done the right thing. How you will achieve this will depend on your joint cooperative efforts. These are my observations.[102]

Afterwards, the king asked Anand (rather than the legislature's nominee, who was an elected MP) to again head an appointed government, which again governed competently.

Analysts are still debating whether, through his intervention,

---

102 Quoted in Handley, *The King Never Smiles*, 355.

Bhumibol was encouraging democracy or protecting the *status quo*. But at the time most of the Thai public saw a wise, fatherly king who protected them by admonishing trouble-making politicians and generals and using his charismatic leadership to restore calm. At that point, he was better and bigger than politicians and generals. He could bring order and harmony. This image of Bhumibol as a political peacemaker, burnished by the palace and governments, persisted for the rest of his reign. In 1992, the monarchy became the supreme mediator and arbitrator of Thai politics, without recourse to the judiciary, legislature or electorate.

Eclipse of the Military

In 1992, for the first time, the military was punished for its abuse of power, especially its brutal massacre of dozens of unarmed protesters. "The military, once viewed in a positive light as the protector of the kingdom, was now seen by many as merely soldiers firing into crowds of unarmed protestors demonstrating for democracy. This image would prove hard to shake, and it gave civilian policymakers leverage over the next several years to formulate and implement policies without fear of soldiers breathing down their necks."[103] The Anand government sacked some senior military officers and deprived others of their lucrative positions in state enterprises. Another source of private income was closed after the government imposed greater scrutiny of military procurement and projects. The military budget was cut.

From Anand to 1997

The post-Anand governments of Chuan Leekpai (1992–95 and 1997–2001), Banharn Silpa-archa (1995–96) and Chavalit Yongchaiyudh (1996–97) were elected, but each of them was a coalition of several

---

103 Paul Chambers, "A Short History of Military Influence in Thailand," in *Knights of the Realm: Thailand's Military and Police, Then and Now*, ed. Paul Chambers (Bangkok: White Lotus, 2013), 232.

parties and therefore perpetually unstable and not always efficient. Ministerial reshuffles were common because coalition survival depended on all parties and factions gaining regular access to the status and spoils of office. The legislature was more a venue for politicking than for policy-making, and again it became a clearing house for business deals.

The bloody events of 1992—and their causes and aftermath— eventually spawned a Constitution Drafting Assembly, comprised of members who had a wide range of professional experiences and who consulted widely during their deliberations. The 1997 Constitution— sometimes referred to as the People's Constitution—introduced reforms aimed at overcoming Thailand's historical predicament of having either entrenched military-dominated governments that restricted civil liberties or short-lived elected multi-party and fractious coalition governments that succumbed to the temptations of "money politics".[104]

The draft of the 1997 Constitution was finalised when Thailand was engulfed in the Asian financial crisis, its biggest economic emergency in decades, which saw thousands of businesses collapse and left millions of Thais unemployed. Naturally, as it was a very new set of written rules for Thai politics, when it was first drafted the new constitution was controversial. But its opponents were silenced because

> the draft's fate became bound up with the economy's slide into the crisis in 1997. Bangkok's businessmen and middle class began to blame the crisis on mismanagement by politicians, and seized on the constitution as a way to bring politics into line with the needs of the globalized economy. White-collar street demonstrations demanded passage of the constitution.

---

104 The instability and ineffectiveness of coalition governments is reflected in the following statistics: from 1988 to 1997 the composition of the governments changed 12 times; over 235 individuals served in the cabinet, sharing 445 separate appointments; and there were 10 finance ministers, 11 foreign ministers and nine interior ministers. See Michael Kelly Connors, *Democracy and National Identity in Thailand* (Copenhagen: NIAS Press, 2008), 153.

> The draft was passed on 27 September 1997, the same day that
> the government concluded an agreement with the IMF.[105]

The 1997 Constitution was different from Thailand's previous 12 constitutions. Like Chulalongkorn's reforms of the 1890s and the constitution of 1932, the constitution of 1997 was an attempt to put Thailand's governance on a new footing. The drafters of the 1997 Constitution tried to answer assorted prayers: the prayers of Thais who were fed up with bullying military governments and ineffectual civilian governments; the prayers of Thais who wanted greater freedom of expression and less corruption; the prayers of business people who wanted a stable government to rescue them from the Asian financial crisis; the prayers of NGOs who wanted greater community consultation on development projects; and the silent prayers of Thais who realised that political stability could not rely forever on King Bhumibol's mediation.

---

105 Baker and Pasuk, *A History of Thailand*, 260.

Chapter Three

REFORMATION UNRAVELLING: SINCE 1997

Nothing can bring me home apart from royal kindness
or the power of the people.[1]

The 1997 Constitution tried to shift Thailand from a five-branch form
of government towards a more conventional three-branch form,
under which political disputes would be mediated and arbitrated
within the legislature and judiciary, or by the electorate. Both houses
of the legislature were fully elected for the first time and, in a bid to lift
the public image of the legislature, all parliamentarians had to have a
university degree. Elaborate arrangements were put in place to elect
an apolitical Senate, which was to play a critical role in overseeing the
selection of principled and capable judges and commissioners to serve
in the courts and independent agencies. The executive was released
from the burdens of unstable coalition governments by an electoral
system that favoured larger political parties. Through party lists, the
electoral system also allowed for the election of 100 MPs who need not
be grass-roots politicians, and who could bring technocratic expertise
to the ministry. In addition, the new constitution strengthened the
powers of the prime minister.

The judiciary was expanded, with the establishment of a
Constitutional Court, administrative courts and a slew of independent

---

1   Thaksin Shinawatra in 2008, quoted in Pasuk Phongpaichit and Chris Baker, *Thaksin* (Chiang Mai: Silkworm Books, 2009, second expanded edition), 335.

agencies, the roles of which are reflected in their names: National Anti-Corruption Commission (NACC), Electoral Commission, Human Rights Commission, Ombudsman's Office and State Audit Commission. The judiciary was also given unprecedented authority to check and balance the power of the executive and legislature, and to protect individual rights and freedoms that, for the first time, were spelled out in the charter.

The military lost its hold over the legislature because both houses of parliament were elected. The power of military courts was curbed and military-controlled media outlets faced stiffer competition. The monarchy, while still "enthroned in a position of revered worship and not to be violated", was expected to play a political role only in extreme circumstances.

Thaksin Shinawatra and Popular Legitimacy

The 1997 Constitution created some of the conditions that led in January 2001 to the emergence of a prime minister, Thaksin Shinawatra, with strong electoral support, or popular legitimacy. In the first election under the 1997 Constitution, he had the political skills and financial resources to gain 248 seats in the 500-seat parliament, and shortly afterwards his Thai Rak Thai Party absorbed smaller parties to give his government a comfortable majority. In the 2005 elections, Thai Rak Thai secured 377 seats. In particular, Thaksin was able to tap into the aspirations of the people variously called middle-income peasants, cosmopolitan villagers and urbanised villagers.[2] His election victory, like most previous Thai electoral victories, owed something to the use of money to gain the support of candidates as well as voters. But in 2001 rural voters of

---

2   Walker, *Thailand's Political Peasants* (Madison: University of Wisconsin Press, 2012), 221; Charles Keyes, *Finding Their Voice*, 185–8; Naruemon Thabchumpon and Donald McCargo, "Urbanized Villagers in the 2010 Thai Redshirt Protests," *Asian Survey*, Vol 51, Number 6 (November–December 2011), 999–1009.

the populous northeast and north, as well as the urban poor who often hailed from these regions, were also won over with Thaksin's well-researched and well-advertised promises of a moratorium on rural debt, a revolving fund for village development and a universal healthcare scheme.

Thaksin's ascendancy, especially in 2001, owed a lot to his ability to convince business-people and the wider community that he could lift the Thai economy out of its post-1997 gloom. In 2000, the CEO of Thailand's biggest business conglomerate, Dhanin Chearavanont, said: "This is an age of economic war. It's crucial that we have a prime minister who understands business and the economy." The CEO of Thailand's biggest bank, Chatri Sophanpanich, said he supported Thaksin "because as a businessman, he understands business".[3]

In 2001, the Thaksin government appeared to represent a dream come true: it had the clearest electoral mandate in Thai history; it was therefore more stable than previous elected governments; it was governing more efficiently than its predecessors; and it was still free of the allegations of corruption that had tarnished earlier governments. In addition, if the health of a legislature is partly measured by participation rates in elections, the legislature was fairly healthy under Thaksin and the Thai Rak Thai Party (and their successors: first the Palang Prachachon Party, then the Pheu Thai Party). In the 2001, 2005, 2007 and 2011 elections, 70 per cent, 73 per cent, 76 per cent and 69 per cent respectively of the voting age population cast a vote. The following graph shows the growing appetite in Thailand for electoral politics.

---

3   Quoted in Pasuk and Baker, *Thaksin*, 70.

Graph 1 Voter turnout for general elections, by Election dates

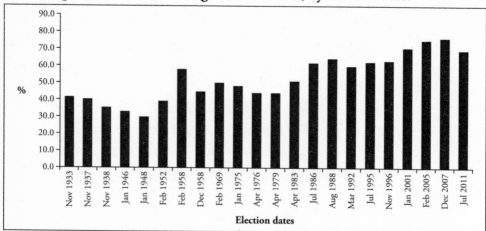

If, as the constitution drafters imagined, the absence of multi-party coalition governments was a sign of a healthy legislature and a more effective executive, the signs were also good. In those four elections Thai Rak Thai and its successor parties secured 50 per cent, 75 per cent, 49 per cent and 53 per cent of the parliamentary seats; its closest rival at each election was the Democrat Party, which secured 26 per cent, 19 per cent, 34 per cent and 32 per cent.[4]

The elected government could focus on policy making rather than politicking, and it could assume some of the power that typically rested with an unaccountable bureaucracy. Drawing on his authority as prime minister—in other words, as the head of the political executive—Thaksin tried to reform the administrative executive, or bureaucracy. He believed the bureaucracy's main task was to implement policies determined by the elected government, so he restructured the bureaucracy and streamlined some of its functions. In keeping with the globally fashionable New Public Management philosophy at the time, he also tried to apply business

---

4   All percentages are rounded. The results of the 2006 and 2014 elections are not included because the Democrat Party boycotted both of them, thereby skewing the results. Also, neither of these elections led to the formation of a new government; both of the Democrat Party boycotts ultimately led to military coups.

principles to public administration, creating "CEO governors" and "CEO ambassadors" who were directed to put the nation's economic interests first and to take risks.

Supremacy of the Law and Judicial Independence

The new constitutional arrangements also had a profound effect on the judiciary. For several years after 1997, the Constitutional Court delivered weighty judgments that would have pleased the drafters of the Constitution. It restricted the powers of military courts. It made well-judged decisions when considering politically-motivated petitions against the elected government's economic policy-making in response to the 1997 financial crisis. Another important decision set a precedent preventing the government from using its lower-house strength to avoid Senate approval of legislation. The court also ruled that the constitution's gender equality provisions meant that married women were no longer legally required to assume the surname of their husbands. And it strongly backed the National Anti-Corruption Commission's efforts to punish wayward politicians; by 2002 Constitutional Court judges had endorsed 17 of 18 decisions by the commission's decisions to disqualify politicians for corrupt practices.

A telling example of the Court's contribution to the new constitutional arrangements was its support for the Electoral Commission's firm stance against fraud and vote-buying during the campaign for the 2000 Senate elections and, in particular, against any candidate who did not meet the new constitution's strict criterion of non-partisanship. "The commissioners had the mettle to disqualify the wife of the Minister of Interior, the chief political advisor of the Minister of Interior, the elder brother of the Deputy Minister of Interior, the wife of the Minister of Justice, the sister of the Deputy Minister of Agriculture, and the wives, siblings, canvassers, and business associates of numerous members of parliament, provincial governors, and the city mayors."[5] As a result, the elections were not finalised for four months, after five rounds of voting. A year later, the Electoral Commission expelled 10 senators, including the President of the Senate, for violations of the electoral law.

Another telling example was the Constitutional Court's unanimous confirmation of the National Anti-Corruption Commission's ruling in 2000 against the politically powerful Major General Sanan Kachornprasart, who had lodged a false statement of his assets and liabilities. Sanan was no ordinary politician; he was Deputy Prime Minister, Minister for Interior and Secretary General of the Democrat Party, and he had been a prominent political figure since 1977. After the Court's ruling, Sanan was immediately dismissed from all his political positions and banned from politics for five years.

The number of cases brought before the new administrative courts, and the quality of their judgments, also met the high standards set by the drafters of the 1997 Constitution, although the courts did not become fully operational until 2001 after implementing legislation was passed in 1999. Between 2001 and 2009, the courts dealt with about 44,000 cases, providing a new and improved avenue for holding state officials accountable. Most cases had limited impact, but they provided ground-breaking protections for ordinary citizens. For example, in 2004 the Central Administrative Court ordered the Office of Atomic Energy and Peace to compensate survivors of a radiation leak. Other cases had wider impact. In 2005 the Supreme Administrative Court ruled against the Thaksin government's major policy initiative to privatise the Electricity Generating Authority of Thailand. The Court accepted the arguments of non-government organizations, labour unions and opposition political parties that no mandated public consultations had occurred, the sale of shares was illegal, and

---

5   James R. Klein, "The Battle for Rule of Law in Thailand: The Role of the Constitutional Court," in *The Constitutional Court of Thailand: The Provisions and Working of the Court*, ed. by Amara Raksasataya and James R. Klein (Bangkok: Constitution for the People Society and Asia Foundation, 2003), 57.

consumers and employees were inadequately safeguarded. In 2009 the same court suspended the development of 65 projects worth $8 billion in Rayong province because health impact assessments were inadequate.

Judicial Independence meets Popular Legitimacy

But a court case against the newly-elected Thaksin exposed a gap between the words in a principled constitution and the deeds of fallible humans. In August 2001, the Constitutional Court had to rule on a NACC decision of December 2000 that while he was a minister in the Chavalit government (1996–97) Thaksin had intentionally concealed assets valued at Bt4.5 billion (approximately US$105 million in early 2001) in the names of his housekeeper, driver, maid, security guard and business colleagues. In nine similar cases against serving politicians, the Court had endorsed the Commission's decisions and all the defendants had been barred from political office for five years.[6] So the signs for Thaksin appeared ominous—and even more so because just a few hours before the decision on his case the judges had ruled by a 12:1 margin against Senator Prayuth Mahagitsiri, whose case was comparable with Thaksin's.[7]

But millions of Thais had voted for Thaksin's party, even though they already knew that the NACC had said Thaksin should be ineligible for political office for five years because he had concealed assets worth billions of baht. Prominent figures, including the highly regarded and conservative social critic Prawase Wasi, who had played a leadership role in initiating the 1997 Constitution, publicly supported Thaksin. After more than three years of gloom following the Asian financial crisis, he and many other Thais saw Thaksin as the answer to Thailand's economic and political malaise. Thaksin's supporters persuaded 1.4 million Thais to sign a petition. Others

6   In the next 14 months, the Court would endorse eight more NACC decisions on the same issue, *ibid*, 70.
7   *Ibid*, 75.

asked the court to postpone its verdict for a year to give Thaksin an opportunity to rescue the country. And 20,000 followers performed religious rites "to purify and strengthen Thaksin's aura so that it would be able to protect him from a guilty verdict".[8] The two men who were ultimately to spearhead the anti-Thaksin yellow-shirt movement— Sondhi Limthongkul and Chamlong Srimuang—openly supported Thaksin at the court. In addition, "Thaksin had deliberately courted popularity, challenging the judges to risk the public discontent that would flare up if he were removed. He dramatized his appearances at the court by arriving on foot and walking through the crowds, shaking hands. He claimed he alone could boost economic growth and rid Thailand of poverty."[9]

The judges of the Constitutional Court ruled in Thaksin's favour by an 8:7 margin. The judges' decision-making and the Court's vote-counting were complex.[10] In brief, in a two-part judgment, four judges said Thaksin wasn't required to declare his assets and four judges said he hadn't intended to conceal his assets. Even though the votes of these judges were in the minority (7:4), they were aggregated, while the votes of the judges in the majority were not. Hence, an 8:7 decision.

A reported remark by one of the Constitutional Court judges, Chumphol na Songkhla, summed up a widely held view at the time: "Who are we to judge that Thaksin is guilty? He was elected by 16 million Thais."[11] Thaksin agreed with Chumphol, but (accurately) said that he had been elected by 11 million Thais. "It's strange," he said, "that the leader who was voted by 11 million people had to bow to the ruling of the NACC and the verdict of the Constitutional Court, two organizations composed only of appointed commissioners and judges, whom people did not have a chance to choose. This is a crucial

---

8   Michael H. Nelson, "Thailand's House Elections of 6 January 2001: Thaksin's Landslide Victory and Subsequent Narrow Escape." In *Thailand's New Politics: KPI Yearbook 2001*, edited by Michael H. Nelson (Bangkok, KPI and White Lotus Press, 2002), 369–70.
9   Pasuk and Baker, *Thaksin*, 2–3.
10   James Klein has written the fullest account. See Klein, "The Battle for the Rule of Law," 71–6.
11   Quoted in Bjorn Dressel, "Judicialization of Politics or Politicization of the Judiciary? Considerations from Recent Events in Thailand," *The Pacific Review*, 23, 5 (2010), 677.

point that we missed. In the USA, only a congressional process can impeach a president."[12]

The day after the judgment, the front-page commentary in the *Bangkok Post* started: "Most Thais are happy with the result because they believe Prime Minister Thaksin Shinawatra is the man with the right policies to alleviate their pain. Businesses are relieved because after months of waiting and guessing, there is political stability and certainty—at least for the short and medium term. A conviction would lead to more months of uncertainty and the economy would suffer even more." But a couple of paragraphs later it warned: "Despite the feeling of euphoria and relief by the majority, a black cloud of uncertainty still hangs over the rule of law under the new constitution. This country and its people have fought long and hard through the decades for a better and more transparent political system where the rule of law prevails over and above that of the individual, no matter who that person may be."[13]

On the same day, *The Nation* concluded that "the verdict was delivered under ambiguous circumstances; and it seems to be a 'political' rather than a 'judicial' decision". The *Bangkok Post* claimed that two judges had planned to vote against Thaksin but changed their minds at the last minute "at the request of a person who has considerable clout". Although no concrete evidence has been produced, the person with considerable clout is reported to have been Prem Tinsulanond, the President of the Privy Council, the king's advisory body.[14] Thirteen years later, an anti-Thaksin figure claimed to this writer that Prem had not intervened; rather, he said, again without any concrete evidence, Thaksin had "promised to look after" at least one of the judges.

---

12 Quoted in Pasuk and Baker, *Thaksin*, 2.
13 *Bangkok Post*, 5 August 2001.
14 Duncan McCargo, "Network Monarchy and Legitimacy Crises in Thailand, *The Pacific Review*, 18, 4 (December 2005), 513; and Thitinan Pongsudhirak, "The Tragedy of the 1997 Constitution," in *Divided Over Thaksin: Thailand's Coup and Problematic Transition*, ed. by John Funston (Singapore, ISEAS, 2009), 33.

Whether these specific stories about behind-the-scenes influence peddling are true matters little. In the Thaksin assets concealment case, the Constitutional Court came under political pressure from a range of sources, and it succumbed. Indeed, in their written decisions, published several weeks later, the judges who cleared Thaksin chose not to rule explicitly on his guilt or innocence. Thaksin and his supporters would argue that the Court succumbed rightly: in a democracy, they would say, why should a few unelected judges have the power to throw out leaders who have been elected? Others would argue that the outcome of the Thaksin assets concealment case was an early sign that the Constitutional Court was not unfailingly independent, regardless of what the constitution might say, and notwithstanding the readiness of the same judges to deliver impartial and cogently argued decisions in other cases.

The Thaksin case was the first major test under the 1997 Constitution of the judiciary's capacity to withstand pressure from the executive, legislature (through pro-Thaksin MPs) and public opinion. The case was a momentous opportunity to demonstrate that the courts, as an independent arbiter of political disputes, could uphold the supremacy of the law. On paper, the Constitution appeared to give the judges greater authority than ever before to protect the interests of the judiciary from political pressure and to advance the rule of law. By a narrow margin, and thanks to a quixotic method of counting votes, the advocates of an independent judiciary—inside and outside the judicial system—were outmanoeuvred. Judges could not, or chose not to, protect the independence of the judiciary and the supremacy of law.

Judiciary under Threat

That said, judges faced a formidable opponent in a challenging environment. For a start, Thaksin's close encounter with the Constitutional Court did not encourage him to respect the authority of the judiciary or to use his authority as a democratically elected prime minister to champion the independence of the judiciary. On the contrary, only a year later he was intimidating the independent institutions and the courts: "Their attitude has to be a correct one. At present we're spending an annual Bt3 billion on independent bodies. If they become antagonistic, I think spending even one baht would be expensive."[15] In 2002, when vacancies arose in the judiciary, Thaksin was able to get people he favoured into these key positions because, over time, he had enticed a sufficient number of notionally independent senators to support his party on most issues, including the selection of a judges and commissioners to serve in the courts and independent agencies.[16] As a result, from 2002, new commissioners on the NACC included a long-time friend of Thaksin's and a former mentor, and new judges on the Constitutional Court included a customs official who had defended one of Thaksin's companies against tax evasion charges, and a former business partner.[17]

CEO Prime Minister

Thaksin's leadership style, electoral popularity, and indifference to the rule of law were not the only reasons he could govern decisively, even brazenly. The new constitution intentionally facilitated strong executive leadership. The framers of the constitution wanted to rid Thailand of unstable, inefficient and corrupt coalition governments, so the new charter strengthened the authority of the elected prime minister vis-à-vis the legislature. First, it required 40 per cent of MPs to agree before a parliamentary no-confidence debate could be launched against the prime minister. Secondly, MPs had to relinquish their parliamentary seats when they became ministers; so if the prime minister sacked them they could not resume their seat in parliament. Thirdly, the prime minister could call an election at 45 days' notice,

---

15   Quoted in Pasuk and Baker, *Thaksin*, 173.
16   For details on how this occurred, see Paul Chambers, "Superfluous, Mischievous or Emancipating: Thailand's Evolving Senate Today," *Journal of Current Southeast Asian Affairs*, 28, 3 (2009), 19–20.
17   Pasuk and Baker, *Thaksin*, 173–6.

but prospective MPs had to have been members of their political party for at least 90 days before the election—so they could no longer threaten to defect to another party.

Thaksin's cabinet felt neither pressure nor obligation to include the parliament in policy development or decision-making. Thaksin "argued that checks and balances, human rights, open debate, and even parliamentary opposition got in the way of his mission".[18] He co-opted and intimidated the media, including through purchasing some outlets and threatening to deny government advertising revenue to others. Thaksin and his cabinet were supreme. Before long, the legislature was again struggling to be relevant; Thaksin rarely attended parliament and parliamentary sessions often lacked a quorum.

Military and Monarchy Provoked

Eventually, Thaksin over-reached. Although untroubled by the rise of Thaksin, the military became upset when he started to interfere in military appointments, promoting his former classmates from the military academy as well as other loyalists and relatives, which included controversially transferring the army commander, General Surayud Chulanont, to make way for them. Most blatantly, in 2003 he elevated his cousin to army commander. These promotions offended Prem. For many years, as president of the Privy Council and as a former prime minister of a military government, Prem had played an active role in military appointments. Prem and the military also resented Thaksin's decision in 2002 to transfer command of security operations in the three southern border provinces from the military to the police.

Most critically, though, Thaksin gave the military political space to oppose him when he left himself open to claims that he questioned the traditional authority of the king. As is the way of politics everywhere, some of these claims were exaggerated or even concocted by political enemies who were keen to bring him down. But some of the claims

---

18   Baker and Pasuk, *A History of Thailand*, 267.

were sustainable. At one end of the spectrum, Thaksin was accused of republicanism. More convincingly, Thaksin's critics alleged that he displayed pictures of himself in poses normally reserved for the king at royal events; appeared without approval at the king's 60th jubilee celebrations; improperly conducted a merit-making ceremony in Temple of Emerald Buddha; and inappropriately appointed an acting Supreme Patriarch in 2004.[19]

Especially after the 2005 elections, which had shown that voter support for Thaksin had grown, supporters of a strong monarchy became more insistent in pointing at Thaksin's alleged failings and flaws, and they claimed that his domestic popularity and international reputation could not match Bhumibol's moral and constitutional authority. Privy councillors—seen as proxies for the king—openly criticised Thaksin and reminded him of the role of the monarchy. Army generals spoke publicly about their duty to protect the monarchy; their voices drowned out murmurings about the benefits of a depoliticised, professional armed forces. Privy councillors and generals publicly accused Thaksin of corruption, mismanagement of the insurgency in southern Thailand, and interference in military promotions.

Street Politics

In 2005, the political tug-of-war spilled on to the street—and the street became a favoured arena for political combat for most of the next decade. As in the 1970s and 1992, the legislature was not considered a fitting venue for resolving political differences. In early 2006 the number of anti-Thaksin yellow-shirted[20] protesters, under the

---

19 Pasuk and Baker, *Thaksin*, 255, and Thak Chaloemtiarana, "Distinctions with a Difference: The Despotic Paternalism of Sarit Thanarat and the Demagogic Authoritarianism of Thaksin Shinawatra," *Crossroads: An Interdisciplinary Journal of Southeast Asian Studies*, Vol. 19, No. 1 (2007), p 69. A decade before Thaksin was prime minister, Nidhi Eoseewong had written: "In Thailand there may be someone who is more 'popular' than the person who occupies position of king ...., but there is definitely nobody more sacred than the king." Nidhi, "The Thai Cultural Constitution." Thaksin's critics would say that he failed to respect this cultural convention.

20 The pro-monarchy protesters wore yellow shirts because yellow is associated with Monday, the day on which King Bhumibol was born. The pro-Thaksin and pro-democracy protesters wore red shirts because red represents the land and people in the tri-coloured Thai flag (white represents Buddhism; blue represents the monarchy).

umbrella of an organization called People's Alliance for Democracy (PAD), grew quickly to several hundred thousand. The numbers rose because Thaksin riled many Thais by selling his Shin Corporation to Singapore's Temasek Holdings for Bt73 billion ($2 billion), after first legislating to raise the foreign ownership limits for telecommunications companies and then allegedly re-arranging his family shareholdings to avoid paying tax on the sale. Thaksin responded to PAD protests by calling for a fresh election in April 2006.

The results of the 2006 election were messy because key opposition parties, including the Democrat Party, boycotted it. In the absence of the main opposition parties, Thaksin's party naturally won (and, based on earlier and subsequent election results, it would almost certainly have done so even if major opposition parties had participated in the election). More critically, the boycott led to a stalemate—parliament could not reconvene because the boycott had left some seats unfilled.

Monarchy Speaks, Judiciary Listens

Throughout this period, the king had resisted calls to use Article 7 of the Constitution, which allowed him to replace the incumbent prime minister in extreme circumstances. On occasions, he also tried to calm the situation, for example by getting the main protagonists to drop legal cases against each other, or by choosing to ignore requests that he intervene. Still, when Bhumibol expressed a view—directly or indirectly—it was invariably directed against Thaksin. He also personally endorsed a popular pro-monarchy tract, which argued that democracy had failed and that all Thais had faith in the king.[21]

Faced with a political system that had become dysfunctional after the 2006 elections, the monarchy intervened in an unprecedented way. During his customary addresses to newly appointed judges, Bhumibol said, first of all, that as a constitutional monarch he could not intervene unilaterally: "If the King did so, he would be

---

21   Pasuk and Baker, *Thaksin*, 256.

overstepping his duty. I have never overstepped this duty. Doing so would be undemocratic." He then told the judges that the issue should be relevant for them and, "You have sworn to work for democracy. If you cannot do it, then you may have to resign. You must find ways to solve the problem."[22]

Afterwards, some of the judges' private conversations were publicised. One of them said, "Yes, but we ourselves when making announcements don't dare to mention the Royal Address because it would be like we just followed what he instructed. The foreigners won't accept it… Don't be afraid. It's better to go out in a dignified manner. Nobody can go against a Royal Address."[23] And they didn't. Following private as well as public consultations involving judges, officials (including palace officials) and anti-Thaksin political activists, the Administrative Court suspended the elections for the 14 unfilled seats, the Constitutional Court invalidated the April election, and the Criminal Court imprisoned the electoral commissioners for malpractice.

Eventually, a coup led by General Sonthi Boonyaratkalin, rather than the judges, ended the crisis in September 2006, but the monarchy's willingness to direct the judiciary was clear. Equally clear was the judges' willingness to oblige their monarch. The monarch (who said he was not supposed to intervene), and his supporters in the judiciary (who were supposed to be independent) and military (who were supposed not to play a political role), were able to match Thaksin at every turn, even though Thaksin had a strong electoral mandate.

Generals and Judges Pursue Thaksin

After the coup, the military installed a government led by the general controversially transferred by Thaksin, Surayud, who had pointedly been elevated to the Privy Council by the king in 2003.[24] Most

---

22 Quoted in Pasuk and Baker, *Thaksin*, 274.
23 Quoted in Pasuk and Baker, *Thaksin*, 276. See pp 274–76 for a fuller account of these developments.
24 In 2001, King Bhumibol had elevated two other officials to the Privy Council who had problems with Thaksin. Duncan McCargo, "Thaksin and the Resurgence of Violence in the Thai South," in *Rethinking Thailand's Southern Violence*, ed. by Duncan McCargo (Singapore, NUS Press, 2007), 65.

observers give the Surayud government low marks; its ministers were not technocrats of the calibre of the military-appointed and monarchy-appointed civilian governments of Anand Panyarachun of 1991–92. Unsurprisingly, though, the Surayud government did help to rebuild the military's stocks. It increased the military budget and put the armed forces back in charge of the southern border provinces. It passed a new Defence Act, which gave the military more autonomy from the government. The Surayud government also resuscitated the Internal Security Act, which re-empowered ISOC. And under its watch the courts kept the electorally popular Thaksin out of Thailand, if not out of Thai politics, by convicting him of helping his wife to buy government property cheaply.

Earlier, the generals introduced an interim constitution, which replaced the pro-Thaksin Constitutional Court with a Constitutional Tribunal. In May 2007, this Constitutional Tribunal, relying on the military government's September 2006 decree that the judiciary could dissolve a political party and ban members of that party's executive from politics for five years, dissolved Thaksin's Thai Rak Thai Party and banned 111 of its MPs (including Thaksin) for five years for malpractice during the April 2006 elections—even though the election results had since been annulled. This decision emasculated the political leadership of Thaksin's political party. It is notable for four other reasons. First, the penalty imposed by the military government's September 2006 decision was applied retrospectively; in other words (and as the Tribunal's president observed in his dissenting opinion), individuals were receiving a punishment that did not exist when the misconduct was committed. Secondly, the day before the verdict was announced the 2006 coup leader, General Sonthi, met the vice-president of the Tribunal, and immediately after the announcement Sonthi proposed that the banned politicians be amnestied. He quickly backtracked, but his actions created a perception of political interference.[25] Thirdly, a few days before the verdict the king referred to the case indirectly, saying, "I have the answer in my heart, but I have no right to say it." His ambiguous comments led some to conclude that he may have wanted a compromise rather than harsh punishment.[26] Fourthly, on the same day that the Constitutional Tribunal dissolved the Thai Rak Thai Party and banned the 111 members of its executive board, it unanimously acquitted the Democrat Party of similar charges. The evidence against the Democrat Party was less compelling, but the exoneration of the Democrats provoked claims of double standards. Collectively, these developments raised further questions about the independence of the judiciary.

The military-appointed government also used the judiciary to target Thaksin personally, including his assets, as well as his political party. It established an Assets Scrutiny Committee, which included several members who had publicly criticised Thaksin and his government, to investigate charges of corruption under Thaksin, with a view to bringing lawsuits before the courts and freezing assets that may have been gained corruptly.

2007 Constitution

The military also established a Constitutional Drafting Assembly, which was heavily populated with coup supporters who, above all, wanted to put the menacing Thaksin genie back in his bottle. Whereas the drafters of the 1997 Constitution sought to make the political executive more accountable to a fully elected legislature and an independent judiciary, the drafters of the 2007 Constitution sought to make the political executive—which, in their opinion, Thaksin had abused—less accountable to the legislature (even though it was no longer fully elected; half the senators were appointed) and more

---

25   Duncan McCargo, "Competing Notions of Judicialization in Thailand," *Contemporary Southeast Asia*, Vol 36, No 3 (2014), 428–9.
26   *Ibid*, 428.

accountable to the judiciary, whose independence was diluted by the increase in its formal powers, including the power to sack a prime minister. These changes to the executive and judicial arms of the government weakened the authority of the legislature—which, in institutional terms, was Thaksin's power base.

In relation to the judiciary, the new constitution sought, first, to lessen the risk of political interference that had marred the reputation of the Constitutional Court after Thaksin gained control of the Senate, which had a decisive role in selecting judges. Selection of judges was depoliticised; judges had to have 30 years of continuous experience, and the five serving judges on the now nine-member bench (previously 15 members) would outnumber the four legal experts and political scientists.[27] Secondly, the new constitution gave the court unprecedented powers, which included "policing political parties, removal from office of members of parliament and ministers, approval of disqualification of election commissioners, approval of organic laws for important institutions, approval of challenges to emergency decrees, and a role for its chairman in committees that select senators".[28] In fact, it wasn't the Chairman of the Constitutional Court alone who was to play a role in the selection of senators; the judiciary generally now had a major say in the composition of the Senate. Under the new constitution, roughly half the Senate was elected on a provincial basis and the other half was appointed by a committee which included the presiding officers of the Constitutional Court, Election Commission, Ombudsman's Office, National Anti-Corruption Commission and State Audit Commission, as well as two judges from the administrative courts. Senior judges also played a critical role in selecting members of the various independent agencies.

---

27   Before the 2007 Constitution came into effect the Surayud government took a leaf out of Thaksin's book and appointed its loyalists as judges and commissioners.

28   Ginsburg, Tom. "Constitutional Afterlife: The Continuing Impact of Thailand's Postpolitical Constitution." *International Journal of Constitutional Law*, Vol 7: 83 (January 2009), 100–1.

Some judges expressed concern that this expanded role would compromise the judiciary's independence.[29] There were also reports of judges declining appointment to the Constitutional Court because it was becoming politicised.[30]

Public consultations on the new constitution were perfunctory. In August 2007, 58 per cent of the electorate turned out to vote in a take-it-or-leave-it referendum (in the 2005 elections, 73 per cent of the electorate had voted). Fifty-seven per cent of those who voted approved of the text. Put another way, over 40 per cent of the electorate chose not to participate. A regional analysis of the referendum results shows that a majority of voters in the northeast and north were opposed to the constitution; in other words, rather than building a national consensus for a new supreme law, the referendum underlined and possibly exacerbated political divisions.

Elections, Sackings and a Funeral

Through court cases against Thaksin and his party, and through constitutional reform, the military tried to domesticate electoral democracy. But Thais continued to value their vote, and Thaksin. Two elections—with high voter turnout—were held under the 2007 Constitution. Thaksin-aligned political parties won both of them.

In December 2007, Samak Sundaravej, whom Thaksin had anointed as the leader of his party (now called Palang Prachachon Party) won after running a "Vote Samak—Get Thaksin" campaign. The election of Samak, and his government's policies to protect Thaksin and amend the 2007 Constitution, inflamed Thaksin's opponents. PAD demonstrators, again dressed in yellow shirts, clogged streets near Government House and eventually occupied the building. The elected government's efforts to get the police, army and courts to move against the demonstrators failed.

---

29   Bjorn Dressel, "Thailand's Elusive Quest for a Workable Constitution, 1997–2007," *Contemporary Southeast Asia*, Vol 31, No 2 (2009), 304.
30   Bjorn Dressel, "Thailand: Judicialization of Politics or Politicization of the Judiciary," 92.

In this highly-charged political environment the judiciary was called upon to deliver judgments that again drew it into the cauldron of political debate. On 3 July 2008, the Supreme Court endorsed an Electoral Commission ruling to ban the Thaksin-aligned Speaker, Yongyuth Tiyaphairat, from political office for electoral malpractice. Six days later, the Constitutional Court sacked the health minister, Chaiya Sasomsap, for failing to properly declare his assets. The next day, the same court forced the resignation of Foreign Minister Noppadol Pattama, who was also Thaksin's personal lawyer, over the Preah Vihear temple dispute with Cambodia. On 12 July, the attorney-general charged Thaksin of using his authority as prime minister to boost the profits of his family-controlled Shin Corp. Other judicial moves during this period that specifically targeted Thaksin included charges that as prime minister he: influenced the Exim Bank to increase loans to Myanmar in order to benefit his family business; breached anti-gambling laws in setting up a new government lottery; and unlawfully approved the expenditure of government funds to purchase rubber saplings.

On 9 September, the Constitutional Court sacked Samak, on the grounds that he had been an "employee" of a television company when he continued to host a television cooking show after he became prime minister. Samak's supporters, and some independent observers, noted that the Court relied on a conventional dictionary, rather than Thailand's civil code and labour laws, to define the word "employee". One judge later described this decision as "judicial creativity".[31]

Parliament decided, by 298 votes to 163, to replace Samak with Somchai Wongsawat, Thaksin's brother-in-law. Samak's sacking did not sate the PAD's thirst for political blood; on the contrary, PAD demonstrators laid siege to Parliament House (forcing Somchai to escape by climbing the rear fence after delivering his prime ministerial policy address) and Government House (forcing Somchai's government to relocate). They also occupied Bangkok's

---

31   Bjorn Dressel, "Judicialization of Politics or Politicization of the Judiciary?," 682.

international airport, forcing its closure for eight days and disrupting hundreds of thousands of passengers. On 2 December, the Constitutional Court dissolved the Thaksin-sponsored Palang Prachachon Party and banned more than a hundred of the party's executives from politics for five years for electoral malpractice. Somchai had to resign as prime minister.

In the midst of this politicisation of the judiciary, the queen attended the funeral of a PAD protester who was killed by a police tear-gas canister, smothering faint hopes in some quarters that the monarchy might try to appear above politics. One of her daughters, Princess Chulabhorn, and the army chief, General Anupong Paochinda, also attended.

It was in between the sackings of Samak and Somchai that the Supreme Court ruled that in 2003 Thaksin had abused his authority by assisting his wife to purchase government-owned land. It sentenced Thaksin, who was overseas, to two years' imprisonment. Thereafter, Thaksin remained in self-imposed exile, claiming he was the victim of a political vendetta, while his opponents counter-claimed that he was evading justice. About 18 months later, in February 2010, the Supreme Court seized Bt46 billion (US$1.3 billion) of the Bt76 billion of Thaksin's assets that the Assets Scrutiny Committee had frozen after the 2006 coup. The court ruled that Thaksin had concealed his ownership of shares in the family-controlled Shin Corp and then committed "policy corruption" by pursuing policies that, while legal and potentially in the national interest, also enriched his family business.

The guilt or innocence of Thaksin and Thaksin-aligned politicians, and the prospect of dispassionate discussions about the role of the judiciary in constitutional government, were overshadowed by triumphalism among Thaksin's opponents and victimhood among his supporters. The PAD and its parliamentary ally, the Democrat Party, with tacit and sometimes overt backing from the military and the monarchy, had used the courts and independent agencies, as well as mob intimidation, to try to banish the electorally popular Thaksin and his influence from Thai politics.

Abhisit Interregnum

After the Constitutional Court disqualified the short-lived Samak and Somchai governments, the military persuaded some MPs previously tied to Thaksin's party to instead support the Democrat Party, led by Abhisit Vejjajiva. In other words, the military was instrumental in determining the shape of an "elected" government. For some months, the newly formed Abhisit government had to operate out of an army base because it was besieged by red-shirted demonstrators, in the same way that Thaksin-aligned governments had periodically been besieged by yellow-shirted demonstrators.

Thaksin's political party and the allied red-shirt movement, whose formal name was the United Front for Democracy Against Dictatorship (UDD), questioned the courts' seeming predisposition to throw out elected governments. Anger over repeated court rulings against Thaksin, and over Abhisit's refusal to hold an election before the scheduled 2012 deadline, fuelled massive red-shirt demonstrations in April–May 2010. Relying on the same intimidatory mob tactics of the yellow shirts, some red shirts occupied public buildings, including parliament and the Electoral Commission, and pressured commissioners to take up a stalled electoral fraud case against the Democrat Party with the Constitutional Court. Following violence by red-shirt demonstrators and heavily armed "black shirt" militants, Abhisit and his deputy prime minister, Suthep Thaugsuban, relying on the Internal Security Act, ordered the army to break up the red-shirt demonstrations. Over 90 protesters and security personnel were killed in the April–May 2010 clashes.

In November 2010 the Constitutional Court dismissed the electoral fraud case against the Democrat Party on a technicality, provoking further claims of judicial double standards. The case was given added piquancy because three judges had to recuse themselves after the release of a video that showed a Democrat Party parliamentarian lobbying court officials in relation to the case, and another video showing an attempted cover-up of improper hiring practices of court staff. To make matters worse for the pro-Thaksin camp, no action was taken against the judges or court officials, but the police launched an investigation into the alleged red-shirt who leaked the videos.

2011 Elections and Yingluck Government

In May 2011, Abhisit announced an early election, which was held in July. The election lowered political temperatures on all sides. The Democrat Party conceded defeat as soon as the magnitude of the electoral victory of the Pheu Thai Party, headed by Thaksin's sister Yingluck, became clear. Pheu Thai won 265 seats in the 500-seat parliament; the Democrats won 159 seats.

During the election campaign, the new army commander Prayuth Chan-ocha, who as deputy commander had played a key role in suppressing red-shirt protesters in 2010, suggested that Thais should not vote for Pheu Thai. After the elections, though, in the face of overwhelming electoral support for the party (including in military-dominated constituencies), the military chose to stay in the background and allow an orderly transfer of power. For her part, Yingluck took the opportunity to develop a respectful relationship with the military. She ensured that the military budget continued to grow and agreed not to meddle in the promotion of senior officers (as well as promoting his favourites to senior positions, Thaksin had cut the military budget as a percentage of GDP).[32] Yingluck tried to constrain Prayuth, and

---

32 James Ockey, "Broken Power: The Thai Military in the Aftermath of the 2006 Coup," in *"Good Coup" Gone Bad: Thailand's Political Developments Since Thaksin's Downfall*, ed. by Pavin Chachavalpongpun (Singapore: ISEAS, 2014), 58.

simultaneously placate red-shirt supporters who wanted him and other military leaders brought to trial, by allowing the police to continue to investigate the army's handling of the 2010 protests.

The military seemed to realise that it would harm itself if it needlessly antagonised the newly-elected government. In addition, the military rebuilt some of its public reputation through impressive and widely publicised relief efforts during massive floods in late 2011. In the following year, it resisted calls for it to unseat the Yingluck government, most notably when a retired army general, Boonlert Kaewprasit, tried to organise a mass rally in Bangkok. Boonlert failed to draw a crowd, let alone awaken the sort of yellow-shirt passion that had derailed Thaksin's government.

In 2013, as the Yingluck government began to attract domestic opposition to some of its policies, the media began to speculate on the possibility of a military coup. From as early as July, Prayuth's response to repeated media questions on this issue invariably included words to the effect: "Don't people who advocate a coup realise that a coup would bring serious bloodshed?" Prayuth was reflecting a widespread view that military intervention would anger the Yingluck government's red-shirt supporters, who would rally on the streets of Bangkok and possibly in provincial towns as soon as a coup occurred; and the military would be able to restore order only by shooting them. In addition, at the time, there was also a widespread view, including in parts of the military, that Thailand's economy and society was now too complex to be governed by the military. The proponents of this view pointed to the ineffectual Surayud government as evidence.

Yingluck also worked assiduously to develop respectful, even personable, relations with the palace, including the influential Prem. During her prime ministership, unlike the prime ministership of her brother, there was no hint of disrespect or tension in her relationship with the king, the royal family more broadly, or the Prem-led Privy Council.

Because Yingluck reached an accommodation with the palace and the military after securing a clear parliamentary majority, from about August 2011 until late 2013 Thailand enjoyed a period of rare political stability—or, more accurately, political equilibrium. Each of the five branches of government was equally strong and equally weak. This stability was, however, fortuitous—and fragile—rather than structural. The five branches of government were balanced because an unambiguous election result had made the legislature stronger than usual. The stability was not the result of the five branches acting as institutional checks and balances against each other in the manner in which this typically occurred in the Western democratic system. The fragility of Thailand's political stability was demonstrated by the ease with which it crumbled when the elected government attempted structural reform.

Judiciary Resists Constitutional Reform

After the Yingluck government felt reasonably secure in its relationships with the monarchy and the military, it set about implementing an election promise to strengthen democracy by amending the military-inspired 2007 Constitution. In 2012, it took its first steps to establish a drafting committee to review the constitution. The Democrat Party immediately brought the matter to the Constitutional Court, arguing that constitutional amendments were an attempt to "overthrow the democratic regime of government with the King as Head of State" (Article 68 of the 2007 Constitution). Rowdy scenes erupted in parliament and protesters blockaded the parliament building. Demonstrations also occurred outside the Constitutional Court. Judges were given police protection and the riot squad was deployed. Pro-Thaksin supporters, fearing that the Court would find against the government and perhaps ban the Pheu Thai Party and its leadership, warned that "civil war" would occur if the Court ruled against the government.

Again, the judiciary was at the centre of political debate. Again, politicians tried to draw the monarchy into politics. Again, parliament was unable to contain a political issue within its walls. Again, mobs of protesters from both sides tried to put pressure on the judiciary. And again the judges were perceived, rightly or wrongly, to have assumed that their responsibility was to read political tea leaves as well as the constitution.

Several observers argued that a strict reading of the constitution would have seen the judges refuse the Democrat Party's application because it was not submitted through the attorney-general's office. Instead, the judges accepted the application but ruled that the proposed amendment of the constitution was not aimed at overthrowing the monarchy. Then, rather curiously, the judges recommended, rather than ruled, that parliament amend only individual articles of the 2007 constitution, not the whole document, which had been adopted in 2007 by a referendum; this constitution, the judges said, could be comprehensively reformed only through another referendum.

The government, in effect, accepted the Court's recommendation as a ruling and put comprehensive constitutional reform to one side. Seemingly in keeping with the Court's view that piecemeal constitutional change was acceptable, in 2013 the government passed through parliament a constitutional amendment that would have restored a fully elected Senate. The Democrat Party again brought the matter to the Constitutional Court and again claimed that the government was contravening Article 68. It also asked the Court to dissolve the Pheu Thai Party. In November 2013, the Court didn't dissolve Pheu Thai but, in a ruling that effectively prevented an elected government from trying to amend the constitution, it ruled that the government had breached Article 68. In other words, it ruled that in seeking to reintroduce an elected Senate (in place of a semi-appointed Senate) the government had attempted "to overthrow the democratic regime of government with the King as Head of State".

The Price of Rice

During the election campaign, the Yingluck government had also promised to introduce a rice subsidy scheme. Under the scheme, the government would pay farmers more for their paddy rice than the Democrat Party government had and, critically, at a price well above the prevailing market price. Because Thailand was the world's largest rice exporter at the time, the Yingluck government thought it could manipulate global prices. It miscalculated, badly, and the scheme cost Thailand billions of dollars. In 2017, Yingluck (whom the Constitutional Court had sacked as prime minister in 2014 for reasons unrelated to the rice subsidy scheme) was ultimately found responsible for overseeing a scheme that was corruptly administered, fined over US$1 billion personally, and sentenced to five years imprisonment. She fled the country before the sentence was delivered.

The Cost of Amnesty

As well as promising constitutional reform and rice subsidies, during the 2011 election campaign the Pheu Thai Party had told its supporters that it would try to bring the self-exiled Thaksin home. Recognising that this undertaking was controversial, party leaders moved cautiously. In November 2013, however, in the middle of the night during the third reading of an amnesty bill with limited scope, a Pheu Thai MP who wanted to curry favour with Thaksin amended the legislation to include all leaders, including Thaksin, as well as grass-roots demonstrators. Massive public opposition, including deep dismay among red-shirts and many Pheu Thai MPs because the amnesty would also have covered political and military leaders who spearheaded the 2010 anti-red shirt crackdown, saw the ill-conceived amnesty bill quickly overturned.

The deputy leader of the Democrat Party, Suthep Thaugsuban, who exploited the anti-Thaksin sentiment in enormous anti-amnesty crowds that had gathered on Bangkok's streets to demand the parliament reject the bill, was unwilling to declare victory and go home. He formally resigned from the Democrat Party (but continued to wield considerable informal influence within it) and established the People's Democratic Reform Committee (PDRC), which called for an unelected government of "good people". For months, Bangkok witnessed massive PDRC-led protests as well as counter-protests organised by the UDD. In various clashes, over 20 people were killed. Over time, the Yingluck government was paralysed—by the demonstrations, an election boycott, and several rulings from the judiciary.

2014 Coup

On 7 May 2014, the judiciary sacked another elected prime minister. The Constitutional Court found that Yingluck had abused her prime ministerial power in 2011 when she transferred a senior civil servant (this transfer was also linked to the appointment of Thaksin's former brother-in-law as the police chief). Nine other ministers and deputy ministers were sacked for their involvement in the decision. On 20 May, army commander Prayuth imposed martial law, followed by a fully-fledged coup on 22 May. He averted potential counterattacks from demonstrators by detaining their leaders immediately, organizing transport to take the demonstrators home, and intimidating anti-military activists in the provinces.

Crisis and Coup: An Institutional Assessment

Reverting to our five-branches-of-government perspective, let us try to assess the 2013–14 political crisis and the 2014 coup. Throughout this period, the monarchy remained in the background. Unlike in 1973, 1992 and 2006, Bhumibol did not try to foster a resolution, although there were calls for him to intervene. It is difficult to know what role the palace might have played behind the scenes. As in the past, the monarchy sanctioned the coup after the event.

Faced with a political crisis and a challenge to its own authority, the political <u>executive</u> responded in a conventional manner for a parliamentary government: it called for fresh elections. The elections were boycotted by the PDRC and Democrat Party. At times, elections were also thwarted by the actions (or inactions) of the Electoral Commission. The administrative executive, or bureaucracy, reflecting the divisions within Thai society as well as its own difficulty in trying to appear apolitical, variously demonstrated against and for the Yingluck government, or kept quiet.

As for the <u>military</u>, from the 2011 elections until the late-2013 mass protests in Bangkok, the troops stayed in their barracks and let politicians tackle Thailand's various challenges through the political system that the military had helped to author through the 2007 Constitution. As mentioned earlier, it did not respond in 2012 when a retired army general tried to destabilise the Yingluck government. Prayuth also seemed genuinely concerned that military intrusion into politics would provoke a red-shirt backlash. And in at least some quarters of the military, there was a feeling that the military's best interests would be better served by professionalization, not re-politicization. From personal experience, I know that these concerns were strongly held by senior military leaders in late November 2013.

Coincidentally, when the large street protests started and the prospect of prolonged disturbances was becoming apparent, the head of the Australian Defence Forces visited Bangkok to receive an official award from the Thai government. At various functions and informal gatherings with the upper echelons of the Thai armed forces, the emerging political turmoil was a natural topic of conversation. In their words and demeanour, Thai generals showed unmistakable annoyance at Thaksin and his supporters for seeking an amnesty and at Suthep and his supporters for calling for intervention by the military or monarchy. They clearly expressed an aversion to another coup, saying it would harm the standing of the Thai military.

The Thai military is not monolithic and some others would have been more willing to resume a political role. As we saw earlier, Prayuth himself openly opposed the Pheu Thai Party before the election. In addition, because of the role he had played as deputy army commander in the suppression of the 2010 protests, he had worked closely with Suthep, who was the director of the Centre for Resolution of the Emergency Situation (CRES), a committee of ministers and security officials that Abhisit established to manage that crisis. Furthermore, as army commander when the 2013–14 protests occurred, Prayuth surely could have exercised more discipline over elements of the armed forces that provided behind-the-scenes support to Suthep's PDRC. He could also have said that the military's role was to support the elected government. And, if Prayuth genuinely did not want to lead a military government, after he declared martial law on 20 May 2014 he could have given the opposing camps of politicians more than two days to produce a political compromise. Instead, he announced a full-blown coup on 22 May.

The point here is not to deny that elements within the military, including Prayuth himself, played a role as the events of 2013–14 unfolded. But if we want to assess, in institutional terms, which branches of government brought Thailand's political system to its knees over this period, the main culprit was not the military. Nor was it the monarchy or executive. As institutions, the legislature and judiciary ultimately played bigger roles in breaking the system.

In the more than eight decades since 1932, the Thai legislature and judiciary have not accumulated stabilising, dispute-settlement responsibilities that are commonly exercised by legislatures and judiciaries in conventional parliamentary democracies. Certainly, the magnitude of the task of reducing the domestic political power of the military should not be underestimated. But, using history as a guide, nor should we overestimate the inclination or ability of MPs and judges in Thailand to consider how the legislature and judiciary might develop into institutional counterweights to the military's political power.

Although voters continued to give Thaksin-aligned political parties a healthy parliamentary majority, the people they elected—the <u>legislature</u>—could not protect either the legislature itself or the elected government from a military coup. Nor could the legislature break a political deadlock through elections. This is partly explained, first, by the underdeveloped party system, especially the absence of sophisticated party organizations that constantly modify policies and strategies. For example, if the Pheu Thai Party had been organized along the lines of political parties in more established democratic systems, in November 2013 the politically suicidal idea to seek an amnesty for Thaksin would have been considered, and almost certainly dismissed, by the party's leadership well before it was introduced into the parliament. Instead, in the middle of the night and without even consulting the office of the party leader (Yingluck), the amnesty was introduced. Until this misstep, the Yingluck government seemed likely to serve its full four-year term, although political and economic pressures caused by the rice subsidy scheme were rising. Similarly, a more developed party system would have prevented Yingluck from re-shuffling senior civil service appointments so that Thaksin's former brother-in-law could become the police chief.

Secondly, the legislature could not match the appeal of the mass political movements, whether they were PDRC or UDD. Aggrieved Thais of all political persuasions have regularly concluded that they are less likely to find satisfaction in a legally constituted parliament (or a court of law), and more likely to find it in mass political movements that resort to often illegal and sometimes violent street protests. For example, after the Senate blocked Thaksin's amnesty in 2013, the Democrat Party was unable to persuade Suthep and his followers to go home and allow parliament to again become the primary venue for political struggle—even though Democrat Party MPs were saying privately that fresh elections and a return to parliamentary politics, and not more PDRC protests, offered the only constitutional and sustainable way forward.

Thirdly, the legislature could not prevent the Constitutional Court from sacking Yingluck and two earlier prime ministers, Samak and Somchai. The legislature did not want Yingluck, Samak and Somchai to lose their jobs; the elected prime ministers had not lost the confidence of the elected lower house of parliament. But the 2007 Constitution made the executive more accountable to the judiciary than to the legislature. Supporters of parliamentary democracy began to say that a "judicial coup" was as threatening to democracy as a military coup.

The judiciary was equally unable to mediate or arbitrate the political impasse—largely because the judiciary broadly defined (i.e. including the so-called independent bodies like the Electoral Commission and NACC) was not perceived by many Thais to be independent. Rightly or wrongly, the Pheu Thai Party believed the judiciary was biased against them. In the same way, many in Suthep's PDRC and the Democrat Party thought the police were biased against them.

From November 2013 until May 2014, some judgments and public statements by commissioners and judges prompted observers to further question the independence of the judiciary. For example, an election commissioner publicly derided the elected government's efforts to resolve the early 2014 political impasse through fresh general elections, and the Election Commission did little to stop anti-government protesters disrupting the registration of candidates and the distribution of ballots for that election. An anti-corruption commissioner publicly implied that members of the government were corrupt in their administration of rice subsidies before any charges had been brought to the Commission, and the Commission fast-tracked an investigation into Yingluck while taking a business-as-usual approach to longstanding allegations against Democrat Party leaders.

The Constitutional Court ruled that the protests led by Suthep, who openly called for the replacement of the elected government with an unelected body, were not an attempt to overthrow the democratic system of government. And within hours of an armed clash that resulted in the deaths of two policemen and four protesters, the Civil Court ruled that the anti-government protesters had demonstrated "peacefully and without weapons" and, therefore, the elected government could not prevent them from occupying public roads and buildings.

In constitutional terms, what Suthep and the PDRC wanted was unconstitutional: to ban a particular family (Shinawatra) from politics, to install an unelected government of "good people" and to delay elections until unspecified "reforms" were implemented. But just as the constitution could not deliver what Suthep and the PDRC wanted, nor could it satisfy Yingluck, the Pheu Thai Party or the red-shirts—because the constitution legitimised the so-called independent institutions which, Yingluck and her supporters believed, were trying to unseat the elected government or prevent a new one from being formed. Nor did the constitution allow the appointment of an "interim" prime minister who might have led a short-term government that could have cleared the way for a political compromise.[33]

From an institutional perspective, therefore, the military prevailed at least partially because the legislature and the judiciary were unable to fulfil the mediating and arbitrating roles in Thailand that they customarily fill in democratic systems.

Prayuth Government

Prayuth decided to lead the post-coup government himself, rather than appoint a civilian administration which might either

---

33 This sort of behind-the-scenes compromise was mooted in the weeks preceding the coup, with possible interim prime ministers including Arsa Sarasin (former Principal Private Secretary to the King and diplomat), Isra Vongkusolkit (successful businessman and Chairman of the Thai Chamber of Commerce and Board of Trade of Thailand), Wisanu Krue-Ngam (former Deputy Prime Minister under Thaksin, and legal expert) and Anand Panyarachun (former Prime Minister, diplomat and businessman).

underperform (like Surayud's government of 2006–7) or clip the military's wings (like Anand's in 1992). He replaced the 2007 constitution with an interim constitution and invoked Section 44 of that constitution, under which the security forces could arrest people without warrant and detain people without charge. Section 44 gave Prayuth full authority over all branches of government while absolving him of any legal responsibility for his actions. In addition to protecting national security and the monarchy and promoting reforms, Section 44 was used to enhance "unity and harmony".[34] In 1958, Sarit Thanarat held, and exercised, similar authority when he was prime minister. Like Sarit, Prayuth also tried to present himself as a fatherly figure who wanted to bring happiness to Thais. Unlike Sarit, he felt obliged to outline a roadmap that included a new constitution and an eventual return to civilian government.

2017 Constitution: Reinventing the Past

Unsurprisingly, the military-appointed drafters of the 2017 Constitution gave the military a supervisory role that pro-military observers argued was aimed at preventing a recurrence of extreme political volatility and the public demonstrations that had been persistent features of Thai politics since 2005. In brief, the military designated itself the supreme referee. The constitution allows the military government to preside over the appointment of a 250-member Senate, in which seats will be reserved for the supreme commander of the armed forces, the chiefs of the army, navy and air force, the secretary of the defence ministry and the police chief. For the five years after the next election (in effect, for the next two elections, given the four-year electoral cycle), it also gives the 250 unelected senators a say in the appointment of the prime minister, and even permits the appointment of a non-MP as

---

34   We will return to this theme in later chapters.

the prime minister. The constitution allows the military government to retain its Section 44 powers until the new government is formed (i.e. for the period between the election and the swearing-in of a new cabinet). In addition, it facilitated a 20-year national reform strategy that has been drafted and overseen by committees mainly composed of generals or people hand-picked by generals. The government is required to report quarterly to the Senate on its progress in implementing this national strategy. If the Senate adjudges any ministers or officials are failing to follow the strategy, it can refer them to the NACC or Constitutional Court. So, even if the government happens to be headed by an elected MP, the shadow of the military will still fall over it.

The 2017 Constitution further strengthened the judiciary, which included giving the Constitutional Court and independent agencies authority to also set ethical standards for themselves, MPs, senators and ministers. These standards should cover "the upholding of national prestige and interest", with judges having enormous discretion to define national prestige and interest. The judiciary's authority is also secured by articles in the constitution that allow 10 per cent of MPs and senators to petition the Constitutional Court to remove from office a minister who does not possess "apparent honesty" or whose behaviour seriously violates "the ethical standard". Again, the court has immense discretion to define ethical standards. In addition, although still untested, the Constitutional Court appears to have the authority to remove individual ministers, or the entire cabinet, if it concludes that they have misused public funds. When considering cases, the Court no longer has to rely entirely on the constitution but can also base its rulings on undefined "constitutional conventions of Thailand under the democratic regime of government with the King as Head of State".

In line with the practice introduced for the 2007 Constitution, the government sought public endorsement through a (firmly controlled) referendum in August 2016.[35] On this occasion, 59 per cent of the electorate voted (75 per cent voted in the 2011 elections) and 61 per cent of voters approved of the text. Fifty-eight per cent approved a second question, which asked whether the appointed Senate might play a role in appointing the prime minister. Like the referendum results for the 2007 Constitution, in 2016 provinces in the northeast and north voted against the new constitution (and second question). In 2016, so did the three predominantly Muslim southern border provinces, because electors there feared the new constitution was shifting towards making Theravada Buddhism the official state religion. So the 2016 referendum, like its 2007 predecessor, laid bare political divisions; its validation of the new supreme law was superficial.

Initially, the drafters of the 2017 Constitution wanted the judiciary to have even more power. No doubt worried by Bhumibol's failing health (he died in October 2016), they had opened the way for a judiciary-led committee to take over the crisis-management role that under previous constitutions had been viewed as a royal prerogative. The newly installed king, Vajiralongkorn, overruled them and restored the provisions of the previous constitution. In doing so, he acted boldly, first of all, in refusing to endorse the draft constitution that had been approved in a referendum; and, secondly, in indicating that he believed the monarchy should be able to play a dispute-settling role during periods of deep political crisis. He had earlier shown boldness in defying protocol by not formally assuming the throne soon after his father's death, saying he wanted to mourn for his father and not concern himself with other matters (he waited until December 2016).

In April 2017, presumably at Vajiralongkorn's request, in a secret sitting, the military-appointed legislature increased the monarchy's

---

35   Duncan McCargo, Saowanee T. Alexander and Petra Desatova, "Ordering Peace: Thailand's 2016 Constitutional Referendum," *Contemporary Southeast Asia*, Vol 39, No 1 (2017): 65–95.

formal power by transferring the custody of five state agencies to the new king. Two of them—the Royal Household Bureau and the Office of His Majesty's Principal Private Secretary—provide the monarch with administrative support. The other three—Royal Thai Aide-De-Camp Department, Office of Royal Court Security Police and Royal Security Command (which has six battalions comprising several thousand troops)—are responsible for security. Since 1932, these agencies had been under the control of the Prime Minister's Office, Ministry of Defence and the police. In July 2017, a law was amended to allow the king to appoint the chairman of the Crown Property Bureau, a position that was previously occupied *ex officio* by the minister of finance. Vajiralongkorn appointed a private secretary, who is a retired air chief marshal, to the post. In February 2019, the king disallowed his sister, Ubonrat, from openly engaging in politics. In summary, under the 2017 Constitution, and through legislative changes as well as personal interventions by the king, the formal authority of the monarchy has been strengthened.

The new constitution allows for an elected 500-member lower house, or House of Representatives; 350 of the elected MPs will be chosen on a constituency basis, and 150 from party lists. The new electoral arrangements (a multi-member apportionment system) are designed to help small- to medium-sized parties to become bigger, which would reduce the chances of a Thaksin-aligned political party gaining a majority. And reflecting public distrust of elected politicians as well as their own ambition to retain control, the military's new blueprint lifts the chances of an outsider, most likely an army general, being appointed prime minister.

Through these constitutional changes, the military may be able to dilute some of Thailand's chronic political instability. However, if history is a guide, the military won't be able to silence elected MPs, who will claim a democratic mandate and legitimacy that the military-controlled Senate and military-controlled national reform strategy committee lack. If MPs follow in the footsteps of their democratically-minded predecessors, over time they will also: criticise the 2014 military coup; baulk at reporting to the Senate on its implementation of a national strategy in which they have had little say; object to the new powers of bodies like the Electoral Commission, Auditor General, NACC and Constitutional Court; demand that more of the budget goes on social programs and less on military equipment; ask questions about military corruption and other wrong-doings; and advocate constitutional reform.

Chapter Four

THE IMPORTANCE OF PERFORMANCE

I had no desire to change from one king to many—
which is a democratic system but only its outer husk. I
am focused on the important point: "improve the well-
being of the people".[1] (Pridi Banomyong, 1933)

Democracy is a good and beautiful thing, but it's not
the ultimate goal as far as administering the country
is concerned.... Democracy is just a tool, not our goal.
The goal is to give people a good lifestyle, happiness
and national progress.[2] (Thaksin Shinawatra, 2003)

Rulers, in Thailand or elsewhere, whether they are kings, generals or
elected, rarely wake up in the morning worrying about legitimacy and
accountability or about how political disputes should be adjudicated.
Nor do most of their subjects or citizens worry about these governance
issues. In their everyday lives, rulers and the ruled tend to be more
interested in results. Thailand may not have had what Western experts
call "good governance", under which the executive is accountable to
the legislature (which represents the people) and the judiciary (which
protects the rule of law).

But Thailand has had enough governance. In other words, the
executive has secured for itself a central role in the economy, society
and nation-building and, moreover, been able to deliver sufficient
economic benefits and government services to earn the support, or at
least the acquiescence, of many Thais. This chapter outlines the main

---

1 *Pridi by Pridi*, 85.
2 Quoted in Pasuk and Baker, *Thaksin*, 171.

socio-economic achievements of the executive branch of government since 1932. It focuses on the outcomes from governance, not the nature of governance.

Commanding Role of the State

We have seen that after the events of 1932 the executive was preoccupied with survival. The new leaders worried about royalist opposition and international acceptance. They also worried about Siam's uncertain economy and the expanding role of migrant Chinese businessmen and labourers. The military and the civilian arms in the government—represented most obviously by Phibun and Pridi—struggled to agree who was best equipped to deal with these challenges; but the civilian and military arms of the government—then and since—have <u>not</u> argued over the role of the state in Thailand. Civilians and soldiers alike have agreed that the state—and especially, in institutional terms, the executive—has a commanding role in defining and pursuing economic and social goals and in cultivating loyalty to the nation.

Both Phibun and Pridi, who dominated policymaking in the first 25 years of the post-absolutist government, favoured deep-state involvement in the economy and society. Initially, Pridi advocated the socialization of agriculture and bureaucratization of the economy; his advocacy was so strong that his political enemies labelled him "communist" and forced him into temporary exile. Later, he moved closer to business: protecting Thai companies with high tariffs; sponsoring joint ventures between government and business; and eventually relying on business to fund his political activities. Pridi also increased government funding for infrastructure, health and education. Phibun, the arch-nationalist, sought to counter immigrant Chinese dominance of Thai commerce by securing government control of critical sectors of the economy in the interests of Thais. And he appropriated for government the right to create an ultranationalist vision for modern Thailand and—through decrees, the education system, all forms of media and occasional physical coercion—the means to persuade Thais, including Sino-Thais, to submit to it.

State-inspired socio-economic reforms and nation-building needed strong bureaucratic support. Phibun and Pridi, and all Thai leaders who followed them, worked hand-in-hand with a bureaucracy that became one of the most powerful institutions in the country.

The Quality of Public Administration

In about 1950, following a comprehensive study of Thailand's public administration, W.D. Reeve came to the following conclusions:

> ... in spite of this inherent difficulty [of governing under a more democratic system] and despite the mistakes that have occurred due to administrative inexperience, despite the disorganizations that have arisen from political jockeying and jealousies, and despite the fact that corruption has sometimes flourished, there is no doubt that the constitutional regime in Siam generally has been a pronounced success... The country's finances and economy are in an enviable position. Thousands of miles of good roads have been built in what was hitherto an almost roadless country. Relations with the Great Powers are, notwithstanding Siam's war-time alliance with Japan, as good or better than they have ever been, and her continued independent status is not in question. Railroads, badly bombed during the war, have been rehabilitated. The administration has been reorganized. Generally, people remain prosperous and contented. The country has undoubtedly advanced during eighteen years of democratic government; that is the true test.[3]

---

3   W.D. Reeve, *Public Administration in Siam* (London and New York: Royal Institute of International Affairs, 1951), 29–30. Reeve's study was conducted under the joint auspices of the Institute of Pacific Relations and the Royal Institute of International Affairs.

Thirteen years later, another comprehensive study concluded:

> With the possible exceptions of Buddhism and the kingship,
> no Thai institutions outrank the bureaucracy as a force which
> has sustained the culture and maintained the vitality of the
> nation during most of the past century .... The modern
> bureaucracy helped project ancient Siam into modern
> statehood. It produced solvency, order, stability, and diplomacy
> sufficient to avoid excuses for Western seizure. Its needs gave
> rise to a system of secular education; and bureaucratic careers
> have fulfilled the expectations of graduates of that system.
> The stable, neutral bureaucracy has carried on the work of
> government without a breakdown in the face of depression,
> war, inflation, and a dizzying succession of political changes.[4]

Whether, as Reeve claimed, Thailand's government was
"democratic" between 1932 and 1950 is debatable, but less debatable is
Reeve's list of Thailand's achievements during these years, to which he
later added: efficiently run state-operated posts, wireless, telephones
and telegraphs; large irrigation schemes; electricity generation; and
impressive public buildings. Reeve also said Thailand's administration
"compared favourably with some of the top-heavy, expensive, and
over-centralized administrations in certain British Colonies" and that
it was "worthy of imitation elsewhere".[5]

Reeve was not blind to weaknesses in Thailand's public
administration. His "defects and recommendations for improvement"
included bribery and corruption, nepotism, failure to take responsibility
for decisions, over-reliance on committees, over-staffing, inadequate
salaries and inefficient local government. Over the next 60 years, any
assessment of weaknesses in Thailand's public administration would

---

4   Quoted in Riggs, *Thailand: The Modernization of a Bureaucratic Polity*, 110.
5   Reeve, *Public Administration*, 78–9.

have included the items on Reeve's list. Equally, though, any assessment would have to include impressive achievements—in absolute as well as comparative terms.

Political Instability and Economic Growth

The previous two chapters have left a strong and accurate impression of political instability. The following graph captures the extent of that instability, if measured in coups, attempted coups, major protests, and number of constitutions. But the graph also shows that since 1951, when reliable statistics became available, notwithstanding this instability, Thailand's civilian-bureaucratic and military-bureaucratic governments have devised a blend of policies that has seen Thailand's economy grow at an average annual rate of 5.8 per cent from 1951 to 2016. Between 1987 and the Asian financial crisis in 1997, the economy grew at a remarkable 9.2 per cent per annum.

Graph 2 Real GDP: at 2010 price (US$ billion)

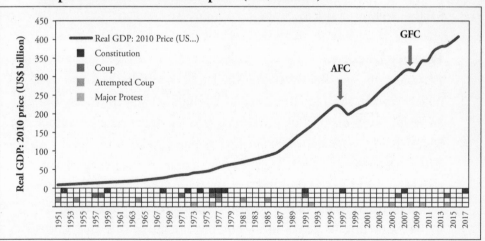

Note: AFC – Asian Financial Crisis
GFC – Global Financial Crisis
Source: World Bank

Graph 3 Thailand's GDP per capita (US$)

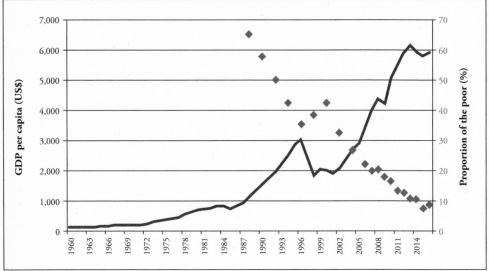

Note: Data for proportion of the poor is available from 1988–2016
Different scale on left and right axis
Source: World Bank and National Economic Social and Development Board (Thailand)

Since 1960, the per capita annual income of Thais has risen from $100 to $5907 (Graph 3).

Poverty Declines

Certainly, the gap between the Thailand's wealthiest and poorest people is wide, although it has narrowed slightly in recent years.[6] But, critically, levels of absolute poverty have fallen dramatically: in 1988, 65.2 per cent of Thais were classified as poor; in 2016 the level had fallen to 8.6 per cent. And the per capita incomes of the poorest 10 per cent increased 5.6-fold from 1975 to 1996. From 1998 to 2016, the per capita incomes of the bottom 10 per cent increased 2.6-fold. Graph 4 gives a picture of Thailand's accomplishments in this area, and a comparison with some selected ASEAN countries.

Put another way, for several decades successive Thai governments

---

6   Pasuk Phongpaichit and Chris Baker, ed., *Unequal Thailand: Aspects of Income, Wealth and Power* (Singapore: NUS, Press, 2016), 9.

Graph 4 Poverty headcount ratio for selected ASEAN members

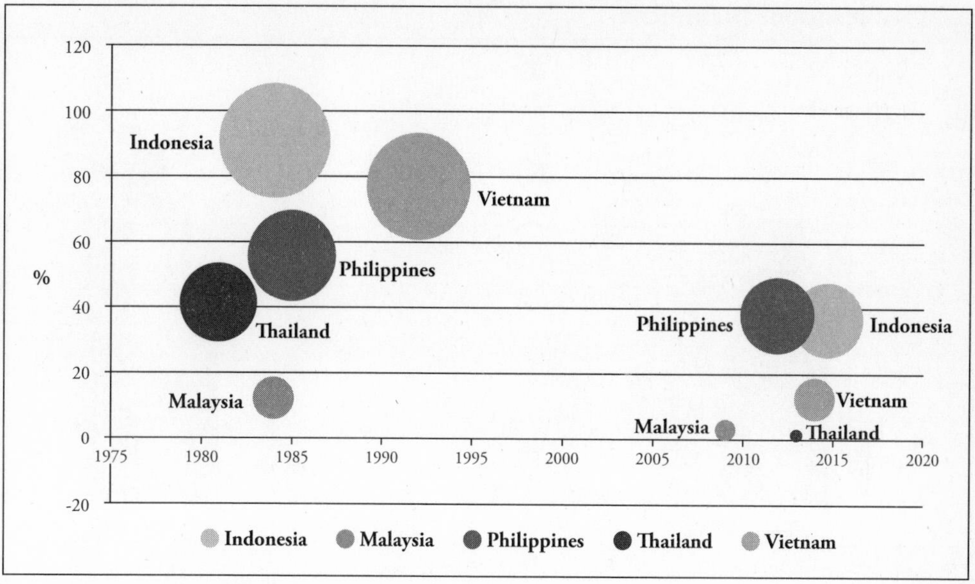

Note: Poverty headcount ratio at $3.10 a day (2011 PPP)
Source: World Bank

have offered Thais opportunities to lift their standard of living, or have not stood in the way of the non-government sector offering opportunities. The incomes of poor Thais as well as rich Thais have grown appreciably.

Physical and Educational Infrastructure

Those opportunities have arisen because civilian-bureaucratic and military-bureaucratic governments have either built impressive physical infrastructure, especially electricity, roads and ports, as well as impressive soft infrastructure, or developed and implemented foreign and domestic policies that allowed the private sector or foreign donors to do so. In 1960, 43.4 per cent of Thais had completed elementary school (six years of education), 3.3 per cent had completed secondary school (12 years), and 0.3 per cent had graduated from university or completed a tertiary qualification. In 2010, those results were 49.1 per cent, 26.7 per cent and 14.1 per cent respectively (Graph 5).

Graph 5 Percentage of population (6 years and over) by educational attainment

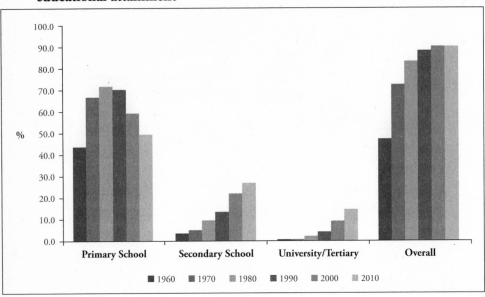

Source: *Thailand Population and Housing Census 1960, 1970, 1980, 1990, 2000 and 2010*

Graph 6 Life expectancy in Thailand by gender

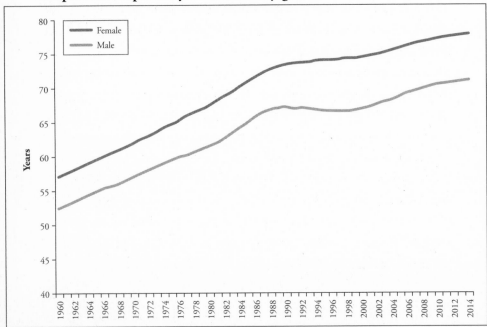

Source: *World Bank*

Living Better and Longer

Because of government policies, Thais are also much healthier and living longer. The infant mortality ratio[7] has decreased from 102.2 to 10.5 in 2015. Estimates of the maternal mortality ratio[8] have also declined, from 40 in 1990 to 20 in 2015. In 1960 life expectancy was 57 years (female) and 52.5 years (male); in 2014 the rates were 77.9 years and 71.1 years (Graph 6).

Graph 7 compares Thailand's performance with that of the other original ASEAN members (Indonesia, Malaysia, Philippines, Singapore).

Graph 8 compares Thailand's performance with that of its two large ASEAN neighbours that followed socialist or quasi-socialist policies: Vietnam and Myanmar.

Family Planning and Property Rights

A couple of other indicators tell us more about the nature of Thailand's socio-economic performance. Few countries have had more effective family planning programs than Thailand. In 1974, the population was growing by 3 per cent and families averaged seven children. Thailand's annual population growth rate is now 0.3 per cent, with less than two children per family. As a result of land reforms, the amount of land attracting strong formal property rights increased from 12.8 million *rai* in 1955 to 126 million *rai* in 2000,[9] and in 2009 Thailand was ranked fifth out of 181 countries for the ease of registering property.[10]

Results Matter

Frequently and justifiably, governments in Thailand have been accused of oppressiveness, corruption and inefficiency. These failings

---

7   Infant deaths per 1,000 live births.
8   Maternal deaths per 100,000 live births.
9   Larsson, *Land and Loyalty*, 108. A *rai* is two-fifths of an acre.
10 *Ibid*, 8.

Graph 7 Real GDP: at 2010 price (US$ billion) compared with original members of ASEAN

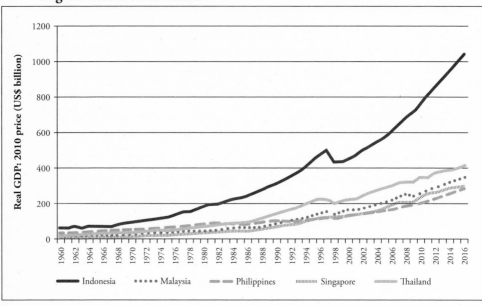

Source: World Bank

Graph 8 Real GDP: at 2010 price (US$ billion) compared with new members of ASEAN

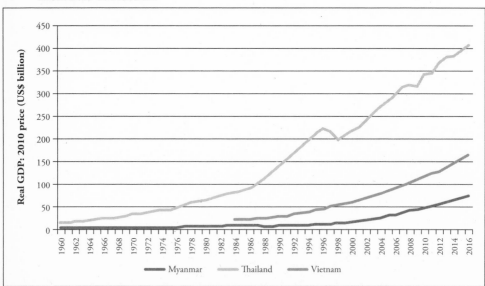

Note: No data available before 1985 for Vietnam
Source: World Bank

warrant all the attention they receive. Certainly, Thailand would be a better place if its people could live under governments that were less oppressive, less corrupt and more efficient.

Equally, for decades, through sound policies Thai governments have contributed to marked improvements in the standard of living of most Thais and protected the security of most Thais, especially in comparison with neighbours who followed a socialist or quasi-socialist path. In personal terms, this means that in their lifetimes most adult Thais have experienced an improvement in their socio-economic conditions or have witnessed an improvement in the socio-economic conditions of many other Thais.

As has been written of northern Thailand (but could be applied generally elsewhere), previously impoverished peasants have reached middle-income levels under the patronage of successive Thai governments, especially over recent decades.[11] Thais have become accustomed to the government providing them with subsidies, credits, construction projects, jobs, land tenure, education, health, welfare and other direct and indirect benefits. In their view, governments have made their lives better.

From 2001, Thaksin extended this state benevolence more deeply into the society, initially because he wanted to stimulate an economy that had over-dosed on IMF medicine. He announced a moratorium on rural debt and provided a continuous flow of funds for village development. In 2002, he introduced a universal healthcare scheme, allowing all Thais access to affordable health services. More than previous governments, he tried to gauge the priorities of the community, which also led to a "war on drugs" that led to about 2,800 extra-judicial deaths.

People found that his populist schemes of public goods and microcredit palpably improved their lives. They felt

---

11   Walker, *Thailand's Political Peasants*, 36–44.

empowered by his offer to espouse their cause against the arrogant bureaucracy and old political elite. Many supporters ignored Thaksin's record on rights, freedoms, and the rule of law because they valued these principles much less than the tangible benefits and sense of empowerment he gave them. Thaksin made ordinary people more aware of the potential of their vote and their voice to overcome the state's persistent neglect of their interests in the past. He brought "the people" into formal politics more firmly than ever before.[12]

The future course of Thai politics will be affected by the extent to which this greater "sense of empowerment" in the electorate can be reconciled with military-sponsored changes to the constitution that are designed to disempower Thaksin—at the personal and political level—and the political executive and legislature—at the institutional level.

Getting Harder

The future course of politics will also be affected by Thailand's tougher economic conditions and tougher economic policy-making environment. If we have another look at graphs 2, 7 and 8, we can see that since 1997 the economy has continued to grow, but it has not grown as quickly as before—and that over the last 15 years some of Thailand's ASEAN partners have performed better than Thailand.

At the same time that governments are struggling to maintain economic growth, they are facing new expectations from Thais who have become wealthier, better educated, more urbanised, more connected to each other and to the rest of the world, and more aware of other ways to organize themselves to protect their interests and pursue their aspirations. These expectations will grow. And NGOs

---

12   Pasuk and Baker, *Thaksin*, 361.

will question government policies more, especially on environmental damage and the uneven distribution of the benefits of development. Others will press for less corruption and greater freedom of expression. The business community will argue for more stable and responsive governments to manage and stimulate the economy.

Thai governments will find it harder to legitimise themselves through performance. Political disputes will become more acute. The need for widely accepted methods for mediating and arbitrating them will become more urgent.

PART II

THE HEART OF
THAI POLITICS

Chapter Five

HIERARCHY, PROTECTION AND PATRONAGE

If there are several Siameses together, and there unexpectedly comes in another, it frequently happens that the posture of all changes. They know before whom, and to what degree, they must keep themselves inclined or strait, or sitting: whether they must joyn their hands or not, and keep them high, or low: whether being seated they may advance one Foot, or both, or whether they must keep them both conceal'd by sitting on their heels. And the miscarriages in these sorts of duties may be punished with the cudgel by him to whom they are committed, or by his orders, and on the spot.[1] (17th century)

You are constantly interacting with other people, and gauging what level you are, and what level they are. You're doing it all the time, like how to address a person, like whether you need the politeness marker, or not, how courteous you have to be to them, how low you have to bow when you walk in front of someone. Everyone does it automatically, and they really don't think about it.[2] (21st century)

---

1   Simon de La Loubère, *The Kingdom of Siam* (Kuala Lumpur: Oxford University Press), 1969. Reprint of 1693 edition, 56. *The Kingdom of Siam (or Du Royaume de Siam)* was an account of La Loubère's visit to Ayutthaya in 1687.
2   An informant quoted in Sophorntavy Vorng, *A Meeting of Masks: Status, Power and Hierarchy in Bangkok* (Copenhagen: NIAS, 2017), 50.

In earlier chapters we have glimpsed the importance and lasting vitality of hierarchy in Thailand's political structure and culture. The continuing authority of the monarchy is an obvious example, including the persistence of prostration and *rajasap*. Other examples include the appeal to paternalism since the 1950s by Prime Minister Sarit Thanarat and his successors and the requirement in the 1997 Constitution that parliamentarians have a university degree. Consider also the idea that "good people" (*phuu dii,* or moral people, preferably with established wealth) rather than elected representatives should govern Thailand—heard during PAD and PDRC demonstrations and expressed in some of the provisions of the 2017 Constitution. All of these examples come after 1932, when constitutional monarchy was introduced, with the promise of equal rights. Some of the examples are post-1997, when equal rights were clearly articulated in the constitution.

The durability of hierarchy tends to surprise newcomers to Thailand. They have usually come from countries where hierarchy no longer matters as much. Outside Thailand, most political systems and political cultures have been more influenced by the ideas of equality and individual rights, even though achievements in these systems and cultures may fall short of aspirations.

The influence of hierarchy on Thai politics owes a lot to Thailand's avoidance of colonial occupation and the durability of traditional political authority. Many of the people who presided over the evolution of Thailand's modern political system—especially King Chulalongkorn, then the civilian and military elite he fostered—were from the upper echelons of the pre-modern political system. Neither colonial rulers nor a colonially-created elite played a role. Nor did the masses. Instead, the Thai monarchy adopted from outside just enough of what it needed to make a pre-modern system modern enough to keep the colonial powers at bay and to help Siam to survive and prosper. When the task became too much for the monarchy, a civilian and military Thai elite took over. That elite was an organic part of an evolving Siamese political structure and culture; it differed from the anti-establishment elites and movements that emerged in many colonized societies.

At times, the surprise of newcomers at the persistence of hierarchy in Thailand, and their uneasiness with it, stems from the conviction that hierarchies are rigid and oppressive. Certainly, Thailand's political hierarchy—traditional and modern—is more rigid and more oppressive than an egalitarian system would be. It is also more rigid and more oppressive than many modern Western observers find comfortable. But there was dynamism within the rigidity of the traditional hierarchy, and moderating checks and balances within its oppressiveness. In other words, though rigid and oppressive, it worked better and less harshly than a modern observer might reasonably expect. Probably for this reason, the hierarchy of the traditional period still echoes loudly in the politics of Thailand of the 21st century.

Historical Setting[3]

Since the Sukhothai period (c. 1239–1438), the king has been at the pinnacle of the hierarchy. In the Sukhothai tradition, he was a *dhammaraja* who ruled in accordance with the cosmic law and teachings of the Buddha and a *pho khun* or patriarch who ruled like a strict but caring father. In the tradition of the Ayutthaya period (1351–1767) he ruled as a *devaraja*, or a semi-divine and more distant figure who was Lord of Land and Lord of Life. A recent study has shown that hierarchy was also a major theme of the Palace Law:

---

3   The following summary draws on the following works: Akin Rabibhadana, *The Organisation of Thai Society in the Early Bangkok Period 1782–1873* (Ithaca New York: Cornell University, 1969); Neil A. Englehart, *Culture and Power in Traditional Siamese Government* (Ithaca: Cornell University Press, 2001); L.M. Hanks, "Merit and Power in the Thai Social Order." *American Anthropologist*, New Series, Vol. 64, No. 6 (Dec, 1962): 1247–1261; Charles F. Keyes, *Thailand: Buddhist Kingdom*; Hong Lysa, *Thailand in the Nineteenth Century: Evolution of the Economy and Society* (Singapore: ISEAS, 1984); Pasuk and Baker, *Thailand: Economy and Politics*; B.J. Terwiel, *Thailand's Political History*; Baker and Pasuk, *The Palace Law of Ayutthaya*; and Baker and Pasuk, *A History of Ayutthaya*.

It prescribes a top-down social order headed by the king, and establishes ways through which this order is dramatized in dress and display. It sets out an annual cycle of ceremonies that present the king as the patron of Buddhism, military defender of the realm, source of agricultural prosperity, fount of charity, and engineer of magical good fortune. It elaborates rules for protecting the king in person, and upholding the palace as sacred space, the large corps of royal women as a symbol of royal power, and the royal elephants as palladia of the realm. It prescribes punishments of death and disfigurement for even minor infractions of these rules. How often such punishments were served is unknown, but the contrast between the protection afforded to royalty and the vulnerability of others lays out a hierarchy of human values. This text is a constitution of its time, a constitution of royal absolutism.[4]

We have seen in Chapter Two how the role of the king was adapted to the modern era. Suffice to say here that the king remains at the pinnacle of Thai society, even though the authority of the monarchy has changed since 1932.

Beneath the king were princes *(jao)*, who had certain legal immunities as well as access to the king, prestigious positions and wealth. Beneath the princes were the nobles *(khunnang)*. In addition to having some access to the king and wealth, the nobles held administrative positions. Beneath the nobles were the commoners *(phrai)*. The commoners were obliged to provide goods and services to the princes and nobles, including *corvée* labour and military service to the king. Beneath the commoners were the slaves *(that)*, who were debt bondsmen or indentured servants rather than chattel

---

4   Baker and Pasuk, *The Palace Law of Ayutthaya*, ix–x.

slaves. (European observers in the 19th century said Siamese slaves were treated as well as servants in France and better than servants in England, which is not to deny the abuse of slaves in Siam, especially the sexual abuse of women. Nor are we assuming that servants in France and England were always treated well).

In the late 16th century Siam's hierarchy was formalised more explicitly when the king assigned numerical rankings—called *sakdina*—to <u>every</u> resident, from princes and officials to beggars and slaves. The highest-ranking prince received 100,000 *sakdina*, other princes received between 1,500 and 50,000, a noble between 400 and 30,000, a commoner between ten and 400, and a slave and beggar received just five *sakdina*. There were over 20 levels of *sakdina*. All recipients held *sakdina* at the will of the king.

Literally, *sakdina* means "power over fields", and theoretically *sakdina* was measured in *rai* (a land measure equivalent to two-fifths of an acre). The literal meaning "power over fields" is misleading. More accurately, *sakdina* reflected resource entitlements.[5] Although theoretically measured in land, the main resource to which people were entitled was manpower. Nobles were "man-lords" rather than land-lords.[6] The implications of this distinctive feature of Siamese hierarchy are considered below.

Sakdina was the starkest manifestation of traditional hierarchy. Hierarchy was also expressed in other ways, including blood relationship to the king; ranks and titles granted by the king; the size of one's retinue; access to the law courts and differentiated compensations and punishments; rules of precedence and protocol; regalia and dress; allegiance ceremonies; numerous other rituals; and tattooing (from the late Ayutthaya period, all commoners and slaves were tattooed on their wrists to show who their master was and where they lived). Hierarchy was captured in language, from *rajasap*

5   Pasuk and Baker, *Thailand: Economy and Politics*, 11.
6   Baker and Pasuk, *A History of Ayutthaya*, 193.

or the language used when speaking to or about royalty to the myriad gradations of personal pronouns and forms of greetings in everyday speech. Respect for people higher in the hierarchy was also expressed through prostration. (In 1873, King Chulalongkorn abolished this practice, but about 90 years later the military government of Sarit Thanarat reintroduced it for Thais who find themselves in the presence of members of the royal family).

Although steeply hierarchical, Siamese society did not develop a rigidly hereditary landed nobility that was a feature of most feudal societies. "The old Thai state extracted labour services and produce taxes directly from the village. This was different from the experience in European history where exploitation in society was exploitation of individual by individual, for example, of the peasant by the landlord."[7] In Siam the king bestowed titles on people but, normally, the children of the title-owner did not inherit the title or benefit from it. The king could also rescind a title at any time. Within the royal family itself, princely ranks reduced with each generation and the great-great grandchildren of a king became commoners.[8]

Philosophically, hierarchy was built on *karma*, the deeply held conviction that one's social status was determined by the merit accumulated in previous lives, or in this life. Within traditional Buddhist cosmology *karma* "gives order and regularity to the universe much as Newtonian laws of Western science give order and regularity to the physical universe".[9] *Karma* "informs behaviour in a way that makes hierarchical social relations seemed normal, natural, and rational",[10] and "the primary goal of politics was to contain as many

---

7   Chatthip Nartsupha, *The Thai Village Economy in the Past*, tr. Chris Baker and Pasuk Phongpaichit (Chiang Mai: Silkworm Books, 1999), 75.

8   Only quite recently (in the reign of King Vajiravudh) were commoner descendants of a king allowed to append "na Ayutthaya" to their surnames to signify their (albeit distant) royal ancestry.

9   Craig Reynolds, "Buddhist Cosmography on Thai History, with Special Reference to the Nineteenth-Century Cultural Change," *Journal of Asian Studies*, Vol 35, No 2 (February 1976), 209. More recently, the American anthropologist, Julia Cassaniti, working in northern Thailand, wrote: "'Karma is like gravity,' I was told more than once: 'It just is.'" Julia Cassaniti, *Living Buddhism: Mind, Self, and Emotion in a Thai Community* (Ithaca and London: Cornell University Press, 2015), 150.

10   Englehart, *Culture and Power*, 25.

people as possible in a single hierarchy. This validated the *karmic* superiority of officials, and ultimately of the king."[11] The king had the most *karma*. He owned all land and, critically, all manpower.

Siam had ample fertile land. People could utilise whatever land they cleared and planted, which was easily accessible along rivers and canals. Manpower, though, was scarce. Siamese kings went to war to bring people (and treasure) they captured back to Siam, not to gain territory. Siamese courts paid more attention to regulating labour and punishing runaways than to registering and administering land. Wealth and authority came from the control of manpower. Through his grants of *sakdina*, the appointment of officials and the allocation of duties, the king exercised power over his people. He rewarded loyalty and competence, but ideally (from his point of view) not to the extent that any rewarded prince or noble could in turn gain control of enough manpower to threaten the throne.

The king assigned to princes, nobles and officials with 400 *sakdina* or more—collectively called *nai*—a designated number of commoners—collectively called *phrai*. The details of the *nai–phrai* relationship were registered. Within the hierarchy, every subject of the king had to have someone who was responsible for them, and a measure of control over them. During war, the king expected the *nai* to deliver *phrai* for military service. During peacetime, the *nai* had to ensure that a certain number of *phrai* were available as *corvée* labour for three to six months each year. For the rest of the year, *phrai* would provide a range of services for their *nai*, for example as guards, personal servants, construction workers, artisans, messengers, administrators and agriculturalists. In addition, the *phrai* were required to give "gifts" regularly to their *nai*, usually rice, other agricultural (and forestry) products and cloth. In cash or kind, a proportion of these gifts made their way up the hierarchy to the king, who also levied a land tax (usually based on the rice yield) and other taxes.

---

11   *Ibid*, 66.

About 99 per cent of the population were *phrai* and upward mobility (from *phrai* to *nai*) was rare, except in wartime, when exceptional service was rewarded. *Phrai* were under the command of *nai*, who had the right to punish *phrai* who refused to obey an order. They depended entirely on their *nai* for protection, without which the *phrai's* property could be stolen with impunity. Military service was feared and *corvée* labour was resented. The penalties for failing to meet a *nai's* expectations were severe, as were the penalties for failing to register as a *phrai*.

Yet the traditional Siamese hierarchy lacked the occupational rigidity of a caste system. *Phrai* could provide the service for which they had the skills and, if they satisfied a *nai*, they could be reassigned to a different, more rewarding or less onerous task. In addition, because land was plentiful, *phrai* were not as territorially constrained as vassals in feudal Europe were. If a *phrai* found a *nai* too oppressive, he could flee and resettle in some previously uninhabited place. Certainly, this step came at a cost for the *phrai*: he could not register his newly-settled land (officials would arrest him for not having a *nai*), his family lived outside the protection of the state, the productivity of his newly-cleared land would be low in the first year or so, and his spiritual life would be unsettled by the long distance from monks and temples.

But the fleeing option was a safety valve within the hierarchical system, not least because the government, which was deeply concerned about the unauthorised movement of scarce labour, would also punish *nai* who oppressed *phrai* so much that they chose to flee. An oppressive *nai* risked failing to meet his main obligations to the king: to provide *phrai* for *corvée* labour and military service and to pay tax based on the number of *phrai* registered to him. "In 1746, [King] Borommakot had two senior nobles flogged for overworking *phrai* engaged to bring a white elephant to the capital, and a royal decree asked: 'Is this the way to help support and sustain the imperial subjects so they can live in happiness?'"[12]

---

12   Baker and Pasuk, *A History of Ayutthaya*, 222.

The system also offered other options for a *phrai* who wanted to ease his burden. He could try to find himself a less demanding (usually wealthier) *nai*, who was willing to pay for the transfer. He could bribe local officials, who were not paid a salary, to escape his obligations. He could become a monk, because monks were not subject to *corvée* labour or military service (although the *sangha* also had a steep hierarchy and initially the fleeing *phrai* would have been at the bottom of it).[13] Or he could become a slave who, in certain circumstances, might have less onerous obligations than a *phrai*.

In practice, of course, the society did not function as effectively as the theory suggested, especially at a distance from the capital (*phrai* outside the central region, for example, paid taxes-in-kind but did not have to provide *corvée* labour).[14] "The villagers' opposition to the state mostly took the form of indifference—slacking and playing around on *corvée* duty, or uprooting the village and fleeing to the forest."[15] There was "evasion and conspiracy at all points of the process and at all levels of the system. This is because it was in the interests of both *nai* and *phrai* to resist the demands of the capital and, paradoxically, it was actually in the interest of the king to tolerate this behavior, at least to a degree.... *Nai, phrai*, and king were all trying to advance their interests while having only limited information about each other's needs and resources."[16] Throughout the Ayutthaya period, "the kings had to contend with ambitious princes and prominent nobles enlarging their entourage by attracting manpower into their service, offering in return protection from the more onerous exactions demanded by the state".[17]

But people who were trying to evade or resist the system, or to conspire against it, understood the hierarchical principles and practices that sustained it.

---

13 Formally, Buddhism ranks a monk higher than a king, regardless of the monk's rank in the *sangha*.
14 Chatthip, *The Thai Village Economy*, 23.
15 *Ibid*, 43.
16 Englehart, *Culture and Power*, 44.
17 Hong Lysa, *Thailand in the Nineteenth Century*, 10.

Pressure for Change

The traditional hierarchy, which, to reiterate, was never as structurally pure or operationally efficient as the summary above might suggest, began to fray in the 19th century when growing international trade and the immigration of thousands of Chinese labourers led to a higher value on property and a lower value on manpower. The king and his administrators could not tightly control Siamese peasants who wanted to spend their time growing rice rather than fulfilling *corvée* labour obligations and who wanted to sell that rice in the market rather than gift a sizeable proportion of it to their *nai*. Nor could the king or administrators tightly control the thousands of largely urban immigrant labourers and traders from China who were already participating in the cash economy. At the same time, Siam was threatened by the imperial ambitions of France and Britain. The choice for Siamese leaders was stark: protect their realm by reforming the administration of it or run the risk of presiding over the demise of Siam as a self-governing kingdom.

They chose reform. The transformation of Siam's governance was initiated by King Rama III (especially tax reform), advanced by Rama IV (Mongkut) and accelerated by Rama V (Chulalongkorn), and their mostly royal advisers. It was not directly imposed by a colonial power; nor was Siam's governance transformed by the middle classes or the masses. The traditional political leadership remained at the helm. Unsurprisingly, kings and princes preserved and, where possible, fortified the monarchy and the principles and practices of hierarchy that underpinned it. In brief, they built a centralized administrative system that strengthened their control over territory as well as subjects. They introduced a tax system that delivered more reliable and higher revenue. And they established a standing army that could meet security challenges and objectives more effectively than the legions of part-time troops and mercenaries upon whom previous kings had depended.

Obligation to Protect

A succession of rulers justified their reforms by relying on their own and their subjects' acceptance of the *karmic* supremacy of the king at the philosophical level, and by seeking to protect themselves and their subjects from the disruptions and uncertainties of a volatile age. Protecting themselves would have been instinctive. In protecting their subjects, they were fulfilling a primary obligation of traditional kingship.

Whether his subjects saw him as a *dhammaraja* in the Sukhothai tradition or a *devaraja* in the Ayutthaya tradition, the king was, above all, expected to protect them: by raising and leading an army to meet external threats; by safeguarding their lives and property from internal threats; by dispensing justice; and by fulfilling religious obligations. The same was true in the more vernacular tradition of *pho khun*, or kind and attentive father. At the apex of the hierarchy, the king was the ultimate protector—of princes, nobles and commoners alike. Cascading from the king, princes and nobles had an obligation to protect commoners.

The final, crowning sentence of the Ramkhamhaeng Inscription of 1292, reputed by many scholars to be the oldest example of Siamese orthography and the foundation stone of the historiography of the Sukhothai period, says the king "<u>protected</u> and reared all these people from all these places and all took pleasure in the *dhamma*".[18] In their study of the Thai folk epic of the Ayutthaya period, *Khun Chang Khun Phaen*, Chris Baker and Pasuk Phongpaichit observe that two of the main items of royal regalia, the sword and the umbrella, are symbols of protection, and that the king is addressed as "lord protector", "divine protector" and "paramount protector".[19] In 1893 King Chulalongkorn, dispirited by Siam's forced surrender of territory to France, expressed fury for not being able to fulfil his protective role: "My people say

---

18 Barend Jan Terwiel, *The Ram Khamhaeng Inscription: the fake that did not come true* (Gossenberg, Ostasien Verlag, 2010), 95. Emphasis added.

19 Chris Baker and Pasuk Phongpaichit, "The Revolt of Khun Phaen: Contesting Power in Early Modern Siam," in *A Sarong for Clio: Essays on the Intellectual and Cultural History of Thailand*, ed. Maurizio Peleggi (Ithaca: Cornell University Press, 2015), 23.

that I cannot protect them!"[20] Less than three years later, he said the aim of all his reforms was "to protect ourselves against internal and external dangers".[21]

Tellingly, the 1932 manifesto of the People's Party justifying the overthrow of the absolute monarchy starts with this question of protection: "When this king [Prajadhipok] succeeded his elder brother [Vajiravudh], people at first hoped that he would govern protectively. But matters have not turned out as they hoped."[22] The king, the new rulers pronounced, had failed to protect. Equally tellingly, and reflecting the revitalization of the monarchy from the 1950s, after the death of King Bhumibol in 2016 many Thais said they felt that they had lost a protector. The idea that the king—and the state—has a primary obligation to protect is deeply embedded in Thai thinking.

Patron-Client Relations: Centrality of Personal Ties

In the traditional hierarchy, in addition to the king having an obligation to protect his subjects, princes and nobles had an obligation to protect commoners. In return, commoners had an obligation to serve princes and nobles while princes and nobles as well as commoners had an obligation to serve the king. As mentioned earlier, the privilege of demanding service from people lower in the hierarchy found its philosophical rationale in *karma*, which explained why people higher in the hierarchy had superior resources, talent and luck. By providing services to their superiors, inferiors also upheld this *karmic* order because it rewarded loyal service with the promise of higher status in the future.

The inclination of inferiors—or clients—to serve also had a worldly rationale: a superior (or patron) might use those *karma*-bestowed resources, talent and luck to help them. Finding a patron, rather

---

20 Quoted in Walter E.J. Tips, *Siam's Struggle for Survival: The Gunboat Incident at Paknam and the Franco-Siamese Treaty of October 1893* (Bangkok: White Lotus, 1996), 122, 124.
21 Quoted in Tej, *Provincial Administration*, 249.
22 *Pridi by Pridi*, 70.

than standing alone, offered a better chance—the only chance—of economic and social well-being, and of protection. It was impossible for an individual to seek help or protection from an agency, for example a police force or judiciary, which was independent of the hierarchical structure. They didn't exist, nor did the idea of them exist. Traditionally, the role of the police was to protect the life and property of the monarchy; the police had no broader public security role. Nobles policed, judged and punished commoners; the king policed, judged and punished princes; he or his personal appointees policed, judged and punished nobles. Explanations were sought, problems were solved, and disputes were settled within the hierarchy. There was no autonomous agency or institution outside the hierarchy.

Because the control of manpower was paramount, because patron-client relations were central, because autonomous agencies and institutions were non-existent, power depended on the quality and quantity of personal relationships. Starting at the top, the king tried to choose people he knew personally, even intimately as members of his immediate family, to fill senior positions where personal loyalty was essential. He tried to consolidate his dynasty through marriages—personal bonds—with the daughters of other princes and nobles, and in turn princes and nobles sought to consolidate their positions through marriages with the king (ideally) and with each other's families. The king depended upon his princes and nobles (*nai*) for, above all, manpower: *phrai* who could serve as soldiers or *corvée* labour. At the lower end of this pyramid, the *nai* had to motivate, persuade, compel or bully his *phrai* to meet his obligations to provide labour, land tax and gifts of rice and other products. The *nai* couldn't turn to a police force or other institutions for support. He relied on personal relations with his *phrai*. In turn, the *phrai* relied on personal relations with his *nai* to minimise his *corvée* labour, land tax and gift obligations, to represent him in any dispute with the government and to lend him money. Often, the only security for a loan was the debtor himself, or his child or wife, who would serve as slaves in the *nai's* household until the debt was redeemed—another indicator of the centrality of personal relations within the traditional system.

Because wealth and authority came from the control of manpower, the more clients a patron had, the greater his power and prestige. A patron increased his "entourage" or "circle"—and thereby increased his power—by increasing the number of clients and sub-clients who were prepared to serve him in some capacity. An early student of this phenomenon, Lucien Hanks, put it this way:

> A patron who summons his clients may also find the clients of these clients responding to the summons. The immediate clients relay the call to their clients, and the call may reach not only to the clients of clients but several stages beyond. Similarly I may respond to the call of my patron, who has responded to the call of his patron, or of patrons several entourages beyond me. The entire range of persons who responded to a man's call, provided it extends beyond his own entourage, makes up his circle. Presumably the king's circle is the largest, the circles of his ministers next largest, and so circles of decreasing size occur in descending the hierarchy. [23]

These patron-client relationships have been variously described as "a complex series of negotiations",[24] a "lop-sided friendship"[25] or a "largely instrumental friendship".[26] A would-be client initiated a "negotiation" or "friendship" by giving a gift to, or doing a favour

---

23   L. M. Hanks, "The Thai Social Order as Entourage and Circle," 202.
24   Englehart, *Culture and Power*, 44.
25   Akin, *The Organisation of Thai Society*, 86.
26   James Scott, quoted in Katherine A. Bowie, *Rituals of National Loyalty: An Anthropology of the State and the Village Scout Movement in Thailand* (New York: Columbia University Press, 1997), 336, n14. More fully, Scott said, a "largely instrumental friendship in which an individual of a higher socio-economic status (patron) uses his own influence and resources to provide protection or benefits, or both, for a person of low status (client) who, for his part, reciprocates by offering general support and assistance, including personal services, to the patron."

for, a would-be patron. Explicitly or implicitly, the gift or favour was a request for protection. Gifts and favours were not short-term transactions; rather, gifts created longer-term obligations, or "enduring, incalculable, and multi-stranded relationships".[27] When the patron responded by providing protection, a reciprocal gift or a favour of some sort, the client was obliged to give another gift or provide another service. Thus, a cycle of reciprocity was nurtured. Because these transactions assumed continuity, "negotiation" and "friendship" are better descriptions than "contract" or "debt". "Contract" and "debt" imply these were one-off transactions, which they normally weren't; and that an autonomous authority would exist to settle disputes, which wasn't the case.

Clients had an interest in attaching themselves to a patron who could protect them. Equally, a patron had an interest in attracting as many clients as possible, because status and authority were linked to control of manpower. If a client felt the protection and favours from his patron failed to meet expectations, he would look for another patron. Equally, if a patron was unimpressed with the gifts or favours offered by a client, or if he no longer had the resources to provide protection or favours in return, the relationship lapsed. Whether as a patron or a client, responsibilities were often lightly worn.

Dilution of Hierarchy

To restate some of the distinguishing features of Siam's traditional hierarchy: the central responsibility of the king to protect his subjects and of other patrons to protect their clients; the interdependence between patrons and clients together with the relative ease with which they could cast aside their relationship; and the dominance of personal connections. And to restate a distinguishing non-feature of Siam's traditional hierarchy: the absence of any autonomous authority outside the hierarchy to settle disputes.

---

27   Walker, *Thailand's Political Peasants*, 199.

But Thailand is not Siam. For almost two centuries hierarchy has been challenged and diluted by new ideas, new ways of doing things, and new institutions. Obviously, nowadays if a Thai needs a loan, he or she can go to a state-regulated bank rather than a patron. Thais are no longer legally subject to forced labour, nor can they legally pay off their debts by becoming slaves. If Thais break the law, the police and judiciary are expected to deal with them impartially; they are no longer at risk of the caprice of a domineering master or an untrained judge. At the political level, there is an understanding that all Thais, regardless of social and economic status, should be subject to constitutional government, not absolutism (monarchical or military). Even military governments have interim constitutions.

Yet hierarchical thinking persists. The rest of this chapter looks at how ideas that traditionally sustained hierarchy still influence Thai politics. Our observations are more suggestive and qualitative than scientific and quantifiable. Our observations are also snapshots, not a full-length documentary. They aim simply to throw a light on the role of hierarchical thinking in modern Thai politics, including its influence on dispute settlement.

Persistence of Hierarchy

First, let's remind ourselves of how traditional hierarchical thinking in Thailand lasted well beyond the reforms initiated by kings in the 19th century and hastened by commoners in the 20th century. Consider the following accounts of Thai villagers in the 1960s on the question of *karma*:

> They readily agreed that a big house, a good deal of money, eyeglasses, good clothes, or good health were all obvious indications of much merit. Such signs make abundantly clear the condition of one's merit. Equally clear, these signs are themselves the natural results of good conduct at some earlier

time. An increase in a person's fortunes would be happily accepted as reward for past merit.[28]

The people of Bang Chan felt they could discern even of themselves who was meritful and who was not according to human circumstances, constitution, and behavior. A meritorious person was healthy, happy, and successful in all undertakings. He enjoyed good health and long life, a kindly personality, many fine children, wealth, high status, intelligence, and luck.... He who lacked merit, because of sins committed perhaps many ages ago ... suffered early death, deformities, unhappiness, poverty, and had a cruel nature. Illness ... struck as part of the suffering brought on by former sin. It was accepted in the conviction that whoever suffered had brought it on himself.[29]

In the 1980s a Thai researcher wrote of Thai villagers: "It's not that farmers cannot see the exploitation or do not feel exploited. Just the opposite. In reality farmers feel exploited. But the farmers explained to themselves that the reason behind this exploitation is that they lack 'merit'."[30]

Far removed from these villagers in education and experience, and far removed from villages geographically, in 1984 officials in the National Cultural Commission and National Identity Office published a book which "pictured Thai society as a pyramid, essentially unchanged since the Sukhothai era. At the top was the king; next came the bureaucracy created when 'the king found it impossible to manage the nation's affairs single-handedly'; and at the base were

---

28 Jasper Ingersoll, "Merit and Identity in Village Thailand," in *Change and Persistence in Thai Society: Essays in Honor of Lauriston Sharp*, ed. G. William Skinner and A. Thomas Kirsch (Ithaca and London: Cornell University Press, 1975), 232.
29 Quoted in Engel, *Code and Custom in a Thai Provincial Court: The Interaction of Formal and Informal Systems of Justice* (Tucson: University of Arizona Press, 1978), 59.
30 Quoted in Chatthip, *The Thai Village Economy*, 42.

peasants living in unchanging, peaceful villages 'where democracy is practised in its purest form.'"[31] At the same time, the Interior Ministry concluded that Thai people were not ready for democracy "because of poor upbringing, an innate lack of ethics or seriousness, or simply a 'disposition to be under the command of others'."[32]

A little over a decade later, in 1997, the most democratic constitution in Thailand's history included for the first time a provision that members of parliament had to hold a university degree—with little debate and less controversy. In other words, Thais seemed to accept that less than 10 per cent of eligible voters should be able to stand for election; or, put another way, that over 90 per cent were ineligible (ironically, King Bhumibol, who sat at the top of the traditional hierarchy, would not have met this test, as he returned to Thailand to take up the throne before completing his degree in Switzerland).[33]

Add another two decades. In 2017 a Thai woman from Isaan who used to work for me was denied entry to a new shopping mall in Bangkok because the guards, acting on instructions from the mall managers, adjudged that she was not of the right class for such a prestigious venue. Tellingly, she expressed annoyance at the waste of her time more than indignation at her exclusion. "That's how it is," she said. A recent book by Sophorntavy Vorng has other examples of this sort of thinking and conduct.[34]

Hierarchy and Modern Electoral and Street Politics

From November 2013 until the May 2014 coup, participants in the Suthep-led PDRC protests against the government of Yingluck Shinawatra and the prevailing democratic system shrilly denounced elected politicians. The PDRC called for a suspension of democracy and rule by "good people", disparaging governments that were

---

31   Baker and Pasuk, *A History of Thailand*, 236.
32   *Ibid.*
33   The 2007 and 2017 constitutions did not retain this provision.
34   Sophorntavy Vorng, *A Meeting of Masks*, see especially Chapter 4.

elected by the "'uninformed' and/or 'bribed' majority".[35] Some called for changes to one-person, one-vote electoral democracy, with the votes of Bangkok electors having a higher value than the votes of rural people. A poll showed that only 30 per cent of protesters agreed that the statement "Thais are not yet ready for equal voting rights" seriously offended the principles of democracy and was unacceptable.[36] Seventy-four per cent of these poll respondents had a university degree and 40 per cent had household incomes of more than THB 60,000 per month (in 2013 the national average monthly income was a little over THB 25,000). Frequently, this suspicion of and contempt for rural voters was tinged with prejudice against Thais from Isaan and northern Thailand, who are nicknamed "water buffaloes" (which Thais have traditionally regarded as stupid and stubborn animals) and other pejorative terms.

Let's compare these largely middle-class and upper-class Thai attitudes to voters' rights expressed at the PDRC rally, and even the decision of the People's Party in 1932 to delay the introduction of universal suffrage because the people were "uneducated", with attitudes in nations that were colonized. In newly-independent India, where only 16 per cent of the people were literate in 1951 (in other words, only one in seven people could sign their name), the middle-class elite accepted universal suffrage without debate—because nationalist leaders had relied on mass support to drive the British out and because they believed universal suffrage would help to overcome entrenched hierarchy and disadvantage. The upper and middle classes of Thailand have never needed mass support to advance or protect their interests. Nor did they ever seriously devalue hierarchy. In Malaysia, where the nationalist movement had neither the mass mobilization nor the decades-long duration of India's movement, and where ethnic differences threatened stable government, the post-

---

35   Charles Keyes, *Democracy Thwarted: The Crisis of Political Authority in Thailand* (Singapore: ISEAS, 2015), 14.
36   Asia Foundation, *Profile of the "Bangkok Shutdown" Protestors*, 18.

independence upper-class and middle-class elite concluded that universal suffrage was a nation-building priority. In contrast, Thai upper and middle classes agreed upon, and imposed, an idea of the nation without feeling a need to consult the masses.[37]

At the same time that PDRC protesters were calling for government by "good people", leaders and participants in counter-protests organized by UDD or the red-shirt movement were denouncing the advocates of a non-elected government in terms that had become familiar since the emergence of the movement after the 2006 coup. Conscious of the hierarchical thinking that fuelled their opponents' reluctance to share political power, red-shirt leaders had revived the traditional term *phrai* (commoner) to describe themselves and their followers. They were arguing that Thai politics remained pre-modern.

Thongchai Winichakul touched on this in a poignant analysis of the last six minutes of an equally poignant speech in 2008 by one of the red-shirts' leaders, Nattawut Saikua. Nattawut blamed the persistence of hierarchy for the grievances of red-shirt sympathisers: injustice; denial of a public voice; neglect; and judicial double standards. Using the metaphors of earth and sky, Nattawut said: "But with the increasing power of the red-shirts ... even when we stand on the earth, speaking from the earth, the sky will hear us."[38] In 2013–14, some red-shirt protesters seemingly saw the Crown Prince as "the sky". They wore "We Love the Crown Prince" T-shirts, implying that they thought this prominent member of the royal family either would offer them support and protection, or could be persuaded to do so.

In a further sign of the persistence of traditional thinking, which weighed political power and status by the number of supporters or clients a leader may attract, in May 2014 as rival PDRC and UDD

---

37   Thai nationalism is discussed in more detail in the next chapter.
38   Thongchai Winichakul, "The Monarchy and Anti-Monarchy: Two Elephants in the Room of Thai Politics and the State of Denial," in *Good Coup Gone Bad*, ed. Pavin Chachavalpongpun (Singapore, ISEAS, 2014), 93.

political groups assembled in different parts of Bangkok, supporters of each group told me that whoever could attract the biggest crowd would prevail.

The traditional idea that social status and political power were determined by the number of one's clients or supporters also helps to explain the relative ease with which the idea of electoral politics has been accepted in Thailand, as well as the greater difficulty in understanding and accepting the other pillars of liberal democracy: equality, individual rights and the rule of law, all of which have been erected over centuries in other societies as bulwarks against hierarchy. Surveys have shown that Thais "conceive democracy in terms of electoral democracy, rather than inclusive of the components of 'liberal' democracy or components of 'substantive democracy'".[39]

Hierarchy and Political Parties

The vitality of patron-client relationships, with their reliance on personal connections, has been reflected in the births, lives and deaths of political parties in Thailand. For most of the period since 1946 when parties were first permitted, they have been formed around leaders, or patrons, who attracted the personal support of various individuals, or clients, who themselves were often patrons of an array of cliques and factions. The would-be MPs offered prospective voters the delivery of state resources in the form of roads, bridges, schools, health centres, subsidies, employment and the like, as well as protection from exploitation by state officials. In keeping with traditional patron-client relationships, candidates for election invariably offered voters money and gifts, too—to establish and maintain their credentials as patrons. Also in keeping with traditional patron-client relationships, voters favoured the candidate who seemed to offer the best protection

---

39   Robert B. Albritton and Thawilwadee Bureekul. *Are Democracy and 'Good Governance' Always Compatible? Competing Values in the Thai Political Arena*. Working Paper No 47 (Chile: Global Barometer and International Political Science Association, 2009), not paginated (quotation appears on the second last page).

or the candidate who was owed a favour, including in return for monetary or other incentives that were distributed more frequently and generously during election campaigns.

Therefore, the primary purpose of the political party was to provide a vehicle for the leader and MPs under its banner to secure cabinet positions. In return, the cabinet ministers were expected to divert state resources to their electors, or clients, and to use the status of minister or MP to moderate their clients' dealings with powerful local bureaucrats. Political parties did not need to offer ideologies or policies; nor did they need to develop organizational structures or impose discipline on their members. If the leader or other MPs of a party thought they had a better chance of gaining cabinet posts by switching parties, they did so. Parties were light-fitting cloaks, not straitjackets.

Voters were loyal to patrons, not a party. And, similarly, MPs were more loyal to their patrons and clients than to their party. In the absence of ideology, policies, organizational machinery and party discipline—which are common features of political parties in other places—Thailand spawned many parties, which formed unstable and often short-lived coalition governments, whose primary purpose was to retain office—and the spoils of office. Policy development and implementation was largely left to the bureaucracy which, luckily for Thailand, has been fairly competent.

Over time, the business community, middle class, and NGOs became hostile towards the narrow focus and short-sightedness of political parties and elected politicians. Their answer—the 1997 Constitution—was designed to reduce the number of political parties and deliver governments that were more stable and efficient and less corrupt.

The 1997 Constitution initially helped to deliver greater stability and efficiency (we will consider corruption later). After the 2001 election, the number of parties represented in parliament shrank from 13 to nine, with Thaksin's Thai Rak Thai Party alone gaining 248 seats in the 500-seat parliament. In the 2005 election, only four parties were successful and Thai Rak Thai gained an outright majority with 377 seats.[40] Partly because they were more stable, the Thaksin-led governments were also more efficient than previous elected governments. For a few years they won plaudits from the business community, Bangkok middle class, and their largely rural support base for their economic policies, social programs and administrative reforms.

To a significant extent, Thai Rak Thai's electoral success reflected a shift away from the previous we-know-best, eve-of-the-election approach of political parties that were formed largely around traditional patron-client relationships. Thai Rak Thai attempted to gauge the longer-term aspirations as well as the immediate local needs of the electorate, especially in rural areas, by consulting widely for over two years before the 2001 election. It then developed policies that sought to respond to those aspirations and needs—rural debt relief, capital for village development, and cheap, universal health care. Then, after a well-funded, sophisticated and successful election campaign, Thai Rak Thai governments implemented their policies quickly. In brief, partly by design and partly in response to voter feedback after the 2001 election, Thai Rak Thai included the views of the rural and semi-urban community in the formulation of policy and gave previously indifferent or cynical voters reason to believe the electoral system could advance their interests. This party-initiated democratization of Thai politics was new.

At the same time, Thai Rak Thai (and its successor parties— Palang Prachachon and Pheu Thai) was the instrument of Thaksin, the patron *par excellence*. Thaksin had enormous resources—he had

---

40   In an (unsuccessful) attempt to prevent Thaksin's party dominating elections, the drafters of the 2007 Constitution designed a system that encouraged more parties, so seven parties gained seats after the 2007 election and 11 after the 2011 election. The same anti-Thaksin motivation prompted the drafters of the 2017 Constitution and electoral law to introduce a new electoral system that encourages even more parties.

become a billionaire largely through government concessions in the telecommunications sector. He funded his party's organization and election campaigns generously. Thaksin was a consummate organizer and dealmaker. He drew other political leaders and parties into his network. Thaksin was charismatic and a gifted communicator. He knew how to connect with voters, whether they were rich or poor, rural or urban, and whether he was dealing with them face to face or through slogans and posters.

And even though Thaksin has been unable to formally lead his party since 2006 and has been out of Thailand since 2008, he remains the *de facto* leader. After he was compelled to relinquish the prime ministership in 2006, Thaksin personally chose Samak Sundaravej as the new party leader and personally settled internal party disputes. The unofficial party slogan in the 2007 election campaign was "Vote Samak, Get Thaksin". After the Constitutional Court fired Samak in 2008, Thaksin put a trusted relative, his brother-in-law Somchai Wongsawat, at the head of the party. A few months before the 2011 election, Thaksin bestowed the leadership of the party on an even closer relative, his sister Yingluck, whom he publicly called a "clone", and from his overseas bases he masterminded an election campaign with the slogan "Thaksin Thinks, Pheu Thai Acts".[41] In other words, Thaksin's party's innovations in policy development and voter engagement did not signal the demise of the traditional political patron. The innovations and the patron co-existed.

Hierarchy and the Legislature

The vitality of hierarchical patron-client relationships, with their reliance on personal connections, has stunted the growth of the legislature as an institution. Certainly, the Thai legislature matters more than before; it can no longer be ignored. But even when the

---

41   Baker and Pasuk, *A History of Thailand*, 279.

legislature has been fully elected, MPs and political parties have rarely demonstrated a loyalty to the institution. Preoccupied with the personal connections that lie at the heart of patron-client relationships, they have not thought in institutional terms. They have not rallied to strengthen the institution when its failings have been identified. Nor have they defended the authority of parliament when the institution has been undermined or attacked by the military, judiciary, government officials or unruly mobs on Bangkok's streets. In other words, they have not concluded that, collectively as legislators, they might better advance the long-term interests of themselves and their clients if they promoted the legislature as an institution, and ideologically or personally demonstrated a loyalty to it.

In contrast, the king is loyal to the institution of the monarchy. Generals have consistently shown a deep loyalty to the military as an institution. Although they may not be as disciplined as military officers, government officials have also loyally defended their individual ministries and the bureaucracy as a whole. Judges are loyal to the judiciary, which has brought them prestige and, increasingly, power.

Playing the Man, Not the Ball

Just as Thaksin's leadership of his political party often typified old-style patronage politics, the responses of Thaksin's opponents often typified the highly personalised politics of Thailand's traditional, hierarchical system. Their main target has been the patron or person. Thaksin's opponents have tried, above all, to deny Thaksin and his successors as party leader a political role. In numerous conversations, Bangkok-based members of the Thai elite and middle class have sought to inform or conclude discussions about the future of Thai politics and any proposals for political reform by telling this writer: "He [Thaksin] must never be allowed back." All other considerations, it seems, are secondary.

Concrete examples of this fixation on the person include the military-appointed government's decision in 2006 to ban Thaksin from politics for five years for alleged malpractice during the April 2006 elections, even though the election results had since been annulled and the penalty was applied retrospectively. In the same year, the military also established an Assets Scrutiny Committee, which included several well-known Thaksin critics and which froze THB 76 billion (US$2.1 billion) of Thaksin's assets, THB 46 billion of which was ultimately confiscated. After Thaksin was sentenced to two years' imprisonment for assisting his wife in purchasing government-owned land, his opponents targeted his personally chosen successor as party leader, Samak Sundaravej, eventually firing him in 2008 over a petty charge in a judgment that one of the judges later described as "judicial creativity". Six years later Yingluck was fired over the transfer of a senior official. A fast-tracked investigation into her party's rice subsidy scheme eventually saw her sentenced to five years' imprisonment and personal liability of THB 35 billion (US$1.1 billion) for dereliction of duty in the management of a policy that was a clear election promise, had been approved by a legally constituted cabinet and a fully elected parliament, and implemented in line with the democratic government's directions by a mostly professional civil service, although evidence of some corrupt practices (by other officials, not Yingluck) soon emerged.[42]

In 2017, Thaksin's opponents drafted new organic laws on political parties and elections with the seemingly primary intention of blocking Thaksin from any role in Thai politics. Under the laws, he is barred from directly or indirectly influencing the party, of which he has remained *de facto* leader, financially or in any other way. If he does, the party can be banned. So Pheu Thai will not be able to publicise its policies as Thaksin-endorsed or have slogans like "Vote Samak, Get

---

42   If this approach to agricultural subsidies were applied to the elected governments of Europe, the United States and Japan, almost all their leaders would be in prison and collectively facing personal liability bills of tens of billions of dollars.

Thaksin" or "Thaksin Thinks, Pheu Thai Acts", or adorn their election banners with portraits of Thaksin (or Yingluck). In addition, as soon as the 10-year statute of limitations expired in 2018 on Thaksin's two-year imprisonment on the land-purchasing case, the military government threatened to activate other pending cases against Thaksin, having earlier deliberately amended the law to remove the statute of limitations applying to them.

In their quest to remove him, anti-Thaksin forces have resorted to the law, which is supposed to treat people equally, and the judiciary, which is supposed to be independent of the traditional hierarchy. Thaksin's opponents re-wrote constitutions and political party and electoral laws to try to thwart him. In addition, through changes to the constitution and the rules for appointing judges, they enlisted the judiciary as a combatant in their highly personalised campaign. And they put public and political pressure on judges, including by allowing the supporters of their political party and the yellow-shirt movement to intimidate the judiciary. In brief, they did not look to the judiciary as an independent, neutral arbiter that could help to advance the public interest and resolve disputes.

The judiciary itself was a willing player in this highly political contest.[43] Judges did not defend the independence of the judiciary. They also admitted to delivering judgments that were influenced by either politics or traditional notions that their primary role was to preserve harmony and restore order in the society, not uphold the primacy of the law.

The purpose here is not to say whether Thaksin was guilty or innocent of the charges brought against him or whether the punishments imposed upon him were fair or not. Rather, it is to point out that the responses of Thaksin's opponents reflected the qualities of the highly personalised politics of traditional Siam; their responses are not consistent with a system where politics is governed by the rule of law and where an

---

43   We will consider the judiciary in more detail in Chapter Eight.

independent, neutral judiciary protects the rule of law. Put another way, they did not see the judiciary as, and did not want the judiciary to become, an independent mediator and arbiter of political disputes.

Nor is our purpose to say that only the anti-Thaksin side of politics conducted itself in this way. Far from it. From the start of his prime ministership in 2001, Thaksin and his supporters put pressure on the judiciary over the assets concealment case he faced. Within a year of controversially escaping a conviction for concealing his assets, Thaksin threatened to cut the budget of the judiciary. And when the opportunity came, he compromised the independence of the Senate and appointed loyalists to the Constitutional Court and independent bodies. Thaksin and his successors at the head of Pheu Thai did not try to restrain supporters of the party and the red-shirt movement when they sought to intimidate the judiciary by occupying public buildings. Also operating within the person-centric politics of hierarchy, they seemingly saw no need to foster an independent judiciary, even though they ultimately claimed that the absence of an independent judiciary disadvantaged them.

Hierarchy and Neutral Referees

The roots of person-centric political thinking are deeper in Thailand than the roots of constitutional government and the rule of law. To a certain extent, the efforts of modern Thai politicians to ignore, manipulate or co-opt the law and judiciary reflect the absence in pre-20th century Thailand of independent authorities, or the absence of even the idea that interests might be advanced or protected, or disputes might be settled, by an independent agency like a police force or judiciary. As we have seen, traditionally, protection and dispute settlement were sought in the hierarchy and were a test of the authority and, ultimately, the utility of one's patron. An independent avenue did not exist. Nowadays, the police force, judiciary, legislature, media and civil society provide a range of new avenues for protecting interests and mediating and arbitrating disputes. But they have not nullified the role of the well-connected patron. The new and the old live side by side. And they overlap—because within the police force, judiciary, legislature, media, academia and civil society patron-client relationships also play decisive roles.

Thais' person-centric approach to politics was illustrated during the turbulent months leading to the May 2014 coup. People tended to look first for an individual to blame for the unwelcomed state of affairs. Anti-government protesters blamed Thaksin, while the pro-government camp said it was all Suthep's fault. Yingluck and Abhisit were also named as culprits; Yingluck for failing to block her brother's bid for an amnesty and Abhisit for boycotting the 2 February election. Having apportioned blame, the next question was: "Who will save us?" Suthep and his followers saw the answer in a government of "good people". Others hoped that the King would intervene, or they hankered after a man on a white horse: an interim prime minister *à la* Anand Panyarachun in 1992–93 or an army chief *à la* General Sonthi Boonyaratglin in 2006—or even the reinstatement of General Prem Tinsulanond as prime minister. In all cases, the focus was on who should govern Thailand. Whether the saviour came to power constitutionally and whether the saviour's government should be subject to the rule of law seemed irrelevant. The question of how Thailand might be governed more effectively did not arise.

Hierarchy and the State

Now we return to our earlier observation that a primary historical obligation of the king was to protect his subjects. The centrality of this notion of protection in traditional Thai political thinking has helped to underwrite the commanding role of the state in modern Thailand. Just as the king within the traditional hierarchical system protected his subjects by deciding what was best for them, post-1932 prime ministers have also protectively decided what was best for their subjects.

The fatherly state decided when Thais were educated enough to elect a legislature and when they were too immature to retain one. With little consultation with the beneficiaries of their largesse, throughout the 20th century paternalistic governments invested heavily in infrastructure, education, health and other social programs, protected Thai business from competition, and subsidised the rural economy. Civilian as well as military governments have agreed that the state should be deeply involved in the economy and the society, and should also cultivate loyalty to the nation, religion and king. To protect their realm (and themselves), since 1932 governments have relied on the civilian bureaucracy and standing army that Chulalongkorn created. Most observers familiar with Southeast Asia would say that only Singapore has a more capable civil service. (Also reflecting a persistence of hierarchical thinking, the Thai armed forces have one general for approximately 200 troops; its US counterpart, by contrast, has one general for approximately 2,000 troops.)

For many Thais the state has been as comforting as it has been threatening. Until the middle of the 20th century the state rarely frustrated their efforts to provide food, clothing and shelter for their families. Since the middle of the century, the state has made it easier to secure these basic necessities. Then, through educational and employment opportunities, the state helped to open new doors for them. Civilian and military governments have also protected, or tried to protect, their subjects from communism, separatism and perceived security threats rooted in social ills, like narcotics. For many Thais, the protection afforded by wars on communism, separatism and drugs seems to have mattered more than the human rights abuses and denial of certain freedoms that have often attended them (and continue in the three southern provinces). And for most of the post-1932 period, many Thais have also seemed to care more about whether their government protected them than whether it was elected by them.

Thailand has a "strong-state tradition", initially absolutist under King Chulalongkorn, then authoritarian under post-1932 civilian and military governments.[44] Within this strong-state tradition, Thai business is closely linked to government and heavily protected by the government. In addition, Thai governments have moved from taxing the rural economy to subsidizing it, to the extent that villagers are now accustomed to, and expect further, state-funded enhancements to their livelihood and well-being.[45]

Although this strong-state tradition is enduring, it is not unchallenged. It has been juxtaposed with another tradition that puts the well-being of the Thai people ahead of the interests of the state.[46] We have seen that from the 1970s the top-down approach of mostly military regimes was challenged by social and political pressures for a more consultative type of government, which eventually led to the 1997 Constitution. The top-down approach was then challenged by the new constitution itself, which opened political and judicial avenues for Thais to voice their views and grievances. Significantly, though, the public pressure was for better government, not less government.

Like his predecessors, Thaksin, the first political leader to gain office under the 1997 Constitution, used the authority of his position to deploy the resources of the state to protect his subjects; in his case, he chose to stimulate the economy (more through government intervention than liberalisation, though some liberalisation occurred), provide social safeguards like health care, support local government, launch a war on drugs, and so on. Like many of his predecessors, he also used the resources of the state to try to protect himself and his personal interests. Less like his predecessors, Thaksin asked his subjects what they wanted from the state and then tried to deliver it. He tried to embrace both the strong-state tradition and the emerging

---

44　Baker and Pasuk, *A History of Thailand*, 282–3.
45　Andrew Walker, *Thailand's Political Peasants*, 220–21.
46　Baker and Pasuk, *A History of Thailand*, 283–4.

well-being-of-the-people tradition. Put another way, he turned the social contract that had developed over several decades between the state and the rural population into "a core political asset".[47] The ensuing struggle between Thaksin and the old elite was a struggle for control of the state, not a struggle between different perceptions of the state's fundamental role to play a commanding, protective role.

Hierarchy and Corruption

In the same way that the king's responsibility to protect his subjects in traditional Siam helps to explain the powerful role of the state in modern Thailand, the traditional interdependence between patrons and clients and the importance of personal connections help to explain the pervasiveness of corruption.[48] We are not interested here in a discussion of corruption in all its complexity; rather, we are interested in how hierarchy, patronage and personal connections contribute to it.

In a sense, governmental corruption as we commonly understand it—illegal conduct for personal gain involving state officials—hardly existed in pre-modern Siam. Before 1932, MPs did not exist. And before Chulalongkorn's administrative reforms from the 1880s it was not illegal for state officials to gain personally from their official positions. On the contrary, they were expected to remunerate themselves by retaining a portion (usually between 10 and 30 per cent) of the taxes they collected and by charging a fee for their services. Officials were considered corrupt only to the extent that they breached accepted limits of remuneration; their right to remunerate themselves in this way was not questioned. A system in which state employers, from the king down, provided a regular income to their employees did not exist.

In theory, the old system was to be superseded by Chulalongkorn's

---

47   Andrew Walker, *Thailand's Political Peasants*, 221.
48   The following observations draw heavily on the first chapter of the illuminating study of Pasuk Phongpaichit and Sungsidh Piriyarangsan, *Corruption and Democracy in Thailand* (Chiang Mai: Silkworm Books, 1996), 1–25.

introduction of a professional civil service in which recruitment and promotion was supposed to be based on merit, civil servants were supposed to serve citizens equally, and civil servants received a regular salary. In reality, the old administrators—drawn from the royal family and nobility—continued to dominate senior positions, so old ways of doing things persisted. Personal connections were still important, and more deeply embedded in the hierarchical culture than ideas of non-discriminatory service for all citizens. In addition, although salaries were initially quite good, over time their real value dropped substantially, and the purchasing power of civil service salaries has still not recovered.[49] Although further reforms after 1932 reduced the role of the monarchy and royal family, and over time the community began to expect more professional conduct from civil servants, change has been shallow and slow. Practices which, as we have seen, were an integral part of the patronage system have been absorbed into the modern bureaucracy and, as it evolved, parliamentary politics: exchanges of gifts and favours; recruitment, promotion and protection of members of one's family and entourage; and diversion of state resources to one's superiors (patrons) and supporters (clients), as well as to oneself.

The 1997 Constitution was designed to deliver governments that were less corrupt, as well as more stable and efficient. The first prime minister under the new constitution, Thaksin, led a government that was more stable and efficient than earlier governments. But he did not lead a government that was less corrupt. The key anti-corruption provisions of the 1997 Constitution—an array of formal checks and balances as well as a quite muscular anti-corruption commission—were ignored or subverted by Thaksin, other politicians, bureaucrats and non-government actors. Although elected post-Thaksin prime

---

49 Peter G. Warr and Bhanupong Nidhiprabha, *Thailand's Macroeconomic Miracle: Stable Adjustment and Sustained Growth* (Washington, D.C.: World Bank, 1996), 21–6.

ministers Abhisit Vejjajiva and Yingluck Shinawatra were not accused of benefiting personally from their positions, ministers and officials in their governments were subject to corruption allegations and convictions. The military government of Prayuth Chan-ocha was also subject to allegations of corruption (including by his brother, sister-in-law and nephew), and the register of personal assets of generals (armed forces and police) and senior officials appointed to various organs of the military government showed that many of them had assets far beyond what they could have accumulated on their official salaries.

In sum, an understanding of the traditional importance of hierarchy, protection and patronage helps to explain the tenacity of corruption in Thailand.

Hierarchy and Monarchy

At various stages since 1932, and especially since 2006, the monarchy has been at the centre of political debate, polarization and conflict in Thailand. At other stages, it has been heralded as a unifying and stabilizing institution. Traditionally, the monarchy was the primary cornerstone of politics. The king's position at the pinnacle of the social order was palpable and impregnated with religious authority and aura. The king defined the social status of every subject. He exercised political control by conferring ranks and titles, appointing officials, allocating duties, dispensing justice, deploying labour and accumulating wealth.

In neighbouring countries, colonial powers largely destroyed the traditional authority of monarchs. Over the same period in Siam, the threat of Western conquest, the monetization of the economy, and the infiltration of new ideas compelled the monarchy to reform and to cede political space—unwillingly and willingly. But in Thailand the monarchy and the principles and practices of hierarchy that underpinned it were able to survive. All governments have relied, informally as well as formally, on the monarchy for their legitimacy. Without the king's blessing they were deficient, less than respectable, less than acceptable. Certainly, political space is now much more contested. The monarchy cannot easily ignore or dismiss the authority of institutions like parliament and the judiciary, the influence of public opinion and NGOs, or a growing appetite for individual rights, equality and accountable government. The monarchy is no longer the primary cornerstone of Thai politics, but it remains an important cornerstone.

The Thai historian, Nidhi Eoseewong, has explained this persisting indispensability of the monarchy in Thailand by showing how the monarchy is a critical institution in Thailand's "cultural constitution". The cultural constitution encompasses "the ways of life, ways of thinking, and values of the society"; or, in other words, "political culture is the state's true constitution".[50] The cultural constitution changes as Thai culture changes; the changes within the institution of the monarchy over the decades—from being the primary cornerstone of Thai politics to being an important cornerstone—reflect profound change, even if the pace of change was sometimes slow and its progression sometimes erratic.

---

50   Nidhi, "The Thai Cultural Constitution."

Chapter Six

IDENTITIES AND NATIONALISM

Today the nation is facing menacing danger.
The flames are rising.
Let us be the ones who step in, before it is too late.
The land will be good soon.
Happiness will return to Thailand.[1]

The idea of the Nation is one of the most powerful
anaesthetics that man has invented. Under the influence
of its fumes the whole people can carry out its systematic
programme of the most virulent self-seeking without
being in the least aware of its moral perversion—in fact
feeling dangerously resentful if it is pointed out.[2]

A deep sense of identity and nationalism usually saturates the modern
political culture of formerly colonized countries, even many decades
after independence. Domination by foreign powers was often a searing
experience. The memory of colonialism and the struggle against it
still colours the national story of the formerly colonized. In addition,
these countries are often governed or influenced by political parties,
movements or individuals claiming links to celebrated nationalists
and freedom fighters.

A newcomer to Thailand soon observes that Thais express a
nationalism and an ethno-centrism, which they label Thai-ness, whose

---

1   General Prayuth Chan-ocha, "Returning Happiness to the People," a song released after the Prayuth-
led coup in May 2014. Charlie Campbell, "The Thai Junta's 'Happiness' Song Is a Hit! (But Who'd
Dare Say Otherwise?)," *Time*, 10 June 2014.
2   Rabindranath Tagore, *Nationalism* (London: Macmillan and Co, 1917) 42–3.

intensity rivals the nationalism and ethno-centrism of the formerly colonized. The Siamese twins of Thai nationalism and Thai-ness were born before 1932 and employed by the traditional elite to justify absolutism and nation-building, suppress opponents and stymie political debate. After 1932, governments employed nationalism and ethnocentrism to justify nation-building, suppress opponents, and stymie political debate.

The Crocodile and the Whale

Although no foreign power annexed Siam, from the first half of the 19th century Siamese rulers could not close their eyes to French imperialism in the east and British imperialism to the west and south, and the real prospect of direct colonization. As the century progressed, France and Britain overpowered Siam's neighbours, one after the other. Foreign powers even vanquished mighty China, to which Siam had paid tribute for centuries. So pressing was the perceived threat of annexation that in 1866, at the height of frustrating negotiations with the French, King Mongkut wrote privately to the British consul saying, if necessary, he could accept Siam becoming a British protectorate.[3] A year later Mongkut wrote that he had to decide whether to "swim upriver to make friends with the crocodile or to swim out to sea and hang on to the whale".[4] Concerned about domestic and foreign challenges, both Mongkut and Chulalongkorn bought "property abroad for use in the event that abdication and exile became necessary".[5] In 1874, during a factional dispute in the Siamese court, Siam requested a British protectorate "of a modified kind".[6]

Almost 20 years and several *contretemps* later, after an exposed Siam had naively tried to defend its interests militarily, crocodilian France anchored two gunboats next to the Grand Palace in Bangkok.

---

3   Terwiel, *Thailand's Political History*, 165.
4   Quoted in Abbot Low Moffat, *Mongkut, the King of Siam* (Ithaca: Cornell University Press, 1961), 124.
5   David K. Wyatt, *The Politics of Reform in Thailand* (New Haven: Yale University Press, 1969), 61.
6   Thongchai, *Siam Mapped*, 108.

Mongkut's successor, Chulalongkorn, had to yield, renouncing Siam's claim to the eastern bank of the Mekong River and agreeing to the withdrawal of Siamese military establishments, vessels and troops from the border region, the payment of reparations, additional extraterritorial privileges for French subjects, and temporary French occupation of Siam's seaborne provinces bordering Cambodia (Chantaburi and Trat). Contrary to Siam's expectations, whale-like Britain offered no protection.

Indeed, in 1896 France and Britain, each of which did not want the other to control the Chao Phraya basin, secretly agreed that Siam could eventually consist of only that basin—testimony to the regional ambitions and power of both Britain and France, and to Siam's vulnerability. Fortuitously for Siam, in the following decade France and Britain put aside their mini-Siam conspiracy because they needed to join forces to meet the emerging threat from Germany closer to home. As late as 1904 Siam's foreign minister, Prince Devawongse, suggested that a British protectorate might be Siam's best defence against France.[7] Even in 1913 the US Embassy was reporting views that Siam could still become a protectorate of the British or French, or a combined protectorate.[8]

In summary, for almost their entire reigns, Mongkut and Chulalongkorn had reasons to believe that France or Britain might want to annex their kingdom, or large parts of it.

Unequal and Uncivilized

From 1855 to 1870 Siam signed unequal treaties with 13 foreign powers, and with two more in 1898 (Japan) and 1899 (Russia). Britain led the way when Sir John Bowring, backed by the threat of force, negotiated the first treaty in 1855. Among other things, the treaties set low taxes on foreign trade, allowed foreigners to own land in parts

---

7   Minton F. Goldman, "Franco-British Rivalry over Siam, 1896–1904," *Journal of Southeast Asian Studies*, Vol 3, No 2 (September 1972), 224–5.
8   Batson, *The End of the Absolute Monarchy*, 20 n15.

of Siam, and exempted the subjects of the 15 powers from Siam's legal system. These subjects were instead judged by consuls according to the domestic law of the non-Siamese treaty partner, or in so-called international courts that dealt exclusively with cases involving foreigners and in which the consul could intercede, or in Siamese courts that were supervised by foreign legal advisers.

To a certain extent, a measure of extraterritoriality was not uncommon in Siam. Historically, when fewer foreigners lived there, Siamese monarchs had preferred an arrangement under which each foreign community settled its disputes internally and appointed a community head with whom Siamese officials could liaise. But the numbers of Europeans in Siam grew rapidly from the mid-19th century, and the treaties were also interpreted to cover the Asian subjects of colonial powers, and eventually any person in Siam who could claim an ancestral connection to territories under control of a foreign treaty partner—in fact, almost anyone the foreign treaty partners chose to enrol.

Although Mongkut readily granted extraterritorial privileges because he and the influential Bunnag family stood to benefit from the increased trade, he had misgivings about the impact of the Bowring Treaty (1855) on Siam's image. He was upset that the British subsequently demanded less in their negotiations with Japan and Vietnam, and he feared the Bowring Treaty would lower Siam's prestige with its Lao and Khmer vassals.[9] Over time, distrust and abuses grew. With the rise in the value of land from the 1880s, foreign ownership became more common, as did land disputes and slights against Siamese sovereignty; for example, in the mid-1890s, farmers in Rangsit (near Bangkok) tried to protect themselves by flying the French flag over their rice fields, and in 1900 Chulalongkorn secretly dissuaded a prince from selling land to an American, arguing,

---

9   Tomas Larsson, *Land and Loyalty*, 35–36.

"The *farang* have extraterritorial jurisdiction, which creates great difficulties for our administration. If they become owners of large plots of land like this, bandits can hide there and it will be difficult for us to capture them."[10] Criminals and reprobates sought consular protection, including defying government efforts to close gambling dens and brothels as well as anti-government newspapers.[11] French, British, American and Portuguese officials flaunted Siam's diminished sovereignty by selling letters of consular protection on the black market, even to soldiers in the Siamese army. In 1893, the French threatened to give extraterritorial protection to Lao war captives and their descendants living in Bangkok.[12] In 1897, Chulalongkorn is reported to have half-joked, "the time may come when there will be only one Siamese subject in my kingdom, and that one myself". In 1901, the Minister for Foreign Affairs is reported to have complained that, "the consular corps in Bangkok would soon have more subjects than the king himself".[13]

At the root of the privileged legal treatment for foreigners was a judgment that Siam's legal system was not modern or civilized. This judgment was informed at least partly by a conviction that white Christians (and their colonial subjects) should not be judged by people who were neither white nor Christian. So, although ultimately escaping formal colonization by France or Britain, for decades Siam lived under the threat of absorption into the French and/or British empires and was subject to Western imperialist thinking, condescension and racism.

Siam sought to lessen the risk of formal absorption into a French or British empire by relying extensively on foreigners for advice and by giving foreigners easy access to its economy. In 1916, there were

---

10   *Ibid*, 53, 44.
11   Matthew Copeland, "Contested Nationalism, and the 1932 Overthrow of the Absolute Monarchy in Siam." PhD diss., Australian National University, Canberra, 1993, 72–3.
12   Edward Van Roy, *Siamese Melting Pot: Ethnic Minorities in the Making of Bangkok* (Chiang Mai and Singapore: Silkworm Books and ISEAS Yusof Ishak Institute, 2017), 129.
13   Both quotations are in Tomas Larsson, *Land and Loyalty*, 37.

208 foreign advisers in Siam.[14] In 1927, there were 124, 64 of whom were British.[15] Before 1932, the number and influence of foreign advisers often frustrated under-promoted Siamese officials. In the late 19th century, approximately 70 per cent of Siam's imports were from Britain and a large proportion of Siamese exports went to British territories. British firms dominated the tin and teak industries—the two biggest exports after rice, and most rice exports went through the British entrepôt ports of Hong Kong and Singapore.[16] Between 1880 and 1899, 50–70 per cent of ships calling at the Bangkok port were British.[17]

Siam's territorial and extraterritorial predicaments were reflected in the lop-sided nature in which they began to be resolved. France and Britain agreed to ease some of Siam's extraterritorial burden in exchange for extra Siamese territory. In treaties with France (1907) and Britain (1909) that defined Siam's borders, Siam was forced to cede Battambang and Siem Reap on the western bank of the Mekong River in Cambodia to France; and Kelantan, Trengganu, Perlis and Kedah in Malaya to Britain—all territory over which Siam had often exercised suzerainty in the 18th and 19th centuries.

Over the next 20 years or so, in further new treaties with France, Britain and the 13 other powers that had secured extraterritorial rights, Siam regained its judicial and fiscal autonomy.

Civilizational Challenge

In addition to surrendering suzerainty over territory that France and Britain coveted on its periphery, and in addition to the indignities that grew as more and more foreigners abused the unequal treaties, Siam faced a civilizational challenge from the West—just like its

---

14 Pasuk and Baker, *Thailand: Economy and Politics*, 259.
15 Batson, *The End of the Absolute Monarchy*, 50.
16 James C. Ingram, *Economic Change in Thailand: 1850–1970* (Stanford: Stanford University Press, 1971), 42, 173.
17 Porphant, *A Regional Economic History*, 8.

directly colonized neighbours. The challenge from the West didn't stem from its military prowess and technological superiority alone. The omnipresent West set new norms and new goals. It represented modernity, progress and civilization. Peoples and nations aspired to be more like Westerners and Western nations. They judged themselves and each other by the extent to which they had, or had not, Westernized; by the extent to which they were, or were not, catching up with the West. This included things as diverse as personal tastes like hairstyles, clothing and other consumption; town planning and architecture; social issues like slavery, polygyny and education; through to systems of government and administration. The West was attractive, alluring, desirable, tempting, successful—and emulated. At the same time, the West was threatening; it aroused apprehension, anxiety, self-doubt, fear—so it was rejected. On one hand the West was craved, on the other it was distrusted. Siam was affected by this civilizational challenge, and the focus on national identity that it engendered, as much as directly colonized countries were. Craig Reynolds has referred to arguments that the Thai elite—royal and commoner alike—was "colonized in consciousness".[18]

Ancien Regime Reinvents Itself

In the directly colonized world, challenges from the West prompted assessments of what it meant to be, for example, Indian, Malay, Filipino or Vietnamese, and what sort of nation an independent India, Malaya, the Philippines and Vietnam should be. In these colonies, largely new elites took on this task, working variously against and with their colonial masters, who tended to ignore, deride or suppress emergent

---

18   Craig Reynolds, "On the Gendering of Nationalist and Postnationalist Selves in Twentieth-Century Thailand, in *Genders and Sexualities in Modern Thailand*, ed. Peter A. Jackson and Nerida M. Cook (Chiang Mai: Silkworm Books, 1999), 263. The civilizational challenge from the West and its varied, complex and subtle implications for Siam are considered in Rachel V. Harrison and Peter A. Jackson (eds), *Ambiguous Allure of the West: Traces of the Colonial in Thailand* (Hong Kong: Hong Kong University Press, 2011), several of the works of Thongchai Winichakul, and the works of both Scott Barmé and Maurizio Peleggi (see bibliography). See also Craig Reynolds, *Seditious Histories: Contesting Thai and Southeast Asian Pasts* (Seattle and London: University of Washington Press, 2006).

nationalism. In Siam, however, the old political elite, led by the king, still had legitimacy. Unsurprisingly, it exercised its legitimacy to retain power and, where possible, to increase both its power and legitimacy. In Siam the *ancien regime* didn't fall, it reinvented itself. It sought to lead and control the debate about what it meant to be Siamese, as well as the debate about what sort of nation Siam would be.

Mongkut, who described Siam as "half civilized, half barbarian", was suspicious of the West, writing that "the British and the French can entertain no other feeling for each other than mutual esteem as fellow human beings, whereas the likes of us, who are wild and savage, can only be regarded by them as animals. We have no means of knowing whether or in what way they have contrived beforehand to divide our country among themselves."[19] Yet Mongkut pursued accommodation—intellectual as well as commercial—with the West, encouraging the study of Western languages, ideas and technology; bringing Western tutors into the palace; adopting a more Westernized dress code for royal audiences; openly consuming Western luxuries; introducing administrative reforms; employing Western advisers; and showcasing Siam in international exhibitions. Some of Mongkut's other reforms were influenced by Western ideas, but they also reflected astute politics in his power struggle with the nobility: introducing the concept of reciprocity into allegiance ceremonies which previously had been a one-way commitment from the king's vassals and officials; allowing the public to see his face and to petition him directly; giving alms directly to the poor; adding Buddhist elements to court ritual and de-emphasizing Hindu elements; introducing ceremonies to honour former monarchs and the present monarch; and making the law and tax obligations more accessible. These changes started to redefine the relationship between the monarch and his subjects.

---

19   Seni Pramoj and Kukrit Pramoj (tr. and ed.), *A King of Siam Speaks* (Bangkok: The Siam Society, 1987), 174.

Chulalongkorn attached attributes of a unified, modern nation-state to Mongkut's kingdom. Fearing colonial incursions, chafing at the unequal treaties, wanting Siam to gain from international commerce, seeking international respect for Siam, and eager to preserve his dynastic rule, Chulalongkorn centralized administration, restructured government finances, established a standing army and equipped it with modern weapons, reformed the judiciary, and improved transport and communications infrastructure. Backed forcefully by his army when required, Chulalongkorn drew previously outlying regions and semi-independent local rulers, as well as their sometimes-non-Thai subjects, under the direct control of his capital. He introduced a standardised curriculum into an embryonic national school system, which was delivered through a standardised Thai language, and he planted the seeds of compulsory primary education. Chulalongkorn's nation-building also saw the *sangha*—or brotherhood of Buddhist monks—transformed from a fraternity of monks occupying a fragmented and autonomous network of temples, often with regionalist leanings, into a Bangkok-controlled, hierarchical, bureaucratic structure, through which institutionalised Buddhism was spread to all corners of the nation.

Chulalongkorn was influenced by Western perceptions of Siam, and Western ideas. He stopped the practice of prostration before royalty, introduced a law on succession, abolished slavery, and educated his sons in Europe. He was also worried by Western ideas, especially the idea of representative government. He emphasised the importance of hierarchy, duties, unity and harmony in Siamese culture. In 1903, he

called upon everyone to recognize that "the only type of unity appropriate for Siam" was "a unity around the middle path of the king." The absolute monarchy was said to be grounded in "Siamese tradition", the people of the kingdom having long accepted the views of the monarch as being "the only correct ones." Moreover, apart from the "handful of people" who had developed the habit of opposing the king's wishes as a result of their "contact with foreigners", he felt that most of the kingdom's people continued to adhere to "the ancient custom of believing the views of the king to be true." Finally, he ... stated his firm opposition to the idea "that people should be permitted to ignore his orders or judge him to be wrong", for such behaviour merely served to indicate that an individual lacked "loyalty ... which is in truth unity."[20]

The king deserved loyalty not only because he sat atop a hierarchy sanctioned by *karma;* he deserved loyalty also because to question the king or to fail to follow the king's wishes threatened the unity of the nation. The problem for Chulalongkorn was, and remained, the "handful" of foreign-influenced people who questioned the king's judgment or ignored his orders. For his successors, this handful would become more than a handful, and eventually a headache.

Vajiravudh built on the foundations laid by his father and grandfather. By the time he assumed the throne (1910), the territorial threat to Siam had eased, but the memory of territorial loss and distrust of colonial powers lingered. The indignity of extraterritoriality also lingered, as did a love-hate relationship with the West. Two other challenges, which Chulalongkorn had mostly been able to sidestep, were becoming more urgent. The first emerged from a growing number of Western-influenced Thai military officers, bureaucrats and authors who pressed for political reforms that would shrink the power of the monarch. The second was the economic weight—in capital and labour—of the large Chinese minority, which also exhibited a strong sense of Chinese nationality. Estimated at about 10 per cent of Siam's population

---

20   Copeland, "Contested Nationalism," 30.

at the time, and over a quarter of Bangkok's population,[21] in 1910 the Chinese affronted the Siamese by organizing a crippling three-day general strike to voice their opposition to a government policy that had brought taxation arrangements for them into line with those applying to the Siamese. In 1911, the community's ethnic and political distinctiveness was again evident when the Chinese celebrated the republican revolution in China, a revolution that Vajiravudh condemned (he also disparaged democracy-inspired nationalist movements elsewhere in Asia).

Vajiravudh claimed the unity of the Siamese nation was under threat. He railed against the advocates of greater freedom because, he said, freedom would lead to disunity, which would lead to destruction, collectively and individually. The unity of the nation and the well-being of its subjects would be preserved through the self-sacrificing and unquestioning fulfilment of one's duties in a hierarchy under the king, who embodied the nation. Vajiravudh deployed nationalism to legitimise absolutism.

The Chinese community were a threat to the nation's unity and prosperity because, Vajiravudh argued, they refused to assimilate with the Thais and they remitted most of their earnings back to China. He vilified them, including through a tract titled *The Jews of the East,* and he threatened discriminatory economic policies against Chinese businesspeople.

In stirring anti-Chinese sentiment, Vajiravudh also stimulated a pro-Thai and pro-Siam consciousness. During his reign, the Chinese, together with non-immigrant but non-Thai people (Lao, northerners, Malays and others) in provincial areas, were cajoled and sometimes forced to accept the primacy of state-sanctioned national values, Central Thai culture and the Central Thai language. To question their primacy carried the risk of being labelled un-Thai and anti-Siam.

---

21   G. William Skinner, *Chinese Society in Thailand: An Analytical History* (Ithaca: Cornell University Press, 1957), 78, 87–8. The estimates include China-born and local-born Chinese.

Vajiravudh extolled the achievements of the Sukhothai period, aiming to convince Thais, and the rest of the world, that Thais were a civilized people and modern Siam was the product of a centuries-old and rich civilization; he decried those who felt they had to ape European ways. For the same reasons, he revived and extolled traditional Thai dance, or *khon*. Vajiravudh also fostered the idea that the Thais were a martial race, boosted the role and budget of the armed forces, and sponsored a paramilitary corps called Wild Tigers, giving military and paramilitary forces a "saviours of the nation" role.

A prolific writer and translator, Vajiravudh wrote plays, novels, short stories, poems, songs, essays and newspaper articles to promote the British-inspired (God, King and Country) triad of "Nation, Religion and King", which identified the nation with the monarchy and gave Buddhist religious overtones to both of them. He used the education system, as well as organizations like the Wild Tigers and Boy Scouts, to reinforce his messages.

Vajiravudh applied harsh security and press laws against Thai critics of his view of the nation, which saw newspapers closed and his opponents prosecuted for libel, sedition and *lèse majesté*. A slight against the king was an insult to the nation and therefore a threat to national security. To offer a different view of the nation was un-Thai.

The Empired Strike Back

The official, state-sponsored, top-down nationalism of Chulalongkorn and Vajiravudh was not unchallenged. Ironically, though, some of the first seedlings of a popular or "bottom-up" nationalism in modern Thai history were planted by Chulalongkorn who, in 1884, asked his senior diplomat in Paris, Prince Prisdang Jumsai, for advice on how Siam might avoid colonization. In early 1885, after consulting three of Chulalongkorn's brothers and seven other Siamese officials who were also based in Europe, Prisdang sent a joint reply which said: "To resolve this problem, Siam must be accepted and respected by the Western powers as a civilized nation."[22] The solution, they said, was "to thoroughly Europeanize ... There is no better path than this".[23] The message to the king recommended the following reforms:

1. change the absolute monarchy to a constitutional monarchy,
2. establish a cabinet system or ministerial government,
3. distribute power to the heads of department,
4. promulgate a law of royal succession,
5. change the payment system for the bureaucracy from the commission system to a salary system,
6. promote equality under the law,
7. reform the legal system on the Western model,
8. promote freedom of speech, and
9. establish a merit system for the bureaucracy.[24]

Their vision of the nation was a long way from Chulalongkorn's. After several months' reflection, he replied politely, firmly and negatively. Among other things, he said:

> Foreign rulers, by which I mean European rulers, have various limitations on their royal power that are due to events that have occurred in their various countries out of the dissatisfaction of the people. So there are regulations to check the power of kings as a consequence of successions of events that have unfolded in their countries... Siam has not yet experienced any event to make it necessary to do as other countries have done... In our country it is the king alone who gives thought to what should

---

22   Quoted in Murashima, "The Origins of Modern Official State Ideology in Thailand," 84.
23   Quoted in Tamara Loos, *Bones Around my Neck, The Life and Exile of a Prince Provocateur* (Ithaca and London: Cornell University Press, 2016), 47.
24   Quoted in Murashima, "The Origins of Modern Official State Ideology in Thailand," 84.

be done. It is he who has thought about acting to bring progress and happiness to the people in general.[25]

For the next 25 years Chulalongkorn continued to rule Siam as an absolute monarch. The significance of the appeal by the princes and senior officials lies in its identifying the nation and the national interest separately from the preservation and expansion of royal authority.[26] Equally pertinently, the petitioners did not advocate elections or a legislature and Chulalongkorn's correspondence with Prisdang was considered so sensitive that it was kept out from public view until 1967.[27] In other words, these first seedlings of popular nationalism were small, survived only briefly and grew in a secret garden. And, if they had been given time to mature, their blossom would not have been parliamentary democracy.

Another event or, as it turned out, non-event, that was a manifestation of emerging popular nationalism was a planned military revolt in 1912.[28] Preparations started in 1910 when Chulalongkorn was still on the throne. The conspirators, mostly junior army officers, used the word revolution *(patiwat)* rather than coup to describe their intended actions, but they were motivated more by frustrated career prospects than a revolutionary ideology. Still, they sought to distinguish between loyalty to the monarchy (especially Vajiravudh, whose personal lifestyle and leadership failures they roundly condemned) and loyalty to the nation, which, they believed, could escape humiliation and oppression by adopting a more Westernized form of government. Their plot, which may have had up to 800 supporters in the armed forces, was uncovered in March 1912, in the second year of Vajiravudh's reign. Twenty-three ringleaders were imprisoned.

---

25 Quoted in Loos, *Bones Around my Neck,* 47–8.
26 Federico Ferrara, *The Political Development of Modern Thailand* (Cambridge: Cambridge University Press, 2015), 53.
27 Loos, *Bones Around my Neck,* 48, 159.
28 This brief account of the 1912 plot is drawn from the comprehensive coverage in Kullada, *The Rise and Decline of Thai Absolutism,* 154–78.

These manifestations of popular nationalism occurred against a background of growing, sometimes strident, criticism of the absolute monarchy and the official nationalism that the monarchy sponsored.[29] Through journalism, cartoons, essays and books, which enjoyed a wide urban readership, the largely Bangkok-based intelligentsia depicted the absolute monarchy and the traditional elite as impediments to the nation's progress, including the progress of their careers, which was thwarted by the traditional elite's stranglehold on senior bureaucratic and military positions. Their arguments often had an economic edge, with the monarchy being criticised for allowing foreigners to control the economy through their ownership of major industries, as well as their dominant positions as highly paid advisers to the Siamese government. In this regard, the critics said, Siam was becoming comparable with directly colonized countries and the Thais risked being transformed into "scrap-eating dogs... like the American Indians, the Malays, the Burmese, the Khmer, the Vietnamese, and the peoples of India... whose mouths no longer have voices, whose guns no longer carry bullets".[30] Initially, the critiques were rather mild, but by the end of Vajiravudh's reign they represented the monarch and his ministers as oppressors and enemies of the nation, with cartoons portraying them as sub-human beings.

The capacity of Vajiravudh and his government to silence their critics was limited, ironically, by the unequal treaties under which Siam

> agreed to refrain from placing restrictions upon the commercial activities of foreign nationals in Siam, making no allowance for the possibility that there might eventually be a need to regulate the foreign-owned publishing concerns of the kingdom. Moreover, in granting Siam's foreign residents

---

29   The following summary of trends draws on the copious material in Copeland, "Contested Nationalism."

30   Quoted in *ibid*, 168.

extraterritorial status, the court inadvertently committed itself to bring libel proceedings against foreign-registered publications in the consulate courts, where a Western standard of journalistic propriety prevailed.[31]

The media reported that, as one of the few remaining absolute monarchies in the world, Siam had one of the world's oldest, least developed and obsolete political systems. In addition to advocating greater Siamese control of the economy and some social reforms (the abolition of slavery and polygyny, greater governmental control over gambling and opium smoking, and the further development of education), the opponents of absolute monarchy variously campaigned for the appointment of a prime minister, a constitution, parliament, elections, and greater equality and freedoms.

Two Rivers Merge

The two nationalisms—official and popular—collided in 1932. Popular nationalism prevailed. Constitutional monarchy superseded absolute monarchy. Siam, however, differed from directly colonized countries, where new elites developed and absorbed nationalist ideas and moulded them to respond to the particular foreign ruler they faced. The critical difference was that in Siam ideas about the nation and the value of nationalism were sponsored by rulers as well as the ruled, by the traditional governing elite as well as an emerging new elite. And the rulers and the ruled spoke the same Thai language, unlike the situation in colonized countries, where native tongues and the language of the colonial elites differed and often conflicted.[32]

So the gap between the new and traditional elites in Siam was not as wide as the gap between new elites in colonized countries and their colonial rulers. The last three absolute monarchs of Siam

---

31   *Ibid*, 16.
32   Maurizio Peleggi, *Thailand: The Worldly Kingdom* (London, Reaktion Books, 2007), 118.

(Chulalongkorn, Vajiravudh and Prajadhipok), who promoted an official nationalism, as well as the new Siamese elite, who promoted a popular nationalism, were inspired by a combination of shared indignation at Siam's powerlessness vis-à-vis foreigners, shared pride in Siam's own history, culture and adaptability, and a shared realization that Siam's prosperity, security and even survival would require the acceptance of some imported ideas and practices.

The collision in 1932 was more like the merging of two rivers than a head-on clash. From 1932, when members of the new elite gained political control and access to career and economic opportunities, they relied on nationalism to help legitimise their regime, just as the traditional elite had in the preceding decades. And, just like the traditional elite, the new elite also relied on nationalism to suppress their opponents and to discourage political debate.

Certainly, there was turbulence; the overthrow of the absolute monarchy signalled a major change in the course of modern Thai politics. Yet the target of the People's Party was absolutism more than the monarchy, whose tacit support it needed for legitimacy. The post-1932 leadership, especially Phibun, who was prime minister for 16 of the 25 years from 1932 to 1957, also sought legitimacy in the idealization of the nation. Phibun was decidedly anti-monarchy. In 1939, he arrested royalists and other opponents, conducted show trials, then executed 15 of them and imprisoned and exiled the others. In his nationalist vision, the monarchy had no place.

Phibun Songkhram: Vajiravudh's Heir

But, in his advocacy of ultranationalism, Phibun was the son that Vajiravudh never had. In January 1940, just a month after executing royalist opponents, Phibun himself fulsomely acknowledged Vajiravudh's pioneering work as a nationalist leader. "The most important and highly beneficial kindness handed down to the Thai country and nation," he said at the launch of a public campaign to raise funds for a statue of the former king, "lies in the fact that King Vajiravudh was responsible in rousing the Thai nation as a whole from its lethargy to realise the importance of carrying out patriotic and other good acts for the betterment and glory of the nation."[33]

Like Vajiravudh, Phibun anchored his nationalism in an extolled Thai past. Relying heavily on the work of a skilled publicist, Wichit Wathakan, Phibun found the roots of Thai culture in the Sukhothai era, just as Vajiravudh had done. Like Vajiravudh, he saw Thais as a warrior race and he sought to assign this martial tradition to the modern armed forces. Phibun established a militarized youth movement, Yuwachon, which was a cousin of Vajiravudh's Wild Tigers and Boy Scouts. Like Vajiravudh, Phibun used literature and cultural performances to extol Thai history and instil patriotism; where Vajiravudh promoted the traditional *khon*, Phibun sponsored a national dance, *ramwong*, as an alternative to encroaching Western dance forms. Keen to use language to unify the nation, Vajiravudh had sought to purify the Thai language and simplify the Thai writing system, and he promoted the use of the Thai dialect of the central region—or Bangkok dialect—in all government schools and discouraged the use of the Lao script in northeastern Thailand. Phibun decreed that Thais in all regions should learn the central region dialect.

Similarly, Vajiravudh had discouraged officials from referring to northeastern Thais as *Lao*, northern Thais as *Thaiyai* or *Thai nua*, and southerners as *Thai tai*; everyone should be called *Thai*. Phibun went a step further and abolished the names of these regional groups of Thai. Vajiravudh had bestowed a new flag and anthem on Siam; Phibun made everyone salute Vajiravudh's flag and memorise Vajiravudh's anthem. Like Vajiravudh, Phibun promoted a cult of the leader; his portrait and slogans were everywhere. Like Vajiravudh, Phibun responded to the economic and political risks posed by the

---

33   Quoted in Walter F. Vella, *Chaiyo: King Vajiravudh and the Development of Thai Nationalism* (Honolulu: University of Hawaii Press, 1978), 272.

large Chinese minority with anti-Chinese rhetoric as well as cultural and economic policies that favoured Thais over foreigners (although directed against all foreigners regardless of race, the economic measures especially affected Chinese enterprises). And like Vajiravudh, Phibun relied on the apparatus of the state to stifle opinions that challenged his view of Thailand's past and future.

Naturally, Phibun's idea of the Thai nation differed in important ways from Vajiravudh's, as did his methods of promoting nationalism. Above all, the monarchy was not central to his vision. On the contrary, Phibun's nationalism was aimed at supplanting the monarchy in the thinking of Thais with first, the idea of the nation; and, secondly, the idea of a non-royal leader, who embodied national sovereignty (unsurprisingly, Phibun thought he was well qualified for the job). Reflecting the shift to constitutional monarchy, under Phibun the national slogan became "Nation, Religion, King and Constitution".

While Vajiravudh's attacks on the Chinese were mostly verbal, Phibun actively discriminated against them, increasing immigration fees, closing banks that profited from remittances to China, arresting and deporting hundreds of Chinese, and closing many Chinese schools and all but one Chinese newspaper. Phibun put a greater emphasis on economic self-reliance than Vajiravudh had. He established state-owned enterprises in strategic industries, imposed monopolies on tobacco and salt, reserved certain occupations and businesses for Thais, and promoted locally-made consumer goods (many of these measures disadvantaged the Chinese community). Where Vajiravudh relied heavily on exhortation, Phibun legislated and imposed penalties for non-compliance. Unlike Vajiravudh, Phibun could disseminate his nationalist messages through radio (which started in 1930) and film.

Furthermore, the international environment had changed by the time Phibun became prime minister. Militarized ultranationalism and fascism were on the rise as Phibun came to power; he was influenced by developments in Germany, Italy and Japan, and he possibly modelled himself on Mussolini. Like European ultranationalists and fascists, Phibun wanted to regain "lost territories" and build a Thai empire. His youth movement, Yuwachon, resembled the Hitler Youth. He saw the military as "the expression of the popular will by virtue of its unique ability to build a stronger nation".[34]

From Multiculturalism to Ethnocentrism

The ethnocentrism in the nationalism of Vajiravudh and Phibun had a lasting impact. Before the racial and national identities of the Thais "mysteriously fused", what we would now call ethnic minorities collectively outnumbered ethnic Thais in all regions of Siam.[35] Within Bangkok, these minorities included Chinese, Mon, Lao, Khmer, Malay, Cham, south and west Asians, Vietnamese, Burmese, indigenised Portuguese communities, and a comparatively small and fragmented community of recently arrived *farang*. They were "refugees from oppression in neighbouring states, war captives from armed conflicts with nearby kingdoms, tribals abducted from the frontier uplands by raiding parties, destitute immigrant labourers from foreign ports, and economic adventurers from near and far".[36] In this plural society each minority enjoyed internal administrative autonomy, so long as they accepted the authority of the ruling Thai elite and contributed to the economy. Because political authority in under-populated Siam was secured through the control of manpower, "ethnic diversity advertised the kingdom's vitality. It spoke to the ruling elite's success in resolving a traditional manpower problem."[37] The same had been true in Ayutthaya. In 1685 the French Ambassador to King Narai said, "There is no city in the East where is seen more different nations than in the capital city of Siam, and where so many tongues are spoken."[38]

---

34 Pasuk and Baker, *Thailand: Economy and Politics*, 274.
35 Van Roy, *Siamese Melting Pot*, 39. This paragraph draws heavily on Van Roy's book, especially 12–41.
36 *Ibid*, 17.
37 *Ibid*, 29.
38 Quoted in Baker and Pasuk, *A History of Ayutthaya*, p 203. For a fuller picture of Ayutthaya's pluralism, see 203–10.

But in the decades of the late 19th and early 20th centuries, "the kingdom's diverse ethnicities were consolidated—at least superficially—through a deliberate, carefully orchestrated political project pursued under the twin banners of opposing Western imperialism and promoting Thai nationalism".[39] Then Phibun imposed a single Thai national identity, "leaving the ethnic minorities little option but to accommodate, integrate, and ultimately assimilate".[40]

Kings and "Prince" Phibun: Overview

Chulalongkorn's handiwork as a nation-maker and Vajiravudh's handiwork as a nationalism-maker have endured. Chulalongkorn's hand can still be seen in Thailand's highly centralised bureaucracy, domestically focused armed forces, instrumentalist judiciary, conformist educational system and state-serving *sangha*. Vajiravudh's hand can be seen in "Nation, Religion and King" persisting as the state ideology; policies that put assimilation ahead of pluralism or multiculturalism; reliance on the military and even paramilitary forces to save the nation in times of perceived crisis; and the silencing of critics of the idealised Thai nation and its symbols, especially the monarchy. Phibun and other leaders of the People's Party were motivated by popular nationalism to gain power in 1932 and to ward off a royalist counterattack. They introduced ideas of constitutionalism into the political culture; but as Phibun gained the ascendancy, nationalism eclipsed constitutionalism and again became the ideology of the state as well as the excuse for outlawing any other ideology. In other words, a modified popular nationalism became the new official nationalism.

Sarit Thanarat: Development and Monarchy

By the time Phibun's successor, military strongman Sarit Thanarat, took over in 1957, nationalism was truly embedded as the guiding

---

39   Van Roy, *Siamese Melting Pot*, 239.
40   *Ibid*, 39.

ideology of the state. Sarit made two major changes. First, he gave economic development a bigger place. He promised that "water will flow, lights will be bright, roads will be good, and there will be work for all".[41] "Our prime objective," he said, "is to strive to make the public aware and agree with the fact that the nation must develop, people must progress, and tomorrow must be better than today."[42] He funded infrastructure (with massive US aid directed to keeping Thailand non-communist) and put highly capable civilians in charge of economic policy and management. "The hardware of industrialized western countries was to be adopted—including asphalt/concrete roads, electricity, technology, and so forth—but they were to be used within a Thai framework. Change was to be accepted, even encouraged, so long as it did not threaten the control of the governing elite and its role as protector of the Thai social and political morality."[43] Secondly, Sarit revived the monarchy as an institution and revered Bhumibol as the monarch. Sarit reunited the monarchy with state-sponsored nationalism. The nation and the monarchy again became indivisible. Official nationalism had come full-circle.

The foregoing summary of the historical development of Thai nationalism—and ultranationalism—has tried to explain why Thai people and the Thai state express their feelings about their nation so intensely and how nationalism has been used to counter political opponents and to stymie political debate. The summary stops in the late 1950s because the main features of Thai nationalism have barely changed since Sarit's time, although the intensity has varied—from high to hyper. The rest of this chapter looks briefly at why and how features of Thai nationalism reveal themselves in modern Thai politics,

41   Quoted in Thak, "Distinctions with a Difference," 66.
42   Quoted in Thak, *The Politics of Despotic Paternalism*, 148.
43   Thak, *The Politics of Despotic Paternalism*, 149.

starting with an account of how some major non-Thai minorities have fared in nationalistic Thailand. We then examine the commanding role of the state in defining the Thai nation and a "good Thai"; the fear of disunity and other "enemies" and the application of the law on *lèse majesté*; and the appeal of nationalism over democracy.

Chinese Minority

Newcomers to Thailand, especially if they are familiar with other countries in Southeast Asia, often assume that ethnic tensions between Chinese and Thais must contribute to Thailand's political instability. Not only newcomers make this mistake. In 1997, the Thai prime minister, Chavalit Yongchaiyudh, emulated his counterparts in Indonesia by trying to save his political skin by blaming the Sino-Thai business community for the economic crisis. In Indonesia, there were anti-Chinese riots. In contrast, in Thailand there was a public outcry and Chavalit apologised, claiming he had been misunderstood.[44] Notwithstanding intense Thai nationalism and ethno-centrism, the experience of Chinese migrants in Thailand differs from other parts of Southeast Asia where they form a sizeable minority.

Chinese have settled in Thailand since at least the 15th century, initially in the south, but with a strong presence in Ayutthaya also, where some served in the government and occasionally entered the nobility.[45] Most were traders, some were refugees. Because Chinese women almost never emigrated, Chinese men married Thais and tended to assimilate. It has been estimated that at least 10,000 Chinese lived in Siam in the late 17th century, at least 3,000 of them in Ayutthaya.[46] A century later the total was probably 30,000.[47] In Ayutthaya, the Chinese fulfilled various roles: merchants, traders,

---

44   William A. Callahan, "Beyond Cosmopolitanism and Nationalism: Chinese and Neo-Nationalism in China and Thailand," *International Organization,* 56 (Summer 2003), 495.
45   This summary paragraph is mostly drawn from Skinner, *Chinese Society in Thailand*, 1–27.
46   Skinner, *Chinese Society in Thailand*, 13.
47   Jeffrey Sng and Pimpraphai Bisalaputra, *A History of the Thai-Chinese* (Singapore and Bangkok: Editions Didier Millet, 2015), 27.

scholar-officials, physicians, artisans, actors, pig breeders and vegetable growers. Most of them assimilated into Thai society rather than establish a hybrid Sino-Thai identity; as late as the early 1900s, the third-generation offspring of Chinese migrants were generally Thai "in culture and identification".[48]

Siamese royalty had Chinese ancestry. After the Burmese invasion in 1767, a Thai with a Chinese father restored Siam's sovereignty and became King Taksin, ruling until 1782 from a new capital, Thonburi. The current Chakri dynasty moved the capital across the river to Bangkok and in the 19th century over half the population of Bangkok was of Chinese descent.[49] The first king (Rama I) of the Chakri dynasty may have had a Chinese mother and, as a result of complex marriage alliances, King Vajiravudh and King Prajadhipok were more than half-Chinese by ancestry.[50] In the current era, most of the Thai prime ministers of the last 40 years had some Chinese ancestors; some of them had a fully Chinese ancestry.

In addition to the trend of Chinese migrants marrying Thai women and their children assuming a Thai identity, there are other explanations for Thailand's success in accommodating large numbers of Chinese migrants. Chinese and Thai have the same racial heritage; the physical differences between them are slight. Chinese religious practices are heavily influenced by Buddhism and Thai religious practices are adaptive enough to tolerate and even incorporate Chinese influences, like ancestor worship. Chinese and Thais speak tonal languages. Both have rice and fish as their staple food. There was another critical reason for the relative harmony between Thais and Chinese: "Whereas in the Dutch East Indies, the British colonies in Malaya, or French Indochina Western colonial domination, especially after Western schools were created, led immigrant Chinese (and also Indians in Malaya) to orient themselves towards Dutch, British, or

---

48   Skinner, *Chinese Society in Thailand*, 134.
49   *Ibid*, 81–8.
50   *Ibid*, 26–7.

French language, culture and society, in Siam, which retained its independence, Chinese migrants felt constrained to orient themselves more toward Thai language, culture and society."[51] In brief, for centuries Chinese migrants advanced economically, socially and politically because they were able to assimilate easily into Thai culture.

From Insiders to Outsider, then Insiders Again

Yet in 1914 Vajiravudh published an anti-Chinese document called *The Jews of the East*, which claimed the Chinese were not only failing to assimilate, but were opportunistic and two-faced, devoid of civic virtues, worshipped money and were parasites on the Thai economy.[52] Although Vajiravudh took few concrete steps against the Chinese, he created an environment of fear and distrust and he urged Thais to assert their identity and sovereignty. Phibun, Vajiravudh's ideological heir, took advantage of this environment and actively discriminated against the Chinese. His favoured publicist, Wichit Wathakan, admired Nazi Germany's Minister for Propaganda, Joseph Goebbels, and said the Chinese "were worse than Jews".[53] (It should be noted that elected members of the National Assembly as well as the press condemned Wichit's racism).[54]

The tensions and periodic confrontations between Thais and Chinese in the 20th century, although seriously unsettling for the Chinese community, were aberrations rather than the norm. They were caused by numbers, nuptials and nationalism. From the 1820s to 1870, each year an estimated 3–7,000 Chinese workers migrated to Siam and stayed, a manageable number.[55] Between 1882 and 1917 about 1.4 million Chinese (mostly labourers) arrived, of whom about 450,000 stayed (on average, more than 10,000 each year).[56] From 1918

51   Keyes, *Buddhist Kingdom*, 48.
52   Skinner, *Chinese Society in Thailand*, 164–5.
53   Quoted in Barmé, *Luang Wichit Wathakan*, 129.
54   *Ibid.*
55   Skinner, *Chinese Society in Thailand*, 59.
56   Calculated from Table 2 in *ibid*, 61.

until 1955, an estimated 2.1 million Chinese (again, mostly labourers) arrived, about 750,000 of whom stayed (on average, more than 20,000 each year).[57]

While the rapidly-growing Chinese population contributed labour and services that Siam needed to expand and commercialise agriculture, forestry and tin mining and construct canals, railways and other infrastructure, it also attracted the suspicion and contempt that often attaches to large numbers of highly visible and hard-working outsiders, especially when some of them are traders, tax farmers and moneylenders (although the view in Bangkok that Siamese peasants were exploited by Chinese moneylenders was "grossly exaggerated" because creditors did not have an automatic right to foreclosed property).[58] In addition, their remittances to China became a drain on the economy. More critically, from 1911 Chinese women, who had almost never emigrated from China before 1893, began to come to Siam in larger numbers. As a result, many male Chinese migrants no longer married Thai women, so the earlier assimilation slowed, and the Chinese became a more obvious and separate ethnic community, forming clan-based associations and secret societies. Finally, from the turn of the 20th century the Chinese migrants and their Thai hosts were increasingly influenced by nationalism and the stereotyping, bigotry and racism that often attend it.

The first cause of tension and confrontation—the unprecedented number of migrants—dissipated after the flow of new migrants slowed from 1948 and eventually stopped in 1954.[59] As a result, "there was no longer a perpetual renewal and reminder of 'Chinese-ness' by the flow of incoming migrants".[60]

Secondly, the end of migration, and the reality that even after more females began to migrate they never comprised more than

---

57   Calculated from Table 6 in *ibid*, 173.
58   Larsson, *Land and Loyalty*, 96–8.
59   Calculated from Table 6 in Skinner, *Chinese Society in Thailand*, 173.
60   John L. S. Girling, *Thailand: Society and Politics* (Ithaca: Cornell University Press, 1981), 77.

about a third of the total Chinese migrants,[61] meant that a reasonable proportion of Chinese men still married outside their own community. Furthermore, as the Thais became wealthier, increasing numbers of rich Thai men married Chinese women or daughters from marriages of Chinese men and Thai women.

Thirdly, Thai nationalism had a cultural rather than a racial base: indeed, the three most prominent proponents of an anti-Chinese strain of Thai nationalism—Vajiravudh, Phibun and Wichit— had Chinese ancestry. For reasons as diverse as ethnicity, religion, language and cuisine, Chinese migrants were able to adapt to Thai culture fairly easily. Integration was also assisted by race-neutral developments such as nationality laws (except for the 1953–56 period) that gave citizenship to everybody born in Siam, regardless of their father's nationality (and full citizenship to the next generation); the requirement for all Thais to have a Thai surname and speak the Thai language; the education of Chinese children in Thai-medium schools and universities; and the growing number of government officials with Chinese ancestry.

Fourthly, the Chinese business elite, Thai bureaucratic elite and Thai royalty gradually developed symbiotic relationships. From the late 1950s the Chinese gained security and protection through cooperation with Thai bureaucrats, politicians and royalty, and the Thais gained access to Chinese wealth as well as Chinese entrepreneurship in the management of state-owned enterprises.

Even before this relationship between Chinese business and Thai officialdom matured, the writer of the finest book on the Chinese in Thailand, William Skinner, concluded in 1956: "It is an interesting feature of Thai psychology that no matter how strong the prejudice against 'those Chinese,' the Thai are never inclined to reject anyone of Chinese ancestry who speaks and behaves like a Thai."[62] Over 50 years

---

61   Table 10 in Skinner, *Chinese Society in Thailand*, 191.
62   *Ibid*, 381.

later, protesters against Prime Minister Thaksin Shinawatra (whose great grandfather migrated from China in the 1860s) proudly wore shirts and badges emblazoned with slogans saying that Sino-Thais loved Thailand and would save the nation. They were demonstrating their Thai-ness by expressing loyalty to the monarchy, which "had helped the *luk chin* (sons of China) to become more comfortable as citizens of Thailand and members of its elite, especially by receiving charitable donations and rewarding them with royal decorations and other marks of status".[63] Although Thai nationalism had earlier been fuelled by anti-Chinese sentiment, the Chinese in Thailand are no longer seen as outsiders and no longer feel like outsiders.

Home-Grown Minorities

Useful insights into Thai nationalism and how it manifests itself in modern Thai politics can be gained by comparing the experience of the Chinese minority in Thailand with the experience of two non-immigrant communities: the ethnic Malay Muslims in the three southern border provinces and the Lao inhabitants of Isaan, or northeastern Thailand.

The southern border provinces of Pattani, Yala and Narathiwat more or less correspond with the former Malay kingdom of Patani, a self-governing kingdom for most of the period from about the ninth to the late 18th centuries. The rulers of Patani paid tribute periodically to Siamese kings to show a measure of respect, but they were never required to concede autonomy. From the late 18th century, Siamese kings forcibly incorporated the region into the Siamese state, initially to establish the authority of the Chakri dynasty after the defeat of Ayutthaya and then to protect Siamese suzerainty from the advances of British imperialism, including by imposing colonial-style control over Patani to showcase their "colonial modernity".[64] Following the

---

63 Pasuk and Baker, *Thaksin*, 323.
64 Tamara Loos, *Subject Siam*, 2–4, 20–1.

Thailand: Main Regions

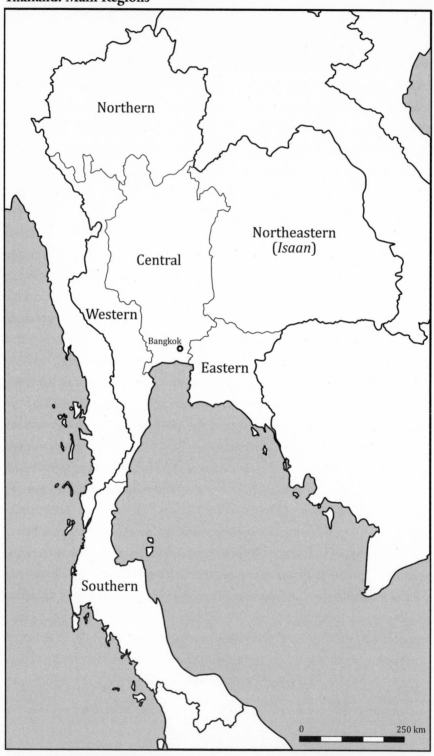

Northern

Northeastern
(*Isaan*)

Central

Western

Bangkok

Eastern

Southern

0   250 km

administrative reforms of Chulalongkorn, Patani became a Thai administrative district (called *monthon*) and later the provinces of Pattani, Yala and Narathiwat. Its raja lost his political power, and the inhabitants became Thai citizens. In 1901, the Malay Muslims rebelled. Following a struggle, in 1902, the Siamese navy and police prevailed. In the same year, in a private message, Chulalongkorn admitted that in this region (and Isaan) the Siamese

> treat the provinces as ours, which is not true; for the Malays and the Lao consider [that] the provinces belong to them. When we say that we are going to trust them, we do not really do so, but send commissioners and deputy commissioners to supervise them. The commissioners and deputy commissioners are then empowered only either to manipulate them as puppets or, if that is not possible, to spy on them and to pass on their secrets. We cannot, however, really protect ourselves against anything in this way. I do not think that an administration, which is so full of deviousness, can result in our mutual trust and peace of mind.[65]

At the end of his letter the King said he was "sorry not to have a solution for the moment".[66]

None of the governments that succeeded Chulalongkorn's have been able to find "a solution for the moment", but none of them have acknowledged the root of the problem as plainly (albeit privately) as he did. The consequent separatist sentiment among ethnic Malay Muslims—which has been expressed violently at various stages, including in the current insurgency that has cost over 7,000 lives since 2004—strikes at the heart of official Thai nationalism, which venerates the territorial integrity of the nation and promotes its cultural unity.

---

65   Tej Bunnag, *Provincial Administration*, 154–5.
66   *Ibid*, 155.

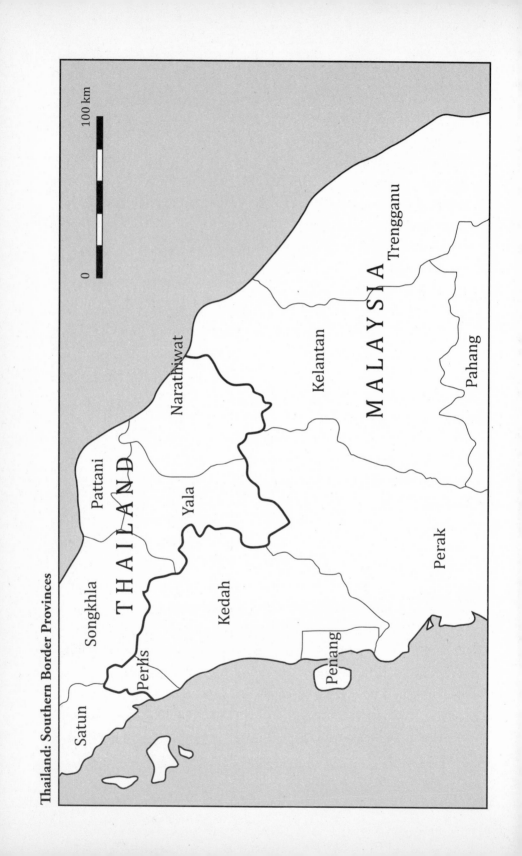

Thailand: Southern Border Provinces

Unlike Chinese migrants, the Malay Muslims have not chosen to migrate to Siam or been forced to move to Siam as refugees or war captives; the southern provinces have been their home since before the Sukhothai period. "The Chinese in Thailand have been willing to subordinate their Chineseness to Thainess, because they saw themselves as immigrants who needed to adapt to the rules and mores of Thai society, and because they suffered from Thai deficiency syndrome. The Malays view themselves as an indigenous people who have been colonized, are immune to the Thai deficiency syndrome, and so are unwilling to play second identity fiddle to Thainess."[67]

Tellingly, the thousands of Muslims who over the centuries have migrated to Thailand from Persia, Arabia, South Asia, Yunnan and elsewhere have assimilated more or less as easily as Chinese migrants have.

Regarding the people of Isaan, as mentioned earlier, to promote their idea of the Thai nation and nationalism, Vajiravudh and Phibun fought against the use of regional names like Lao, which had traditionally been used to refer to the people of northeastern Thailand, and tried to impose Central Thai culture and the Central Thai language. But these exhortations from Bangkok-based leaders did not stop the people of Isaan still seeing themselves as *khon Isaan*, people of Isaan, or "Lao within a Thai nation-state".[68] Their Isaan identity was traditionally built around the village, where peasants cooperatively struggled with poor soils and cycles of drought and flood, and centred their religious life on the local Buddhist temple and shrines to village spirits. They also sang distinctive songs in their local dialect, played distinctive music on local instruments, and enjoyed a distinctive local cuisine. From the 1960s, as economic opportunities grew in Bangkok, more and more people from Isaan found work there. This work eased their poverty, but exposure

---

67   Duncan McCargo, *Mapping National Anxieties: Thailand's Southern Conflict* (Copenhagen: NIAS Press, 2012), 125.

68   Charles Keyes, *Finding Their Voice*, 3. The following paragraphs rely heavily on this excellent study of the history, ethnography and politics of northeastern Thailand.

to the outside world also made them more aware that the people of Bangkok and the central plains had higher incomes, better amenities and more opportunities. In addition, their urban cousins scorned the rural accent, customs and poverty of Isaan people.

For several decades the burden of this Central Thai chauvinism was lightened by steadily-rising incomes in rural areas during Thailand's pre-1997 economic boom, a belief that the more democratic system of government would give people from Isaan a bigger say in national affairs and a bigger share of national resources, and a conviction that the charismatic King Bhumibol viewed them benevolently. As well as denting the incomes of Isaan people (migrants and villagers alike), the economic gloom of the 1997 Asian financial crisis threw a spotlight on the unequal distribution of wealth in Thailand, where incomes in Bangkok are three times bigger than incomes in Isaan. After the crisis, Isaan voters overwhelmingly supported the governments of Thaksin and Yingluck Shinawatra. So they saw the 2006 and 2014 military coups as a deliberate attempt by Bangkok to silence Isaan voices and block Isaan aspirations, not least because many sponsors and supporters of the PAD and PDRC movements openly called Isaan people ignorant and stupid. And unquestioning faith in the monarchy was reassessed after Queen Sirikit attended the funeral of a PAD demonstrator in 2008 and other signs emerged of the monarchy's partisanship.

Charles Keyes, who has studied Isaan for decades, has written about the Isaan people having a schizophrenic relationship with the Thai state in the 1960s. "On the one hand, they had come to see themselves as Thai citizens, even if they were culturally Lao.... On the other hand, the actual interactions north-easterners had with government officials, which increased significantly in the 1960s, were often very far from positive."[69] Government officers often treated villagers arrogantly, and sometimes corruptly.

---

69   *Ibid*, 110–11.

Fifty years later Isaan attitudes remained schizophrenic. During visits to several villages from 2010 to 2014 people would tell me that their sense of Thai identity was, or had been, deeper than their sense of Isaan identity. They said they were (or had been) proudly Thai; but some of them went on to speak movingly about the actions of "Bangkok" and the *ammat* (aristocrats)[70] stimulating a loyalty to Isaan that was, to their surprise, overshadowing their attachment to Thailand. They added that this feeling was especially intense after the shooting of red-shirt protesters in May 2010.

The experiences of the large Chinese minority and Muslim migrants show that Thai nationalism has been both flexible and forceful enough to accommodate migrants in enormous numbers, as well as migrants from vastly different cultural backgrounds. They have assimilated. Yet Thai nationalism has alienated Malay Muslims in the south and Thai ultranationalism has troubled the people of Isaan. The experiences and expectations of the unassimilated Malay Muslims and now warily assimilated people of Isaan will continue to influence the course of Thai politics. If history is a reliable guide, the course of Thai politics will also continue to be influenced by firmly entrenched Bangkok-centric views about Thailand and Thai-ness.

Learning to Love your Protector

For over a century the Thai state has been inculcating a state-endorsed view of the Thai nation as well as a state-endorsed view of how Thais should express their feelings about the nation. The education system, which still relies heavily on direct instruction and rote learning rather than enquiry-based learning, has been a primary

---

70   The villagers' use of this terminology was another reflection of the red-shirt movement's revival of feudal terms to explain modern Thai politics. See Thongchai, "The Monarchy and Anti-Monarchy," 89.

vehicle. Through the school curriculum and through extra-curricular opportunities provided through educational institutions, every Thai is instructed from a young age to love the Thai nation and its symbols enthusiastically and unquestioningly, and to prove this love through their public and private conduct. The parents, grandparents, great grandparents and great-great grandparents of Thai children have been instructed in the same way, also from their first day at school. For generations, the messages of teachers have been echoed at home.

In addition to inculcating nationalism through the education system, all Thai governments have defined and promoted the state's vision of the Thai nation and the Thai way of life through the media (some of which it owns), public campaigns, ceremonies, commemorations, national holidays, festivals and performances. About five million Thais were initiated into the ultranationalist Village Scouts.[71] And every year a significant proportion of Thai men receive further indoctrination when they are conscripted into the armed forces. The state's century-long effort to inculcate a nationalist ideology has helped to create a market for popular culture infused with nationalist themes.

Little wonder, then, that Thais from all walks of life have a broadly shared affection for the nation, broadly shared knowledge of what the nation represents, and broadly shared habits and rituals for demonstrating their affection and knowledge. Critics claim that these state-sponsored conventions and norms of Thai nationalism are confected. Certainly, like the conventions and norms of other nationalisms, they were confected. But following a century of inculcation they are now woven into Thailand's social fabric and political culture.

Broad acceptance of this orthodoxy is not the result of propaganda alone, or of a fear that questioning orthodoxy carries the risk of being shunned socially for a lack of Thai-ness and possibly accused of *lèse*

---

71   Bowie, *Rituals of National Loyalty*, 1–2.

majesté. The state-endorsed views on the nation and how to serve it also took hold because for decades Thais could reasonably conclude that nationalistic government policies helped Thailand to meet many of the challenges it faced: imperialist pressures from France and Britain; lax control over its territory and peoples; the commercial dominance of a large Chinese minority; a communist insurgency; a financial crisis; and, most recently, the passing of a revered monarch. The constancy of nationalism as the state ideology, coupled with the constancy of broadly pro-market economic policies, regardless of what sort of government was in power, have helped Thailand's economy to grow, providing opportunities for advancement for a large proportion of the population.

Disunity, Other Enemies and *Lèse Majesté*

Thai nationalism has put a high value on unity. We have seen how Chulalongkorn emphasised the importance of unity with the king as its centre, and Vajiravudh argued that unity would be preserved through self-sacrificing fulfilment of duties in a hierarchy under the king. Similarly, Bhumibol said that unity depended on responsibilities and duties being taken seriously, that the absence of unity led to subversion and crime, and that no individual was separable from the societal whole, which served the common good.[72] For Bhumibol also, the indivisibility of the monarchy and the nation was essential to unity. "The King and People become one," he said. "The Throne and the Nation become one, and a profound meaning is thus given to the Throne. It becomes the personification of Thai nationhood, the symbol of the Nation's unity and independence, the invariable constant above the inconsistencies or politics."[73]

Even in the intense struggle that has dominated Thai politics since about 2005—between the traditional elite and its most adroit

---

72   Kevin Hewison, "The Monarchy and Democratisation," in *Political Change in Thailand: Democracy and Participation*, ed. Kevin Hewison (London and New York: Routledge, 1997), 65–66.
73   Quoted in Hewison, "The Monarchy and Democratisation," 61.

adversary, Thaksin—the protagonists on both sides have appealed to nationalism. Thaksin named his political party "Thai Rak Thai", which means "Thai Love Thai", and the party's slogan, "Think new, act new, for every Thai", projected an "inclusive nationalism".[74] The "new nationalism" of the party de-emphasised ethnic identities, blamed foreign advice and global capital for Thailand's post-1997 economic misery, and advocated stronger national government management of the economy.[75] After Thailand repaid its IMF loan two years early in 2003, Thaksin gave a televised "independence speech".[76] This nationalist vision underpinned Thaksin's election victories in 2001 and 2005.

The high value placed on unity has been joined by a preoccupation with—even a national neurosis about—the historical experience of its opposite, disunity. In 2006, the military justified its coup to oust Thaksin as a response to "conflict, partisanship, and <u>disunity</u> on a scale unknown in the history of the Thai nation".[77] Although nationalistic, Thaksin did not equate the nation with the monarchy. His opponents did. They alleged that Thaksin had affronted the monarchy and thereby affronted the nation. Their vision of a monarchy-led nation underpinned their coup, and the monarch's endorsement of it.

Thais have an ingrained fear of disunity. Disunity, more than any other factor, led to Ayutthaya's shattering defeat at the hands of the Burmese in 1767, according to historical accounts as well as folklore, legends and myths, all of which have been incorporated into the school curriculum and popular culture. For 250 years, leaders have argued that a repetition of the horror and humiliation of 1767 can be avoided if Thais unite against external threats like France and Britain and internal threats like the Chinese minority and communism. In the 1970s, instructors of the anti-communist Village Scouts staged

---

74   Pasuk and Baker, *Thaksin*, 78.
75   *Ibid*, 79.
76   Duncan McCargo and Ukrist Pathmanand, *The Thaksinization of Thailand* (Copenhagen: NIAS, 2005), 181–2.
77   Pasuk and Baker, *Thaksin*, 285. Emphasis added.

historical dramas to show villagers that Ayutthaya had fallen to the Burmese because the Thai people had not been united. Communism and its causes were not seriously discussed. "Communists were presented primarily as foreigners recruiting Thais willing to betray the country by destroying its unity." Similarly, the Burmese were a proxy for the "contemporary alleged enemy, the Vietnamese".[78]

The alleged sponsors of disunity—Burma, France, Britain, unreliable vassals, the Chinese minority, communists, global capital, Thaksin—are depicted as enemies. One of Thailand's most eminent historians, Thongchai Winichakul, has written: "The creation of otherness, the enemy in particular, is necessary to justify the existing political and social control against rivals from without as well as from within. Without this discursive enemy, all the varieties of coercive force ... would be redundant."[79] Thongchai added: "To confirm Thainess, it does not matter if the enemy is relatively abstract or ill-defined. The enemy must always be present."[80]

The enemies of Thai-ness who "must always be present" are now critics of the monarchy—real and imagined. *Lèse majesté* has become "perfectly suited to serve as a weapon against political opponents... The insinuation—and quite often a direct accusation about Thaksin, the red shirts, and those who opposed the [2006] coup—is that they are somehow involved in a conspiracy to overthrow the monarchy. Discussions of reforming the monarchy or even analyses of power structure in Thailand have typically been depicted as acts of treason."[81] Strict judicial protection of the monarchy is not new. In the 17th century, Jeremias Van Vliet, the head of the Dutch East India Company in Ayutthaya, observed: "Of all crimes, none are so heavily

78   Bowie, *Rituals of National Loyalty*, 241.
79   *Siam Mapped*, 167.
80   *Ibid*, 168. Pavin Chachavalpongpun has also written perceptively about the role of "enemies" and "otherness" in Thai politics. See "The Necessity of Enemies in Thailand's Troubled Politics," *Asian Survey*, Vol 51, No 6, November/December 2011, 1019–41.
81   David Streckfuss, "Freedom and Silencing under the Neo-Absolutist Monarchy Regime in Thailand, 2006–2010," in *"Good Coup Gone Bad:" Thailand's Political Developments since Thaksin's Downfall*, ed. Pavin Chachavalpongpun (Singapore: ISEAS, 2014), 127.

punished as sinning against the authority of the king, against the priests, or the temples. If anyone should try to usurp any honor due to the king secretly or in public, should act against him or his state, or should show any disrespect, should treat the priests badly, rob their properties, profane churches or idols, he or the suspected would be punished with a cruel death without trial [while other offences are submitted to court process]."[82]

In modern times, what was new was the increase in both the penalty for *lèse majesté* and the number of cases. When a new Criminal Code was adopted in 1908, the maximum penalty for *lèse majesté* was increased from three years to seven years' imprisonment, with no minimum penalty. In 1976, after student protesters were accused of *lèse majesté* and communism, the maximum penalty was increased from seven years to 15 years, and a minimum penalty of three years was introduced. As a result, the penalty for *lèse majesté* under the constitutional monarchy is more severe than it was under the absolute monarchy of Chulalongkorn, Vajiravudh and Prajadhipok, and more severe than current punishments for contempt of court and insulting religion.[83] Anyone can file a *lèse majesté* accusation and all accusations must be formally investigated. Details of the accusations have seldom been publicized for fear of repeating the alleged offence. The accused have often not been granted bail, and have rarely been found innocent, and their trials have been conducted in secret. A guilty plea tends to attract a halving of the penalty and open the way to seeking a royal pardon. The number of *lèse majesté* cases has increased from less than one per year from 1947 to 1957 to a little more than five per year from 1992 to 2005, and to more than 100 per year from 2006 to 2009.[84] The number of cases remained high after the 2014 coup until 2018 when, reportedly on the instructions of King Vajiralongkorn, who was persuaded that over-use of the

---

82 Quoted in Baker and Pasuk, *The Palace Law of Ayutthaya*, 3.
83 Streckfuss, "Freedom and Silencing," 115.
84 David Streckfuss, *Truth on Trial*, 101, 111–112.

lèse majesté law damaged the monarchy, the military government virtually stopped charging its opponents with the offence (relying instead on sedition and computer crime laws). Since the 2006 coup the targets have changed from largely politicians to "a vast array of common people".[85]

Nationalism versus Democracy

Alleged perpetrators of *lèse majesté* are at one end of the spectrum of the "enemies" of state-sponsored Thai nationalism. At the other end of this spectrum are Thais who simply want to continue the struggle for a more democratic political system, especially elections and civilian rule. In 1932, it was advocates of democratic ideals who toppled the absolute monarchy and its monarchy-centric official nationalism. For the next 25 years democratic ideals remained alive, and were often advocated most strongly by elected MPs. But these ideals were resisted by the royalism of wounded monarchists and the ultranationalism and militarism sponsored most strongly by Phibun and Wichit. Supporters of a more democratic system then struggled under the despotic paternalism of Sarit, but grew quickly in numbers and influence from the 1960s as educational levels rose and the media became bolder.

Following the violent political conflicts in Bangkok in 1973 and 1976 between military governments and royalist paramilitaries on one side and students, farmers and workers on the other, most Thais accepted the idea that, to be legitimate, governments needed a level of popular support. The massive demonstrations of 1992 in Bangkok and the ensuing 1997 Constitution were further signs of momentum towards greater democracy. Nowadays, even the leaders of military regimes say soon after their coups that they will write a fresh constitution and organise an election as soon as possible. That

---

85   Streckfuss, "Freedom and Silencing," 124.

said, few observers of Thai politics would say that democratic ideals have taken deeper root than nationalism. Why is this?

Siam's comparatively benign political and economic conditions—a political system that was home-grown, not imposed externally, and an economy that gave subsistence affluence to many and opportunities to the elite and growing middle class—did not rouse the anti-establishment fervour that fuelled democratic-nationalist movements, and even revolutions, in other places. In the 1930s, when Siam's political system began to break under the weight of accumulated rigidities, it was easier to repair it with nationalism, including nation-building economic policies, than with democracy. Since 1932 most governments have claimed that the interests of the nation mattered more than democratic principles. The People's Party showed the way when it decreed that the electorate was too unsophisticated for democracy, disallowed the formation of political parties, quashed media freedom through a strict Press Control Act, and exiled, imprisoned and occasionally executed its political opponents.

In Thailand, democratic principles, unlike the communitarian principles of nationalism, don't appeal intuitively or effortlessly. Democracy implicitly rejects the idea that a harmonious hierarchical utopia is possible. Democracy accepts that reasonable and well-intentioned people can disagree, and that public discussion can resolve conflicts, as well as create them. Democracy can't exist without debate, which is often noisy and disruptive. In addition, the rule of law, which is essential to a fully functioning democracy, is impersonal, often coldly so. Rules, regulations and laws treat everybody equally; properly applied, the rule of law allows no exceptions.

Democracy is therefore handicapped in a society that traditionally gives precedence to order, harmony, hierarchy, community, loyalty and personal relationships, which are preserved through the observance of duties, responsibilities and rites, not through the exercise and protection of rights. Nationalism has put down deeper roots than democracy because it hasn't challenge traditional beliefs about the state's protective role; the primacy of hierarchy and the community over equality and the individual; the value of harmony over debate; the importance of observing duties rather than exercising rights; and the danger of disunity. For all these reasons, most of the time the advocates of Thai nationalism have been pushing against open doors.

In 1987, King Bhumibol said: "We Thais ... need not follow any kind of foreign democracy and should try instead to create our own Thai style of democracy, for we have our own national culture and outlook and we are capable of following our own reasoning."[86] The generals who ruled Thailand after 2014 and their supporters talked of Thai-style democracy. The 2017 Constitution is their most recent attempt to describe it, and perpetuate it.

---

86   Quoted in Hewison, "The Monarchy and Democratisation," p 68.

PART III

THE RULE AND ROLE OF LAW

Chapter Seven

THE RULE OF LAW:
WESTERN CONCEPTIONS

For as in absolute governments the king is law, so in free countries the law ought to be king, and there ought to be no other.[1]

Most foreigners and Thais seem to agree that Thai politics would be more stable if the "rule of law" were observed more consistently. These notions about the rule of law spring to the foreigner's mind as soon as protesters occupy public buildings or prevent people from voting; police and other security forces refuse to implement the law or ignore the directions of a lawfully elected government; elected politicians and other national leaders advocate a military or judicial coup; members of the elite or bullying mobs try to influence or intimidate the judiciary; wrong-doers grant themselves an amnesty; or judges and "independent" commissioners comment publicly on domestic politics or deliver decisions that are influenced by politics rather than the law. Just as frequently, Thai political activists say they rue the absence, or weak application of, the rule of law. Red accuses yellow of failing to respect the rule of law and yellow levels the same accusation against red. Unsurprisingly, colour-blind Thais accuse both sides of breaking the law or of benefiting from the failure of officials, judges, commissioners, the police and the military to observe the rule of law.

---

1   Thomas Paine, "Common Sense," in *Paine's Political Writings During the American and French Revolutions*, ed. by Hypatia Bradlaugh Bonner (London: Watts and Co, 1909), 25.

For decades, the leaders of every shade of Thai government have said they favour the rule of law; none of them have said they oppose it. The consensus that the rule of law is a good thing is not unique to Thailand. It is a global phenomenon. Brian Tamahana has argued eloquently that this "apparent unanimity in support of the rule of law is a feat unparalleled in history. No other single political ideal has ever achieved global endorsement."[2] He shows that the ideal has been sanctioned by leaders from a range of societies, cultures and economic and political systems. He acknowledges that they might support the rule of law for different reasons: "some in the interest of freedom, some in the preservation of order, many in the furtherance of economic development, but all identify it as essential".[3]

Tamahana further acknowledges that political leaders and activists, journalists as well as theorists, have struggled to define precisely what the rule of law is. "The rule of law thus stands in the peculiar state of being *the* preeminent legitimating political ideal in the world today, without agreement upon precisely what it means."[4] In his view, three themes run through the rule-of-law tradition: first, the government is limited by the law; secondly, a rule-bound order is established and maintained by the government; and thirdly, the law, not man, rules.[5]

Subsequently, an eminent British jurist, Tom Bingham, has said that the core of the existing principle of the rule of law is that "all persons and authorities in the state, whether public or private, should be bound by and entitled to the benefit of laws publicly made, taking effect (generally) in the future and publicly administered in the courts".[6] Bingham advanced eight "suggested principles" which help us "to explore the ingredients of the rule of law a little more

2   Brian Z. Tamahana, *On the Rule of Law: History, Politics, Theory* (Cambridge: Cambridge University Press, 2004), 3.
3   *Ibid*, 3.
4   *Ibid*, 4.
5   *Ibid*, 114–26.
6   Tom Bingham, *The Rule of Law* (London: Penguin, 2010), 8.

thoroughly".[7] These principles, which have been acclaimed for their breadth and clarity, are:

1. The law must be accessible and so far as possible intelligible, clear and predictable
2. Questions of legal rights and liability should ordinarily be resolved by application of the law and not the exercise of discretion
3. The laws of the land should apply equally to all, save to the extent objective differences justify differentiation
4. Ministers and public officers at all levels must exercise the powers conferred on them in good faith, fairly, for the purpose for which the powers were conferred, without exceeding the limits of such powers and not unreasonably
5. The law must afford adequate protection of fundamental human rights
6. Means must be provided for resolving, without prohibitive cost or inordinate delay, bona fide civil disputes which the parties themselves are unable to resolve
7. Adjudicative procedures provided by the state should be fair
8. The rule of law requires compliance by the state with its obligations in international law as in national law.[8]

Most people would not think or speak about the rule of law in these precise, technical terms. It is the language of an expert. But many people would understand what Bingham was talking about because they have been brought up in a system and a culture where these principles are valued and generally applied.

---

7   *Ibid*, 37.
8   *Ibid*, 37–129. Bingham devoted a chapter to each of these suggested principles.

These people have also absorbed the idea that powers of government are shared among the legislature, executive and judiciary (and that in a federal system powers can be shared with state and local governments). They understand that parliament makes the law, the government executes the law and the judiciary determines whether the parliament, government and individual citizens have abided by the law. They also understand that no branch should dominate; instead, each branch has a role to play in checking and balancing the power of the others.

From the perspective of settling disputes, in countries where the rule of law applies an elected legislature creates new laws to resolve disputes (or to avert possible disputes), and an independent judiciary is available to adjudicate disputes, if required.[9]

Essential to the separation of powers and to the settlement of disputes is the independence of the judiciary. An independent, neutral judiciary offers the best protection against a repressive or tyrannical government; the best protection against general lawlessness; and the best avenue for adjudicating disputes when a binding decision is required. A judiciary that is not independent and neutral can become a helpmate of a repressive or tyrannical government, as well as both a sponsor and a victim of general lawlessness. A judiciary that is not independent and neutral cannot protect the executive and legislature from each other or from themselves; nor can it protect individual citizens from the excesses of an unchecked executive or legislature.

Essential to the independence and neutrality of the judiciary is a respected and protected legal profession. Judges, including commissioners of independent agencies and regulatory bodies, should not be open to accusations that their rulings and judgments are based on anything other than the law. The executive and the legislature

---

9   In some jurisdictions, alternative or additional means of resolving disputes, like mediation, conciliation and arbitration, have emerged outside the formal judiciary. The independence of the mediator, conciliator or arbitrator is also critical to these additional means of dispute resolution.

therefore normally establish rules and observe conventions, first of all, to appoint judges in a non-partisan way; and, secondly, to enable judges to perform their functions without fear of intimidation or victimization. And judges themselves are jealous of their independence and neutrality; in particular they avoid commenting publicly on domestic political issues, which are the domain of the executive and legislature. Judges, and lawyers generally, also earn public respect by developing and demonstrating a deep knowledge of the law and, critically, a deep commitment to the values of legality.

In practice, of course, these principles are not always observed. And in practice the conduct of judges and lawyers sometimes disappoints. But in the minds of many people, these principles and these standards of conduct embody the rule of law. They are the fruits of centuries of debate, struggle and bloodshed since Aristotle argued that society should be ruled by law, not men.

Chapter Eight

THE ROLE OF LAW:
THAI CONCEPTIONS

The constitution is said to be the supreme law, but only because foreigners said this already. We copied their textbook and memorized it like a parrot. It has no real meaning in Thai culture. If it had real meaning, the constitution could not be torn up often, and laws, ministerial orders, regulations, and so on could not contravene the constitution. But in Thailand the constitution is torn up often, and more easily than the various rules and regulations of ministries and departments. Besides, there are many laws, ministerial orders, regulations, and so on, which contravene the constitution. Yet neither those enforcing these rules, nor those subject to them, feel any embarrassment at all.[1]

In Western societies and in societies heavily influenced by Western ideas, usually during periods of colonial rule, the law has assumed a dominant role. These societies are, or aspire to be, governed by law rather than by men. Each individual citizen in the society, regardless of rank (including monarchs, generals, ministers, parliamentarians and judges), is supposed to be subject to the law. The law is supreme.

In Thailand the law is sometimes supreme; at other times men triumph. Sometimes they triumph for nefarious reasons. Sometimes,

---

1   The opening sentences of Nidhi, "The Thai Cultural Constitution."

though, they triumph because, in certain circumstances, many Thais still prefer to be ruled by men than by the law. In other circumstances, some Thais also prefer to be ruled by laws of causation—like *karma* and astrology—that aren't easily reconciled with Western notions of the rule of law. And, on occasions, some Thais believe that guardian spirits can protect them from laws as well as outlaws.

Western Law and Thai Law: Principles Compared

Thailand has never wanted for laws. Over the centuries, Thailand, like other societies, has relied on laws to articulate accepted standards of conduct, maintain order and settle disputes. But the principles underlying those laws differed from the principles underlying Western law. Underlying Western law is the belief that each individual has a right to life, liberty and property. Without laws, only the strongest members of society would be able to protect these rights; without laws, society would be brutal and conflict-ridden. Furthermore, these individual rights and liberties need to be protected from the state, whose role is to maintain the rule of law while placing minimal limits on the rights and liberties of individual citizens.

To help understand how the principles underlying traditional or Siamese law differed from Western principles, let's look briefly at the nature of Siamese law before King Chulalongkorn's reforms in the late 19th century.[2] The first point to make is that, although Siam never wanted for laws, the law may not have been important in the thinking and daily lives of many Thais.

---

2   The following overview of traditional Siamese law draws on: Prince Dhani Nivat, "The Old Siamese Conception of the Monarchy;" R. Lingat, "Evolution of the Conception of Law in Burma and Siam," *Journal of the Siam Society*, 38 (1), (1950), 9–31; R. Lingat, *The Classical Law of India* (Berkeley, University of California Press, 1973); Engel, *Law and Kingship*; Engel, *Code and Custom*; Sarasin Viraphol, "Law in Traditional Siam and China: A Comparative Study, *Journal of the Siam Society*, 65 (1), (1977), 81–135; Hooker, *A Concise Legal History*; Apirat Petchsiri, *Eastern Importation of Western Criminal Law: Thailand as a Case Study* (Littleton Colorado: Fred B. Rothman and Co, 1987); Neil A. Englehart, *Culture and Power*; William Klausner, *Transforming Thai Culture: From Temple Drums to Mobile Phones* (Bangkok: The Siam Society, 2004); and Baker and Pasuk, *The Palace Law of Ayutthaya*.

Traditionally, in rural Thailand the social order and solidarity of the village was maintained by recognized and accepted norms of appropriate behaviour. Deviations were kept at a minimum through a complex web of family, communal, Buddhist and animist constraints. When conflicts arose they were settled by compromise and consensus, using the charisma and mediation skills of monks, clan heads and spirit mediums. A voluntary restitution of wrongs committed against persons and property followed. Dissatisfaction, or "grievance tension", resulting from the resolution of conflicts, was kept to a minimum.[3]

The overriding priority was social harmony, which was secured through negotiation and compromise. Recourse to officials for dispute resolution was discouraged and "when legal decisions were required, they were made by local officials who had little or no training in the law, who may never have seen a law book, and who prepared for the position by watching a prior officeholder at work".[4] More recent scholarship has challenged notions that the law was inaccessible and officials were untrained,[5] but that does not contradict the observation that Thais normally preferred not to involve the state in the resolution of their disputes.

At a philosophical level, traditional Siamese law was influenced by the Indian tradition, especially Buddhism.[6] Law was the rules of conduct and duties that upheld the universal cosmic order or *tham* (the Thai transcription of Sanskrit *dharma),* including the teachings of the Buddha.[7] This cosmic order was eternal and preordained.

---

3   Klausner, *Transforming Thai Culture*, p 124.
4   Englehart, *Culture and Power*, 29.
5   Baker and Pasuk, *The Palace Law of Ayutthaya*, 6, 8–12.
6   The extent to which the Indian tradition influenced Siamese law has been questioned recently by Baker and Pasuk, *ibid*, 26–31.
7   Robert Lingat has written: "Dharma is a concept difficult to define because it disowns—or transcends—distinctions that seem essential to us, and because it is based upon beliefs that are as strange to us as they are familiar to the Hindus [and Buddhists]." He goes on to say that "*Dharma* is what is firm and durable, what sustains and maintains, what hinders fainting and falling… Applied to the universe, *dharma* signifies the eternal laws which maintain the world." *The Classical Law of India*, 3.

By observing *tham* (which also means "living righteously"), this cosmic order—which entailed justice, social harmony and general well-being—was preserved. The universe and morality were coeval. In contrast, in Western thought order was established through the development of law. Order was not eternal. It did not pre-exist; nor was it preordained. According to Western thinking, if law was absent, conflict and chaos were inevitable.

Siamese law texts were laden with duties, obligations, privileges, truths, virtues, morals, instructions, rites, rituals and punishments. If these principles and practices were observed, justice would prevail and harmony would be preserved. In essence, traditional Siamese laws outlined duties, how duties should be observed and the consequences if duties were not observed. They did not outline the rights of individuals, which lie at the heart of Western law.

Just as rights did not lie at the heart of traditional Siamese law, nor did individuals. The law emphasised the duties and interests of individuals <u>within the community</u>. The purpose of the law was to preserve and promote harmonious social relations. The individual was defined by the social group to which he or she belonged, starting with the family, which was usually dominated by fathers and husbands.[8] Family obligations were pervasive.

Another major difference between the principles underlying traditional Siamese law and the principles underlying Western law was hierarchy. In traditional Siamese thinking the cosmic order that was upheld by law was hierarchical. "Without hierarchy, order cannot reign."[9] An individual's status within the hierarchy (and within the cosmic order) was determined by one's *karma*, or the merit an individual had accumulated through generosity, virtue and mental discipline in previous lives or earlier in this life.

---

8   Male domination was less common in urban, commercial society than in the nobility or agrarian society. See Baker and Pasuk, *History of Ayutthaya*, 193–8.
9   L.M. Hanks, "Merit and Power," 1249.

In contrast, according to Western thinking everyone is equal before the law and the law should treat everyone equally. This idea of equality also fostered the development of an adversarial system in many Western courts, where the prosecutor and defendant engage in a contest to convince the judge (or jury) of the justice of their claims. In contrast, the traditional Siamese system put a premium, first, on conflict avoidance—disputes should not arise, let alone be enlivened by an adversarial system of justice; and, secondly, on the preservation of social order—disputes should be settled quickly through negotiation and compromise.

In addition to explaining hierarchy, *karma* explained actions or events that affect an individual in this life. A fortunate event may be caused by good *karma* or accumulated merit; an unfortunate one by bad *karma* or accumulated demerit. As we will see later in this chapter, this traditional law of moral causation *(karma)* does not always sit easily with the application of Western law, which tries to establish more worldly causes of events.

Traditional Siamese law was also punitive and pedagogic. Because the primary purpose of law was to preserve harmony, "any violation or transgression, no matter how mild or severe, must be regarded as disruptive".[10] For example, close relations (and even friends) of offenders were liable to punishment and had a duty to report the offender's whereabouts to the authorities or to apprehend the offender. Punishment was corporal and instructive (for the miscreant and the broader community alike). And because harmony relied on the observance of hierarchy, hierarchy applied to punishments: the higher the social status of a miscreant, the heavier the punishment.

To summarise the principles underlying traditional Siamese law and how they differed from Western notions of the law: in Siam the law reflected cosmic order, which was eternal, pre-existing and

---

10   Sarasin, "Law in Traditional Siam and China," 116.

preordained; the law was not a man-made response to worldly disorder; Siamese law emphasised duties, not rights; the community, not the individual; hierarchy, not equality; and negotiation and compromise, not debate and victory versus defeat. When the law had to be applied, penalties were severe and had a pedagogic purpose. The cultural roots of traditional Siamese law and Western law were deep and different.

Pressures for Change

In the early 19th century, King Rama I (reigned 1782–1809) became concerned that traditional Siamese law had been contaminated or was being misinterpreted because the Burmese had destroyed about 90 per cent of legal texts when they sacked Ayutthaya in 1767. He commissioned specialists to cleanse the existing texts—the *thammasat* and the *rajasat*—of the Ayutthayan period (1351–1767) and incorporate them into a new legal code. The result was the Three Seals Code[11], which was promulgated in 1805. The surviving pre-1767 legal texts have since been lost, or may have been deliberately destroyed to enhance the validity of the new code.[12] In addition to clarifying the law, the Three Seals Code served the broader objective of consolidating and legitimising the kingship of Rama I, the founder of the Chakri dynasty. The Code remained the primary law of Siam until King Chulalongkorn's reforms in the 1890s; parts of the Code remained extant until the Civil and Commercial Code of 1935 was promulgated.

When the Three Seals Code was completed only four copies were made: one for the king's bedchamber, one for the court of justice, and one for the palace library, and an additional copy a little later— evidence of the hallowed status of the written law, though extracts were available for provincial officials.[13] In 1849–50, an American medico-

---

11 It was called the Three Seals Code because the original royal edition carried the seals of the interior, defence and finance departments.

12 Klaus Wenk, *The Restoration of Thailand under Rama I, 1782–1809* (Tucson: University of Arizona Press, 1968), 37.

13 Baker and Pasuk, *The Palace Law of Ayutthaya*, 11–12.

missionary and Thai noble, who faced a legal battle over inheritance, printed the Three Seals Code, partly because the noble realised that ignorance of the law could lead to legal difficulties, and partly because publication might be financially rewarding.[14] Authorities immediately seized and destroyed all copies on the grounds that the Code was a sacred text; distributing a printed version would rob the Code of its sacredness and be disrespectful to the king, then Rama III (reigned 1824–51).

In addition, for most of the century after the finalisation of the Code, the administrative writ of the Chakri dynasty was weakly applied, or hardly applied at all, beyond the central plains and upper south of the country. "The authority and jurisdiction of Bangkok's courts and codes likely decreased with distance, measured both in terms of geography and kinship ties, from the capital and its major ministries."[15] Before Chulalongkorn's reforms, the north, northeast and Malay south of what we now call Thailand had their own administrative and judicial systems, untouched by the Three Seals Code.

Within a few decades of the completion of the Three Seals Code, Siam was being transformed by economic, social and political changes that demanded new systems of governance. In response to Western traders, envoys and the occasional gunboat, the Siamese economy, which had been touched only lightly by the written law, developed a bigger and more diverse export market and became monetized. More and more Siamese, a growing number of migrants from China, as well as European and American merchants, missionaries and diplomats, lived outside the subsistence economy and its traditional governance arrangements. Time-honoured methods of regulation did not have ready answers to the unprecedented administrative demands associated with port and warehouse facilities, commercial offices,

---

14   Thanapol Limapichart, "The emergence of the Siamese public sphere: colonial modernity, print culture and the practice of criticism," *South East Asia Research*, Vol 17, No.3 (November 2009), 370–2.
15   Tamara Loos, *Subject Siam: Family, Law, and Colonial Modernity in Thailand* (Chiang Mai: Silkworm Books, 2002), 34.

mechanised rice and sugar mills, financial institutions, exchange rates, taxation, and new infrastructure like canals, roads, railways, ports, posts and telegraphs. Foreigners brought new ideas and new technology, stirring an apprehension that Siam needed to catch up, as well as an appetite for Western education. In addition, Siam had new and powerful neighbours: Britain and France, who had unseated the traditional rulers of Burma, the Malay peninsula, Laos, Cambodia and Vietnam. King Mongkut and King Chulalongkorn were afraid that they would be added to this list.

Traditional methods of governing, including the role of the law, had to change. A little over a decade after authorities had forbidden the publication and distribution of the Three Seals Code, Mongkut printed a two-volume version and distributed it widely. At the same time, Mongkut "did not feel bound at all by old provisions of law whenever they appeared to him no longer suitable for modern times".[16] He also published a Government Gazette to disseminate the increasing number of government decisions, including laws, in the fast-changing environment. As soon as Chulalongkorn reached his majority (1873), he attempted judicial reform—a special court to clear a backlog of cases, clearer judicial procedures and the creation of a Privy Council and Council of State with some legislative powers. Initially, he was thwarted by ministers and officials, who remained powerful and stubborn until the 1880s. When, finally, he had the opportunity to implement reform, he moved quickly and systematically.

Chulalongkorn's Reforms

Chulalongkorn was motivated by fear of colonial incursions and humiliation at the extraterritorial status Siam had already been forced to grant 15 foreign powers. He reasoned that the colonial powers might

---

16   Lingat, "Evolution of the Conception of Law in Burma and Siam," 30.

think twice before trying to grab territory he considered Siamese if he could demonstrate that Siam controlled it. And they would lose their justification for extraterritorial protection if Siam could introduce Western laws and a Western judicial system. Chulalongkorn also wanted Siam to benefit from international commerce, which a modern legal system would facilitate. Finally, he concluded that the traditional legal system was unsuited to modern Siam's domestic needs, including his need to make the monarchy more powerful.

By 1935, the reforms initiated by Chulalongkorn—heavily influenced by foreign advisers and foreign models—had delivered Siam a European system of legal codes and law courts. The codes were based on Western ideas of state sovereignty rather than Siamese ideas of the *thammasat*. The courts, previously spread across several government bodies, were brought under the administration of the Ministry of Justice, and the ministry and courts were given the judicial power that previously resided with the monarch.

In theory at least, the new legal system transformed the relationship between the government and the governed. "The king had effectively granted to the people a right against arbitrary and capricious applications of the law, against the taking of liberty or property without proper notice as to the legal justification for such action by the state. King Chulalongkorn had created a new legal standard requiring that the law function in a predictable and foreseeable manner in its regulation of the affairs of the people."[17]

On the surface, Chulalongkorn's reforms provided a stark alternative to the *thammasat* as the foundation of the law; but below the surface, his reforms did not dislodge the *thammasat* from Siamese thinking regarding preserving cosmic order. Notwithstanding the new theoretical relationship between the government and the governed, in reality Siamese law and Siamese courts—the visible manifestations of the justice system—were restructured much more

---

17   Engel, *Law and Kingship*, 104.

easily than the values and ideologies underpinning Siamese notions of justice. "New laws had seemingly created new legal rights, and the relationship between the government and the people appeared to have undergone a remarkable transformation."[18] As discussed in more detail below, introducing a new legal consciousness and a new political culture was qualitatively harder than introducing new laws and new courts.

1932 Constitution

After Chulalongkorn's reforms, the next major development was the 1932 Constitution, which spelt the end of absolute monarchy. The promulgation of a constitution, in a ceremony replete with the beating of gongs and blowing of conch shells, was act enough in itself to signal a bigger and different role for the law in Siam. The manifesto issued by the People's Party to justify the overthrow of the absolute monarch had said that the new government would "not act like a blind man as the government which has the king above the law has done" but would follow principles, including "equal rights (so that those of royal blood do not have more rights than the people as at present)".[19] The 1932 Constitution said all Thais were equal before the law, enjoyed a full range of freedoms and liberties, and had a duty to respect the rule of law.

Like Chulalongkorn's reforms, the constitution was more imposed from above than conceived from below; it was also largely imported, not locally grown. For most Thais a constitution was an alien concept, as was the democracy it was supposed to facilitate. Some people reportedly thought the constitution was a relative of Phahon Phonphayuhasena, the prime minister, and that democracy was the brother of the king.[20] In the same vein, there were reports of villagers, accustomed to personal rule, asking: "Whose child is *rathathammanun*

---

18   *Ibid*, 119.
19   "Announcement of the People's Party No 1," 24 June 1932, in *Pridi by Pridi*, 72.
20   David Wyatt, *Thailand*, 239.

[constitution]?"[21] Others ascribed a religious significance to the document. The Thai writer, Kulap Saipradit, observed that among the general population "it was said that the constitution deity was most holy and to be respected ... Everybody ... even the king who was considered to be god, was subject to its authority ... All activities in the kingdom were to be in accordance with its commands".[22]

To accommodate this type of thinking, the government "decided to promote the constitution not as a practical code defining the relationship between the people and the state, but as a revered object of national importance".[23] Miniature copies of the constitution were anointed and monks chanted over them, and the Department of Fine Arts made special cabinets for the miniatures, which were distributed to each province. In 1934 the head of the British legation described a ceremony to mark Constitution Day, which the government elevated above the king's birthday as the premier national holiday, where the constitution was placed on the largest and centre-most of three altars, with the image of the Buddha and portrait of the king on the other two. Candles and flowers—"semi-divine honours"—were offered to the constitution, as well as to the Buddha image and portrait of the king.[24] In 1935, in a remote village, another observer saw the constitution "reverently placed on a lacquer bowl ... raised on a litter, and carried off to be deposited in the temple", after watching "the expressions of the assembled peasants as they listened unemotionally. Faces remained blank and uncomprehending. The meaning entirely escaped them."[25] On another occasion, it was placed on top of a replica of Mt Meru, the sacred mountain of Buddhist cosmology.

---

21   Wendell Blanchard, *Thailand: Its People, Its Society, Its Culture* (New Haven: Hraf Press, 1970), 167.
22   Kulap Saipradit, quoted in Barmé, *Luang Wichit Wathakan*, 111.
23   Barmé, *Luang Wichit Wathakan*, 111.
24   *Ibid*, 112.
25   Wales, *Years of Blindness*, 282–3. These rituals resemble the rituals surrounding the recitation of the Vessantara Jataka, which in Thailand is the most famous and popular tale of the Buddha's past lives, where the text is elaborately and respectfully transported in a specially crafted box to the place where it is to be recited. In the case of the Vessantara Jataka, though, the audience does not listen unemotionally, and the meaning does not escape them. See Jory, *Thailand's Theory of Monarchy*, 26–7.

The previous national dictum of "Nation, Religion and King", sponsored by the ultranationalistic King Vajiravudh, was recast as "Nation, Religion, King and Constitution". In 1936, in his concluding remarks in a radio address to mark the fourth anniversary of constitutional government, Pridi Banomyong, the brilliant Paris-trained lawyer who was the strongest promoter of constitutional government, said:

> The constitution is the highest dhamma to enable the Siamese people to survive as an independent nation. For those of you who abide by the constitution, who abide by the dhamma, good things will result…. [Pridi then quoted a Pali verse which translates as: "Dhamma always protect those who practice dhamma"]. May you all be resolute to sustain the constitutional system for ever. May I request the power of the three jewels— that is, the Buddha, the Dhamma, and the Sangha—and all the sacred things in the world to protect you all to have happiness and prosperity under the constitutional system at all times. Any wish that you have which is legitimate within the scope of the constitution, may that wish be fulfilled in all respects.[26]

To try to convey the meaning and significance of the constitution to an audience that was largely unfamiliar with imported Western law, Pridi had to resort to the symbolism and vocabulary of traditional Siamese notions of the law—to equate the Western-style constitution with Buddhist *dhamma* (or *tham*) even though, as we have seen, the principles underpinning each were far apart.[27]

---

26 *Pridi by Pridi*, 196. *Dhamma*, like *tham*, is an alternative Thai-language term for *dharma*. The "three jewels" (also called the "Triple Gem") are the three things in which Buddhists take refuge or seek guidance (the Buddha, *dharma* and *sangha*).

27 This was not the only occasion on which Pridi linked ostensibly secular matters to Buddhist beliefs. His radical economic plan of 1933 ended with references to *si-ariya* and *phra si-ariya* (the future Buddha) and the *kalaphapruk* tree which, according to Thai Buddhism, will grow in the future world of *si-ariya* and yield fruits containing anything one may wish for. The handbill announcing the overthrow of absolute monarchy on 24 June 1932, which Pridi authored, also ended with references to *si-ariya*. *Pridi by Pridi*, 72, 114.

Pridi and his colleagues also resorted to draconian legislation. Under the Act for the Protection of the Constitution (1933), drafted by a committee headed by Pridi, anyone found guilty of challenging the constitution faced up to 20 years' imprisonment. The "crime" of challenging the constitution was defined very broadly; it covered any act that might "lessen the people's appreciation of the same [i.e. constitution], or causes alarm in regard to the administration of the state by way of the Constitution of Siam, even though such an act is only a conspiracy or the making of an agreement or preparation to act".[28] People were charged for this offence, imprisoned or sentenced to "restricted residence".[29]

In 1939, a bronze version of the constitution formed the centrepiece of the Democracy Monument in central Bangkok, with 75 cannons at the base of the monument symbolically protecting the constitution. The cannons and the Act for the Protection of the Constitution were symptoms of the People's Party's anxiety about the life expectancy of its government and constitution.

Thailand's first constitution had an ungainly birth, and subsequent constitutions have often lived ungainly lives. Thai constitutions have not radiated the ideological fervour of the revolutionary American or French constitutions. Nor have they radiated the regenerative sentiment of the constitutions of newly independent countries in the post-colonial period. And only in 1997 (see below) did a constitution reflect the results of a dialogue between its drafters and its subjects.

In 1932, the People's Party certainly needed a constitution to legitimise its government internationally. But domestically it needed more; a constitution wasn't enough. To legitimise their government in the eyes of most Thais—and to a certain extent in their own eyes— the new leaders had to cloak the constitution in the symbolism of

---

28   Quoted in Barmé, *Luang Wichit Wathakan*, 110. See also Stowe, *Siam Becomes Thailand*, 66.
29   Barmé, *Luang Wichit Wathakan*, 110.

pre-constitutional law. Above all, to legitimise their government the usurpers of the king's power had to get the king's blessing. King Prajadhipok gave his blessing, and his successors have given their blessing to subsequent governments. But since 1932, traditionalists have not conceded fully that the monarchy itself is subject to the constitution. No one talks openly any more about Prince Dhani's constitution of the *Thammasat*, but the idea that the home-grown monarchy is somehow bigger and better than the imported constitution still resonates in Thai society.[30]

1932–1997

The 15 written constitutions from 1932 until 1997 were not the supreme law of the land; they were tools in the hands of the political elite of the day.[31] Successive elites ignored or discarded inherited written constitutions with impunity and either ruled without a constitution or wrote a new one aimed at improving their chances of retaining power. Depending on the demands of the time, on paper these constitutions gave less or more power to the monarchy, military or bureaucracy and made occasional concessions to advocates of a more democratic government; but they rarely constrained the elite and rarely captured the imagination of the public.

1997 Constitution

The 1997 Constitution was different. Like Chulalongkorn's reforms of the 1890s and the constitution of 1932, the constitution of 1997 was an attempt to recast Thailand's governance.

But unlike the drafters of Chulalongkorn's reforms and the drafters of the 1932 Constitution, the drafters of the 1997 Constitution consulted the Thai public. A 99-member Constitutional Drafting

---

30   Nidhi Eoseewong has written eloquently about this "cultural constitution". Nidhi, "The Thai Cultural Constitution."
31   The dates for these constitutions were 1932 (2), 1946, 1947, 1949, 1952, 1959, 1968, 1972, 1974, 1976, 1977, 1978, 1991 and 1997.

Assembly (CDA) was formed, comprising 76 elected representatives from each province and 23 experts. The CDA was an elitist body; for a start, all members had to have at least a bachelor's degree. It drafted a constitution, which naturally reflected elitist CDA views on how Thailand should be governed, but it then sought public submissions and comment through meetings with business associations and NGOs, public surveys and public hearings across the country, all of which received widespread coverage in the media.[32] In other words, the CDA didn't first canvass views across society and then draft a constitution, so the 1997 Constitution was not a "grass-roots constitution" (but which constitution is?). But the CDA did engage the community and publicise the CDA draft and, ultimately, this engagement gave the draft a measure of legitimacy because NGOs and the community supported the changes it foreshadowed. In addition, if parliament hadn't endorsed the document in September 1997, the draft would have been put to a referendum.[33]

The new constitution also tried to safeguard judicial independence and the separation of powers between the judiciary, executive and legislative branches of government. The administrative, budgetary and personnel arrangements for the courts were separated from the Ministry of Justice and an independent judicial commission was established to oversee the promotion of judges as well as any disciplinary procedures. Judges of the superior courts had fixed terms. Once assigned to a case, judges could not be taken off it. Judges had to declare any potential conflicts of interest and they were barred from holding positions in government, business or the professions. The salaries of judges were set at reasonably high levels compared with other Thai officials (although the judges did not always agree

---

32 For more on public consultations on the 1997 Constitution, see Michael Connors, "Framing the 'People's Constitution,'" in *Reforming Thai Politics*, ed. by Duncan McCargo (Copenhagen, NIAS, 2002), 37–55.
33 With the benefit of hindsight, an open, democratic referendum (unlike the tightly controlled referendums of 2007 and 2016), rather than parliamentary endorsement, may have promoted greater social consensus in favour of the new rules of politics.

that their salaries were high enough) and they continued to receive the health and retirement benefits that have historically attracted Thais to public sector employment. Finally, and critically, elaborate arrangements were devised to try to protect judicial appointments from political interference.

In summary, the 1997 Constitution instituted itself as the sole supreme law; spelled out the rights and liberties of citizens; established administrative courts so citizens could challenge government decisions; launched Thailand's first fully elected bicameral parliament; outlined a clear separation of powers between the executive, legislature and judiciary; put in place checks and balances, including through the establishment of a constitutional court and a range of independent agencies; and promoted the independence of the judiciary.

2007 Constitution

The 1997 Constitution was annulled after the military coup of 2006 and replaced by a constitution that was drafted by a military-nominated committee which had to follow military-endorsed drafting guidelines. Public consultations were perfunctory, and in August 2007 the constitution was passed in a heavily controlled referendum.

The 2007 Constitution boosted the judiciary, vesting it with the authority to dissolve a political party and ban party members from politics for five years (and thereby formalised the power the military government had already exercised after the 2006 coup, when it dissolved Thaksin's Thai Rak Thai Party and banned 111 party members). It also gave the judiciary additional authority over MPs and ministers, organic law-making, emergency decrees and the selection of senators. While making both the legislature and the executive more accountable to the judiciary (and thus increasing the opportunities for a "judicial coup"), the 2007 Constitution also attempted to strengthen the judiciary's independence by lessening the risk of political interference in the selection of judges and commissioners.

2017 Constitution

In turn, the 2007 Constitution was annulled by the military coup of 2014, and in 2017 it was replaced by another military-sponsored constitution. The drafting of the new constitution was tortuous. The appointed military-dominated legislature rejected a first draft, which had been finalised by another military-appointed body and focused heavily on promoting morality and fighting corruption. The military assigned a new drafting committee and in August 2016 its draft was endorsed in another heavily-controlled referendum. As in 2007, public consultations on the new constitution were perfunctory.

To recap the likely effects of the 2017 Constitution on the roles of the monarchy, military, executive, legislature and judiciary: the legislature will be comprised of a 500-member elected lower house and a fully appointed and military-dominated senate. The electoral system will limit the scope for the most popular party, which since 2001 has been pro-Thaksin, to form a majority. For five years after the next election, appointed senators will be able to play a role in appointing the prime minister. The 2017 Constitution further strengthens the political role of the judiciary.

After the constitution was passed in the August 2016 referendum, it was submitted in the normal way to the king for royal endorsement. Unlike his father, the new king, Vajiralongkorn, amended the document.[34] He restored provisions of the previous constitution, giving the king a potential role if a political crisis arose. He also changed the arrangements for the appointment of a regent in his absence and cancelled the need for a parliamentary counter-signature to royal orders. In April 2017, he presided over an elaborate ceremony in which he formally granted the new constitution to the people of Thailand.

---

34   See Chapter Three.

1997 Yardstick

Post-coup governments used the constitutions of 2007 and 2017 to improve the chances of the traditional, conservative elite retaining power. In this regard, these documents resemble Thailand's 15 constitutions between 1932 and 1997.

Because both the 2007 and 2017 constitutions moved away from the 1997 model, many Thai observers and a higher proportion of foreign observers tend to view them as utterly backward steps. They use the 1997 Constitution as a benchmark against which to judge Thailand's constitutional development.

This 1997-centric view is understandable. The 2007 and 2017 constitutions fall short of their 1997 predecessor. But the 1997-centric view has two shortcomings. First, it tends to overlook the durability of some of the ideas that underpinned the 1997 Constitution and some of the institutions and practices it spawned.[35] The idea that governments need to be legitimised by a constitution survives; immediately after coups military governments say that a new and better constitution will be drafted. So does the idea that all political action needs to be cast in constitutional terms; even the PDRC, which wanted to replace a legally elected government with an appointed government, took pains to claim (albeit disingenuously) that it was acting in accordance with the constitution.[36] The idea that the public should have a role in legitimising the constitution also survives, even if it is largely through a referendum that offers a take-it-or-leave-it choice.

Military governments and their hand-picked constitution drafters have not abolished the major guardian institutions established under the 1997 Constitution: the constitutional court, electoral commission, anti-corruption commission, human rights commission, state audit commission, ombudsman's office and administrative courts. The survival—and occasional blossoming—of the administrative

---

35   Tom Ginsburg has written that the 1997 Constitution had a "constitutional afterlife". See "Constitutional Afterlife," 83–105.
36   Ferrara, *The Political Development of Modern Thailand*, 284.

courts, in particular, is noteworthy; these courts have given citizens unprecedented opportunities to contest government decisions, which they have taken. Post–1997 constitutions continue to allow citizens, through petitions, to sponsor a bill in parliament. The 2007 Constitution preserved the requirement that the prime minister be an elected MP, a major change introduced in 1997; and, while re-opening the possibility of an unelected prime minister, the 2017 Constitution puts a five-year limit on this option. And since 1997 there has been a consensus that, ideally, governments should be elected. Even the PDRC advocated the eventual return to elected government, after a period of rule by "good people". And immediately after coups, military governments say they want Thailand to return to elected, civilian governments as soon as practicable.

Secondly, a 1997-centric view tends to see what is written in the constitution—whether it is the 1997 Constitution or another one— as a demonstration of either a commitment to, or even evidence of, democracy and the rule of law. Notwithstanding the survival of ideas, institutions and practices of democratic government after the demise of the 1997 Constitution, gaps continue to exist in Thailand between constitutional words and political thinking and deeds, especially in the eyes of observers from societies where the principles underpinning constitutional government and the rule of law are embedded in the political culture. Since 1997, Thais from different quarters have variously contradicted the text of the 1997 Constitution, defied the intentions of the drafters of that constitution, and belied notions that the law was paramount.

How Supreme is the Supreme Law?

Even Constitutional Court judges have been unable or unwilling to accept that the constitution is the supreme law in <u>all</u> instances. Since 1946, every Thai constitution had proclaimed that the constitution was the supreme law but, at the same time, these constitutions had stipulated that Thai citizens enjoyed their rights and liberties "except where laws stated otherwise", or words to that effect. As a result, statute law and executive decrees routinely took precedence over the constitution, especially in cases touching on national security, public safety or morality.[37] The 1997 Constitution, though, was unequivocal: the constitution was the highest law in the land and it stipulated that statute law and executive decrees, as well as administrative rules and regulations, could not take precedence. The constitution further allowed for the amendment of existing laws, rules and regulations to bring them into line with the new supreme law.

An early high-profile case to raise concerns about inability or unwillingness of Constitutional Court judges to fully comprehend the supremacy of the constitution involved the Deputy Minister for Agriculture, Newin Chidchob, who in 1999 had been found guilty of defamation and sentenced to imprisonment for six months, suspended for three years. According to the letter of the constitution and the clearly stated intention of the constitution's drafters, Newin should have lost his cabinet position because he had been sentenced to imprisonment. But, in a complex decision, the Constitutional Court ruled that an earlier decision of the Supreme Court had determined that a suspended jail term was not imprisonment and, therefore, Newin could remain in the cabinet.[38]

Another oft-quoted case that illustrated the difficulty some Constitutional Court judges had after 1997 in accepting the supremacy of the constitution involved Sirimit Boonmul and Boonjuti Klubprasert, who had been disqualified by the Judicial Commission from applying to become assistant judges because they had polio-related physical disabilities. The Ombudsman brought their case to the Constitutional Court; in 2002 it ruled, in an 8/3 decision, in favour of the Judicial Commission, even though the

---

37   William Klausner, *Transforming Thai Culture*, 159, 165–66. James R. Klein, *The Constitution of the Kingdom of Thailand*, 15–16.
38   Klein, "The Battle for Rule of Law," 61–4.

1997 Constitution expressly prohibited discrimination on the grounds of physical disability. The Judicial Commission had ruled that, according to the Justice Personnel Law, judges must inspire public awe and respect, and judges who walked with a limp did not meet this criterion.[39]

The drafters of the 1997 Constitution had realised that many existing Thai laws, rules and regulations would not meet the standards of the new constitution. So they put in place transitional arrangements that offered the Constitutional Court an opportunity to bring these laws, rules and regulations into line with the rights and obligations embodied in the new supreme law. On the whole, though, judges chose not to take up this opportunity, especially in relation to rules and regulations, which they said fell outside their jurisdiction.[40] As a result, in these areas also the constitution was not always the supreme law.

At times, some judges also seem to have been swayed more by traditional *thammasat* notions that the primary purpose of the courts is to preserve harmony, than by newer notions that the primary purpose of the courts is to settle disputes in accordance with the law. For example, a former President of the Constitutional Court has admitted that the Court's ruling in 2008 to dissolve the Palang Prachachon Party, ban its executives from office for five years and thereby force the resignation of a prime minister "was based not on the merits of the case, but on the court's desire to restore 'order' in society".[41] An earlier example of the durability of traditional thinking is reflected in the comment by a judicial official in 2006 that judges cannot go against the wishes of the king. In yet another example of a reluctance to accept that, in a democracy, the law is supreme, a Constitutional Court judge reportedly said in 2001 that the court was not in a position to decide whether Thaksin was guilty or innocent because he had just won an election.

---

39   *Ibid*, 45.
40   *Ibid*, 43–4.
41   Ferrara, *The Political Development of Modern Thailand*, 245.

Judges have left themselves open in other ways to claims that they have not acted independently. For example, in 2008 a judge openly described the decision to sack a prime minister for hosting a cooking show as "judicial creativity",[42] and in 2014 the Constitutional Court ruled that a call to replace an elected government with an unelected council was not an attempt to overthrow democracy. The independence of commissioners serving on various independent agencies established under the 1997 Constitution and retained under the 2007 Constitution has also been questioned. For example, in 2014 the Electoral Commission helped to thwart an election and a National Anti-Corruption Commissioner seemed to adjudge officials corrupt before charges were laid.

With judges and commissioners of independent agencies unable or unwilling to accept the supremacy of the law and promote the independence of the judiciary, non-judicial officials and political activists have felt little pressure, or inclination, to do so. At times, political leaders of all persuasions have not observed the 1997 Constitution, the 2007 Constitution that replaced it, or basic principles of the rule of law. Thaksin threatened to cut the funding of independent bodies if they became antagonistic. On another occasion he said: "One weakness of the nation is a tendency to prioritise law as a way to solve problems, management principles should be used instead and law treated as only one supporting element." He interfered in the appointment of judges and commissioners.[43] Supporters of Thaksin's political parties and the red-shirt movement threatened judges and the courts, including by publishing the home addresses and personal phone numbers of judges who were about to rule on sensitive cases. Thaksin and other leaders sympathetic to him did not try to persuade their supporters or the general public that in a democracy judges, courts and the rule of law must be respected.

---

42   Bjorn Dressel, "Judicialization of Politics or Politicization of the Judiciary?" 682.
43   Pasuk and Baker, *Thaksin*, 64.

The military government that ousted Thaksin in a coup in 2006 annulled the 1997 Constitution, amnestied itself for breaking the law and then imposed a new constitution on the nation, with minimal consultation with the public on its contents. Contravening another central tenet of the rule of law, this government imposed retrospective penalties on Thaksin and his political allies. In 2008, Abhisit Vejjajiva was prepared to take office as prime minister in the knowledge that the military had cajoled a minor party to shift its allegiance to his Democrat Party. A Democrat Party MP was caught on video lobbying court officials on a case involving the party. In 2014, the party decided to boycott an election that the elected government, in accordance with normal democratic practice, had called in order to break a political deadlock, and members of the Democrat Party actively obstructed citizens who wanted to vote. Supporters of Abhisit's party and the PDRC, led by the recently retired Democrat Party stalwart, Suthep Thaugsuban, threatened judges and the courts. Abhisit and other leaders sympathetic to him did not try to persuade their supporters or the general public that in a democracy judges, courts and the rule of law must be respected.

The military government of Prayuth Chan-ocha that ousted the Pheu Thai government in a coup in 2014 annulled the 2007 Constitution, amnestied itself for breaking the law and imposed a new constitution on the nation, with minimal consultation with the public on its contents. At will, it invoked the authority of Article 44 of the interim constitution it wrote for itself, which granted the prime minister absolute powers.

Role of Law: Some Conclusions

The drafters of the 1997 Constitution were unequivocal in saying in the text of the document that the law was supreme; the rule of law was to apply in Thailand in the same way it applied in other constitutional monarchies influenced by Western concepts of the law.

Secondly, the 1997 Constitution gave the judiciary a moderating role akin to the role the judiciary plays in Western legal systems in checking and balancing the power of the executive and legislature.

Thirdly, "this elaborately structured edifice of constraints on politics"[44] did not constrain politics as much as the drafters of the constitution intended. In institutional terms, Thailand did not become the conventional three-branch government the constitution assumed; at various times since 1997 the military and the monarchy have again played roles, including in settling political disputes, that are conventionally the responsibility of the executive, legislature and the judiciary. In addition, the 1997 Constitution did not constrain politics because judicial officials often failed to understand the rule of law or knowingly ignored it, and political leaders and political parties have not been fully committed to the rule of law.

Fourthly, the 1997 Constitution did, however, introduce ideas, institutions and practices that have survived and continue to influence thinking about the role of the law as well as the conduct of politics.

Fifthly, since 1997, the law and the courts have played a bigger role in Thai politics. The 2007 and 2017 constitutions expanded that role, bestowing unprecedented political power on the courts. The judiciary now acts more as a check on the authority of the executive and legislature than as a counterbalance to their authority. The judiciary risks becoming a servant of the monarchy and military.

Liberty and/or *Issaraphap*

In much the same way that, on the surface, Chulalongkorn's reforms in the 1890s provided a stark alternative to the *thammasat* as the foundation of the law, the reforms of 1997 and since provided an alternative to prevailing norms and practices. The alternatives now are less stark than they were over a century ago because the ideas underpinning the reforms of the 1890s, 1932 and 1997 have seeped

---

44 Ginsburg, "Constitutional Afterlife," 84.

into Thai institutions and practices and into much Thai thinking about the role of law in the society. And, as noted in the last chapter, support for the rule of law now has global endorsement. Yet, in much the same way as, below the surface, Chulalongkorn's reforms did not dislodge the *thammasat* from Siamese thinking about law and cosmic order, imported ideas have struggled to dislodge some traditional values and ideologies that still underpin Thai notions of law and justice. Introducing new laws, including constitutions, and new courts has been much easier than introducing a new legal consciousness and a new political culture.

A study by Tamara Loos on the translation of the English word "liberty" into Thai by legal experts in 1908 illustrates the hazards that were involved in importing a Western idea into Siam and in trying to render it in terms that were meaningful in Siamese legal and political culture.[45] Wanting to rid Siam of the humiliation of extraterritoriality, Chulalongkorn introduced Western laws. To finalise a penal code along Western lines, he engaged advisers from Europe and Japan who worked with Thai experts who had studied abroad. After reviewing the penal codes of 10 foreign jurisdictions, they completed a draft code in their *lingua franca*, English, which they then translated into Thai under the supervision of four minister-princes. One of them, Minister of Justice Prince Ratburi, summarised the hurdles facing the translators: "The rhetoric is not very precise," he said, "since the *farang* [White Westerner] terms and Thai terms are not identical. Each has their own habits and disposition. To select accurately [a term] without excessive or incomplete meanings is, then, a supremely difficult task."[46]

Because the Thai language did not have a ready-made word that captured the Western idea that liberty was enjoyed <u>equally</u> by each individual, the translators chose the Thai word *issaraphap* for "liberty".[47] In Siam's traditionally hierarchical society, however,

45   Loos, "Issaraphap: The Limits of Individual Liberty in Thai Jurisprudence," *Crossroads: An Interdisciplinary Journal of Southeast Asian Studies*, 12, No 1 (1998), 35–75.
46   Quoted in Loos, *Subject Siam*, 67.
47   *Issaraphap* was also chosen to translate "independence", "freedom" and "autonomy".

"*issaraphap* described a relationship between unequals and referred to the supremacy *over*, not independence *from*, another individual".[48] *Issaraphap*, unlike liberty, was not enjoyed equally by each individual. "Rather, *issaraphap*'s meaning depended on whether the term was used in reference to one of superior or one of subordinate status. For subordinates, *issaraphap* was conceptualised in negative terms: it described the condition of not being subject to the power of a superior. For superiors, *issaraphap* consisted of the sovereignty, authority, or supremacy held over themselves and their subordinates."[49] As Loos points out, the Thai legal experts were elite males with a substantial degree of personal *issaraphap*, so it is not hard to understand why they chose *issaraphap* as the Thai term that best captured the concept "liberty".

Drawing on court cases before and after 1908, Loos shows how *issaraphap* struggled to become an egalitarian right because traditionally it had carried an hierarchical meaning. In one case, army officers were charged with violating the *issaraphap* of a female servant. After passing through three courts, in 1914 King Vajiravudh imprisoned the officers because they had damaged the honour of the royal army and failed to respect the martial *esprit de corps*, offences with which they had not been charged. In putting its recommendation to the king, the Supreme Court did not even mention the allegation of *issaraphap*, presumably because at some stage during the appeals process the judges had concluded that a commoner woman could not have *issaraphap*. Nor, unsurprisingly, did the king mention *issaraphap* in his judgment. Equally, Loos shows that the new penal code, by introducing the concept that depriving someone of his or her *issaraphap* was a crime, eventually made it possible for people to assert their *issaraphap*. She concludes: "The attempt to map Western liberal ideas onto the Thai legal landscape

---

48 Loos, "Issaraphap," 37.
49 *Ibid*, 41.

did not eradicate the history of *issaraphap* as an indigenous concept, but it did begin to narrow *issaraphap*'s meaning and reify the gender and status differentials in society."[50]

Loos's study shows that, over time, the legal culture began to absorb imported ideas. Still, nowadays when foreigners talk about liberty and Thais talk about *issaraphap*, are they talking about the same thing? Or when English-speaking Thais talk about liberty, do they mean liberty or *issaraphap*?

The Meanings of Law and Justice

The role of law vis-à-vis the rule of law in Thailand has been further illuminated by two other scholars, David Engel and Jaruwan Engel, who have looked at how people in northern Thailand in the 1990s felt about the law in their everyday lives, especially after they have been injured in accidents.[51] Before looking at the results of the ethnographic studies that are the main focus of their inquiry, in keeping with Loos's focus on the meaning of the words "liberty" and *issaraphap*, it is useful to look quickly at what Engel and Jaruwan say about the Thai words for "law" and "justice". The word for "law" is *kotmai*, which literally means "rule" or "regulation". "*Kotmai* is somewhat narrower than *law*. Although the term was readily understandable to our interviewees, when asked about *kotmai* they tended to confine their responses to criminal prohibitions and the police rather than the entire range of legal institutions and practices that injury cases might implicate."[52]

The words for "justice" are *khwam yuttitham* and *khwam pen tham*, with *yuttitham* being used colloquially. *Yutti* means "to conclude" or "to finish", so justice is the concluding or finishing of *tham*—which, as we have seen, equates to the universal cosmic order. "To regard *tham, khwam pen tham,* or *khwam yuttitham* as simple cognates for the English word *justice* is to ignore fundamental differences

---

50   *Ibid*, 71.
51   David M. Engel and Jaruwan S. Engel, *Tort, Custom, and Karma: Globalization and Legal Consciousness in Thailand* (Chiang Mai: Silkworm Books, 2010).
52   *Ibid*, 124.

between Hindu-Buddhist and Anglo-European philosophical and jurisprudential traditions."[53]

So when foreigners and Thais agree that Thais should observe the rule of law, are they agreeing to the same thing?

Faults and Remedies

To return to Engel and Jaruwan's ethnographic work. When we have an accident, we normally look for a cause and, having established the cause, decide who might be liable for any compensation and whether we will pursue a remedy. Engel and Jaruwan's interviews with 35 accident victims in Chiang Mai province found that victims would attribute accidents to a range of causes, including bad *karma*; ghosts; fate; sexual impropriety of a relative (who was not involved in the accident but whose actions upset an ancestral spirit who visited when the victim's stars were weak); the victim's forthcoming birthday was for an odd number of years (which is bad luck for a female; even numbers are bad luck for males); working above a shrine to a local spirit (thereby disrespectfully having his head higher than the spirit's head); urinating or defecating in a forest without asking permission of the forest spirits; astrological stars in decline; and having a name that is inappropriate to the day, month or year of one's birth. Usually, victims referred to multiple causes for a single accident.

Victims did not rule out negligence by the other party, but in its colloquial meaning the Thai word for "negligent" *(pramat)* "carries some connotations that are lacking in English. When individuals cite the injurer's negligence as one cause of their injury, they usually hastened to add that they themselves had also been negligent. Negligence on the part of both parties—injured and injurer—appear to be linked conceptually in the minds of ordinary people in Thailand."[54] Both parties are negligent because both parties lacked *sati*, or mindfulness—a mind that is focussed, calm, aware and undistracted.

---

53   *Ibid*, 125.
54   *Ibid*, 73.

This is another illustration of how the Hindu-Buddhist tradition still influences legal consciousness. (A prominent Thai intellectual, Sulak Sivaraksa, has suggested that Western law may be incompatible with the Buddhist principle of mindfulness.)[55]

When Thais lived in their ancestral village, after an accident, justice (or *tham*) would have been restored by customary law. Respected elders, who knew both the victim and the injurer, would apportion blame and determine compensation, which would normally involve payments for rituals and other costs. An overriding priority was to retain community harmony by getting both parties to accept the outcome.

As economic opportunity and disruption have prompted people to move away from their ancestral villages, injured parties now tend to cite Buddhist principles rather than village belief systems to explain their accident and their response to it. All injuries are subject to the civil and criminal codes, but accident victims find the state's legal system incompatible with their Buddhist principles, even though their adherence to Buddhist principles means that they will not gain compensation.

> They explain such outcomes by pointing to their own karmic responsibility for the harm and by emphasizing their pursuit of a virtuous course of conduct as defined by Buddhist doctrine. In the end, they maintained, karma will ensure that justice prevails, although it may take some time. If not in this lifetime, then in a future life, the consequences of the injurer's action will be apparent. In the meantime, the injury victim must observe the Buddhist teachings, follow the eightfold path, and respond to wrongdoing with forgiveness, generosity, and compassion.[56]

---

55   Munger, Frank W., "Global Funder, Grassroots Litigator—Judicialization of the Environmental Movement in Thailand." (1 September 2012). NYLS Legal Studies Research Paper No. 12/13 #38. Available at SSRN: https://ssrn.com/abstract=2145543, 39.
56   Engel and Jaruwan, 135.

Engel and Jaruwan found that people were aware of state law; indeed, one accident victim threatened to take the other party to court if he did not fulfil his promise to reach a private settlement. But, on the whole, people were suspicious of the government officials and believed that the law tended to favour the rich and powerful. In addition: "In their minds, law was tainted not only by the sometimes-suspect character of its institutions and officials but more fundamentally by its emphasis on short-term, tit-for-tat vindication rather than the Buddhist virtues of forgiveness, generosity, compassion, selflessness, and nonattachment."[57]

People in Chiang Mai were rarely relying on the courts to settle personal injury cases, and the trend was downwards. Justice and the law were unrelated. When Engel and Jaruwan asked Thais about justice they never mentioned law, lawyers or the courts in their responses; a few mentioned the mass media as a possible provider of justice sometimes. Their images of justice were "rooted in religious beliefs and practices that do not correspond to their perceptions of the law".[58]

> They believed that a virtuous—and therefore *efficacious*—response to wrongdoing required them to avoid legal action and instead to adhere to the teachings of the Buddha. By doing so, they might forego their legal rights, and they might even forego the compensation to which they felt entitled, but they would resolve the root cause of their suffering and would ensure that the conflict would not continue to disrupt their lives and the lives of their children. Piety, compassion, generosity, and selflessness might lead to justice even if the law does not.[59]

---

57   *Ibid*, 154.
58   *Ibid*, 20.
59   *Ibid*, 139. Another scholar has observed that Thai consumers are reluctant to confront sellers or manufacturers of faulty products; they prefer to avoid conflict. Munger, Frank W., "Revolution Imagined: Cause Advocacy Consumer Rights and the Evolving Role of NGOs in Thailand." (20 May 2014). *Asian Journal of Comparative Law*, 2014, DOI: 10.1515/asjcl-2013-0054. Available at SSRN: https://ssrn.com/abstract=2439377 11, fn 38.

Engel and Jaruwan acknowledge that over several decades foreign concepts of law and justice have influenced the consciousness of Thais, but they show that these concepts have not "displaced dharmic and other understandings of law and justice that were long familiar in Thai communities".[60]

Let's leave aside for a moment the victims' suspicions about government officials and their doubts about the moral efficacy of the law practiced in Western-style courts. Instead, let's consider the perspective of the committed advocates of the rule of law and the conscientious custodians of the courts who are supposed to facilitate the rule of law. Is it possible for them to apply something as secular, and coldly impersonal, as the rule of law in cases where a plaintiff or defendant believes that an accident had a religious or supernatural explanation? How can they consider evidence from gods and ghosts? How can they weigh the good and bad *karma* of plaintiffs and defendants? How could they demonstrate that a natural explanation to the plaintiff or defendant is, in their eyes, supernatural?

When foreigners and Thais advocate the rule of law for Thailand, how do they propose to make ideas underpinning Western concepts of the rule of law more appealing than the ideas about justice people in, for example, Chiang Mai, already hold deeply? Can rights trump *tham*? Should rights trump *tham*? Can rights and *tham* live side-by-side?

Western Law in a Non-Western Setting

Another American scholar, Frank Munger, has been interested in "cause lawyers" or "lawyers guided by a 'vision of the good society'".[61] Over several years he interviewed more than 200 Thais engaged in legal affairs and consulted extensive written material.[62] Although Munger's

---

60   Engel and Jaruwan, 126.
61   Frank W. Munger, "Trafficking in Law: Cause Lawyer, Bureaucratic State and the Rights of Human Trafficking Victims in Thailand," *Asian Studies Review*, Vol 39, No 1 (2015), 70.
62   Munger, "Revolution Imagined," 4.

main purpose has been to illustrate how "cause lawyers" operate in Thailand, he has made several observations that are pertinent to our discussion on the role of law in Thailand vis-à-vis the rule of law as it is generally understood.

Munger recognises that notions of equality and democracy have attracted growing support in Thailand, for example in the rejection of military government in 1992 and subsequent constitutional reform, which reflected "a long history of 'bottom up' pressure for democracy and the 'right to have rights'".[63] Similarly, NGOs in Thailand are increasingly relying on the legal system to defend human rights and protect the environment. To quote Surachai Trong-ngam, an NGO lawyer and one of Munger's respondents: "Ratification of the Constitution in 1997 including the trend toward development of administrative law, these make it easier for the people to oversee the state's power ... Until now, the legal process has been employed to limit the people's rights. Now, people have their own rights to assert in the legal process. The legal process is a channel for people to fight. And we think we can back them up on this part."[64]

Yet in his pursuit of justice for his clients Surachai does not emphasise individual rights; he "employs the concept of rights to express the responsibilities of the State and limitations placed on its power. For him .... rights empower <u>communities</u> by giving them a legal status which they previously lacked".[65] In another case, slum organisers trusted their lawyer because, like them, he believed that "empowering <u>communities</u> is more important than winning legal cases or developing legal policy".[66]

---

63 Frank Munger, "Culture, Power, and Law: Thinking About the Anthropology of Rights in Thailand in an Era of Globalization," *New York Law Review*, Vol 51 (2006–07), 832–3. In 1991, Nidhi Eoseewong had also noted two trends: the government was guaranteeing more rights for the people as well as changing laws and regulations to impose more duties on itself. If a growing recourse to the law continued, the rule of law would gain a bigger place in Thailand's "cultural constitution". Nidhi, "The Thai Cultural Constitution."

64 Quoted in Munger, "Global Funder, Grassroots Litigator," 31.

65 Munger, "Revolution Imagined," 34. Emphasis added.

66 Frank Munger, "Cause Lawyers and Other Signs of Progress: Three Thai Narratives," in *An Unfinished Project: Law and the Possibility of Justice*, ed. by Scott Cummings (Palo Alto, California: Stanford University Press, 2010), 257. Emphasis added.

Religion also influences attitudes to rights. As feminist lawyer, Malee Pauekpongsawale, wrote:

> The other influence would be Buddhism. I was very much into it. You're not so radical in your way of thinking. You look at things, trying to identify what is the root cause. I think one of the things is kindness. You don't start to accuse people and try to understand. I think that you have to take this kind of approach in our society because it's different from American society. Everyone [in America] has to protect their own right; individualism is very strong and justifiable. But in ours, we aren't at that level yet.... I think Buddhism speaks to the roots and the cause.[67]

Respect for hierarchy and traditional authority also remains important. One human rights lawyer said her work was "for the King and the law".[68] Respect for tradition also seems to explain a continuing reluctance of rural Thais in particular to rely on the law when they have a grievance. They prefer to appeal directly to government officials through petitions and demonstrations, in the time-honoured tradition of appealing to the king or his representative. Even the legal fraternity's peak body, the Lawyers Council of Thailand, encourages traditional appeals to government paternalism rather than redress through the courts.[69]

The value placed on hierarchy, tradition, community and Buddhism has encouraged Thai lawyers to put a higher premium on networking, collaboration, negotiation and accommodation rather than on confrontation and litigation, which is more common in Western societies. To promote and protect their clients' rights,

---

67   Quoted in Munger, "Cause Lawyers," 252–3.
68   Quoted in Munger, "Trafficking in Law," 84.
69   Frank Munger, "Constitutional Reform, Legal Consciousness, and Citizen Participation in Thailand," *Cornell International Law Journal*, Vol 40, Issue 2 (Spring 2007), 471.

lawyers develop networks of reciprocal relationships inside and outside government. Although they occasionally resort to litigation, lawyers prefer to try to shape government policies and practices in ways that alleviate their clients' grievances. "Lawyers who work in this environment use the symbolic and moral power of the law to educate, instruct, and guide the government officials themselves, and function (among other things) as trainers of the lower-level bureaucrats."[70] Lawyers are partly motivated by the government's own failure to observe the rule of law but, unlike their counterparts in Western societies, they "often devote as much effort to changing the government from the inside as they do to assisting confrontation between the government and outsiders".[71]

Munger also draws attention to the lack of independence of lawyers and the courts in Thailand, which we have noted earlier. He attributes this in part to Thailand's adoption of the civil law tradition, under which lawyers are "subordinate to judges as a professional group. Judges in turn are bureaucratic, civil servants schooled in a conservative legal methodology-statutory construction, and not given to displeasing superiors. They are unfamiliar with policymaking under broad common law or constitutional mandates. Litigation to make new policy is far less common in the civil law world."[72] The Thai judiciary "has traditionally been bureaucratic, concerned about career advancement, conservative, and unlikely to thwart the government's purposes".[73] Because Thailand has remained a kingdom, "the moral force of the monarchy, patron-client relationships and other customary relationships makes establishing the authority of law more complex".[74]

70　Munger, "Cause Lawyers," 264.
71　Frank W. Munger, "Globalization, Investing in Law, and the Careers of Lawyers for Social Causes—Taking on Rights in Thailand," *New York Law School Law Review*, Vol 53 (2008–9), 799.
72　Munger, "Trafficking in Law," 71.
73　Munger, "Revolution Imagined," 22 fn 73.
74　Munger, "Trafficking in Law," 71.

Subjects, not Objects

More starkly than other scholars, Tyrell Haberkorn has shown how the authority of the law threatened traditional power structures, but it could not defeat them.[75] In the period of comparative political freedom between the 1973 student uprising and the 1976 coup, some tenant-farmers in northern Thailand demanded that landowners obey, and the government enforce, a 1974 law that would have reduced tenants' land rents. In other words, the tenant-farmers sought to exercise the legal rights that Chulalongkorn's reforms had created in theory and that, over time, had begun to seep into the legal and political consciousness. They did not seek a remedy in the dispute resolution mechanisms within the traditional hierarchy, which automatically favoured the landowners, who had higher status. Nor did they seek a remedy through the communist insurgency, which had attracted considerable farmer support elsewhere. Rather, the farmers became subjects, not only objects, of the law, "and forced landowners and the state to become accountable to them".[76] "For a brief time, farmers and landlords seemed to be on the path towards becoming equal in the eyes of the law, each a partner in a contractual relationship overseen by the state."[77]

Before long, though, the landowners were "cornered, afraid, ashamed, and losing power".[78] State officials responded by colluding with these landowners and intimidating the tenant-farmers. They rejected the claims of the tenant-farmers as well as their methods. In brief, the state was unwilling to enforce the law. Ultimately, 33 tenant-farmers were assassinated, another eight were seriously injured, and five "were disappeared".[79] No one was charged for this extra-judicial violence.

---

75   Tyrell Haberkorn, *Revolution Interrupted: Farmers, Students, Law, and Violence in Northern Thailand* (Madison: University of Wisconsin Press, 2011).
76   *Ibid*, 6.
77   *Ibid*, 20.
78   *Ibid*, 121.
79   *Ibid*, 106.

During conflict between the tenant-farmers and authorities, which occurred through a period of general lawlessness, approximately 100 protesting and drunken police officers in uniform looted the Bangkok home of the prime minister, Kukrit Pramoj, demanding that he say "whether Thailand was going to be ruled by the law or by the mob" (the mob they had in mind was protesting tenant-farmers and their supporters, not themselves).[80] Kukrit forgave the protesting police because, he said, many members of his family were in the police force.[81] He chose to defuse tension and restore social harmony by allowing the police to break the law with impunity.

Legal Culture and Consciousness

The foreigners and Thais who lament the seeming absence, or the weak application, of the rule of law in Thailand have a point. The rule of law as understood in Western societies (and societies heavily influenced by Western ideas) does not always apply in Thailand. As we have seen, at times even judges have either chosen not to follow Western notions of the rule of law or been unaware of them. So have prime ministers. The judiciary has not been allowed to become, and seemingly not wanted to become, an independent avenue for settling political disputes.

Furthermore, no judge, academic, media commentator, politician or other public figure in Thailand has championed the rule of law, including the notion that the constitution is the supreme law, in a sustained manner. Nor has any attempt been made to introduce ideas about the rule of law into the school curriculum, which is routinely used to inculcate all sorts of other values into Thai schoolchildren.

Yet the rule of law cannot be turned on like a light switch. When the light switches of history and ethnography are turned on, we can

---

80 *Ibid*, 147.
81 *Ibid*, 146.

see more clearly the different principles underlying Western and traditional Siamese law, the sheer ambition of efforts in the 1890s, 1932 and 1997 to introduce Western laws and legal systems into Thailand, and the emergence of a modern legal culture and consciousness in Thailand that is distinctly Thai.

We can also see how the role of law in the governance of Thailand has changed under the influence of Western notions of individual and equal rights and Western legal systems. Equally, we can see how these notions and systems are influenced, and sometimes resisted, by the value that many Thais continue to place on order, social duties, hierarchy, community, negotiation and compromise, and on religion and the supernatural. These values are more familiar and can be more appealing, including in the settling—and avoidance—of disputes.

CONCLUSIONS

In modern times, when Westerners think about opposing power, they arrange for several independent powers to oppose one another. But the Thai think that power is indivisible. (1991)[1]

The cultural constitution has started to accept that power, once considered indivisible, can be divided into several parts, and that there should be institutions, mechanisms, and processes for creating a balance among these powers, rather in the Western fashion. (2014)[2]

Now to return to the reader who has to explain to their employer, client or professor what is going on in Thai politics. Quite often, these employers, clients and professors seem to be asking, "When is Thailand going to be like us, or more like us?" "When is Thailand going to be more democratic, or more Western, or more modern?" They tend to assume that Thailand should be, or should want to be, on a trajectory to be more democratic, Western or modern. Or they are asking implicitly, "Why is Thailand failing to be like the West?" From this viewpoint, not to be more Western is a disappointment or a setback.

Foreigners are not alone in asking when Thailand will be more democratic. Many Thais also want this. Other Thais, though, would argue that their country is doing well enough, and being truer to itself, without becoming more democratic—or by moving in this general direction but at a slower pace.

---

1 Nidhi, "The Thai Cultural Constitution."
2 Nidhi Eoseewong. "Understanding the Cultural Constitution." *Bangkok Post*, 13 August 2014.

Co-existing Legitimacies

Because Siam was not directly colonised, Thai politics is easier to understand if we view Thailand as the site of both a traditional political legitimacy and a modern political legitimacy. Each of these legitimacies is dynamic, not static. Both can be found within the overall body politic, within political movements and parties and, most critically of all, within the thinking and values of individuals engaged in Thai politics.

Thai politics is also easier to understand if we view the traditional and modern political legitimacies as co-existing rather than competing. Competition can create an impression of well-defined competitors, one of whom will eventually be victor, and the other vanquished. Certainly, the traditional and modern sources of legitimacy compete with each other, but the contest is as unwinnable as it is unstoppable. There will be no V-Day on which one defeats the other. This contest will proceed slowly and unevenly, sometimes erratically, for many decades.

Furthermore, because both the traditional and modern legitimacies are firmly rooted in Thai history and political culture, the idea of co-existence better conveys that, in the minds of many Thais, both legitimacies are valid. A Thai who genuinely prostrates himself or herself before the king can firmly believe in the rule of law, and a judge who has pledged to uphold the supremacy of the law can firmly believe that he or she should sometimes make a judgment for extra-legal reasons.

Traditionally, political order was built around hierarchy, with the king at its apex. Because Siam was not directly colonised, hierarchy and monarchy are still tightly woven into the fabric of Thailand. Many Thais, including the king himself, still believe that at times the king should play a direct political role. Or they believe that governments—civilian and military—should rule with the king's blessing. Many of them are also comfortable with the idea that Thailand as a nation and Thais as individuals would be better protected if "good people" (*phuu dii,* or moral people, preferably with established wealth) governed, and that the quality of protection a government provides and the quality of the order it imposes matter more than whether it was elected or whether it abides by the law. They believe in a moral hierarchy, based on the *karma* that individuals have accumulated in previous lives or earlier in this life. Within this moral hierarchy, power relations are determined between patrons and clients on a personal basis, not through elections. When disputes arise, they are best mediated and arbitrated by the king, his representatives (appointed or self-appointed *phuu dii*), or the military, not in courts of law or legislatures or through elections.

Because Siam was influenced by the West, many Thais now resist this traditional moral hierarchy because it conflicts with the idea of equality that underpins electoral democracy and the rule of law. They want to, and believe they have a right to, participate in politics. They believe that governments should consult the governed and be open to challenges from the governed. They argue that elected rather than appointed governments can better protect the nation and individual Thais, and that all Thais should be equally subject to the law. Sovereignty, they say, belongs to the people; the parliament, government and judiciary should exercise power on behalf of the people without undue influence from the military or monarchy. When disputes arise, they are best mediated in an elected legislature or, if need be, by the electorate through an election or referendum. Or, again if need be, disputes should be arbitrated by an independent judiciary.

The preceding two paragraphs over-simplify the political landscape, but they say enough to give an idea of the defining values of each legitimacy. These paragraphs are silent on the extent to which political actors seek power by preying on, rather than sharing, their fellow Thais' attachment to these values. But that mystery bedevils politics everywhere.

Individuals, classes, political movements, political parties and other social groups are more aligned with one legitimacy than the other. But none fully exemplifies either the traditional legitimacy or the modern legitimacy. For example, although King Bhumibol naturally symbolised the traditional legitimacy, in the late 1960s he began to goad the military to introduce a constitution and hold elections—so adherence to a particular legitimacy can shift temporarily. We have seen that in the 1970s some tenant-farmers understood the rule of law more deeply than some Constitutional Court judges have since 2001— so educational levels and occupations are not always reliable guides. In 2013–14, elected politicians abandoned parliament, boycotted elections and called for government by unelected "good people"— so we cannot assume that "democrats" favour electoral democracy, which is a vital part of the modern legitimacy. Commitment to a legitimacy can also vary over time: in 1992, Bangkok's middle class demonstrated against the military's grab for power after an election; in 2006 and 2014, they welcomed military coups against elected governments. Some politicians now claim that the judiciary is prejudiced against them and they strongly advocate for an impartial judiciary, but when they were in power the same politicians openly opposed judicial independence.

Yet, in this confusion, the traditional and modern legitimacies are still discernible. They co-exist and will continue to co-exist within the thinking and values of each Thai engaged in politics—and in the political movements and parties, as well as the institutions, that they support.

Undoubtedly, though, the contest between these two conceptions of legitimacy is unequal. Advocates of the traditional legitimacy have usually been able to rely on the coercive power of the military, which has usually gained the endorsement of the monarch. Challenges against the traditional legitimacy have been led by protesting university students in Bangkok in 1973 and 1976; by Bangkok's protesting middle classes in 1992; and by a protesting rural and semi-urban constituency from 2001 (through elections as well as street protests). On all occasions, traditional political authority re-grouped and then found or created enough political space in which to reassert itself.

Even though the traditional legitimacy has more easily held the upper hand, and is currently in the ascendancy, election participation rates and election results suggest that most Thais favour a political system that is more democratic. And some of the formal features of a democracy now either exist in Thailand or, during periods of military rule, are recognised as norms to which the country should return. In other words, some of the formal features of a democracy are either in place or likely to return in some form—for example, a constitution, elections, parliament, judiciary, and greater freedom of expression.

Certainly, for the foreseeable future the constitution will be more imposed than consented; the electoral system will impede as well as express the popular will; the parliament will not be fully elected or sovereign; the judiciary will not be fully independent; and the media, though parts may be independently owned, will be constrained by sweeping laws on defamation, sedition and *lèse majesté*. But these formal features are underpinned by a political culture that now says politics should be more participatory, governments should be more consultative, public opinion should be heeded, constitutions and the law should play a bigger role, checks and balances should exist, and individual rights should be protected.

Because these voices are now louder, and more people want to listen to them, military governments can no longer get away with some of the excesses and human rights abuses that were common in military governments in Thailand before the 1980s. Certainly, human rights are still abused. The Prayuth military government arrested and detained people arbitrarily, prompting some of its political opponents to seek refuge overseas, and some of them may have been pursued and even killed. It prohibited assemblies of five people or more and suppressed free speech through laws on sedition, computer crimes and *lèse majesté*. Some *lèse majesté* detainees died in custody. No one is excusing abuses. But the Prayuth military government mostly detained its political opponents for a few days for "attitude adjustment", and required them to sign agreements to refrain from further critical comments and political activities and not travel overseas without permission. More serious "offenders", in the eyes of the regime, were charged with sedition, computer crimes and *lèse majesté*.

This pales in comparison with earlier practice. On paper, as prime minister of a military government, Prayuth had as much dictatorial power and immunity under Section 44 of the interim constitution of 2014 as Sarit Thanarat had under Section 17 of the interim constitution of 1959, but he did not invoke Section 44 to execute anyone. Sarit ordered the summary execution of five suspected arsonists, one suspected heroin producer, one suspected messianic leader and four suspected communists—eleven people in total, five of whom he adjudged guilty of political offences.[3] Under the preceding Phibun regime, members of parliament were killed extra-judicially. In 1949 four pro-Pridi MPs from Isaan who had been arrested for alleged treason were assassinated by their police escort; in 1952 an anti-Phibun MP from Isaan was murdered in police custody; and in 1954 another MP was found murdered after he alleged the police chief was corrupt. The post-coup government of 2006–07 and the military government since 2014 could not—and showed no signs of wanting to—deal with political opponents in the cavalier manner of Sarit or Phibun and their henchman.

Co-Existing Legitimacies and the Rule of Law

The gap between the two legitimacies has narrowed since the late 1970s, but Thai politics remains chronically unstable. This instability

---

3   Thak, *The Politics of Despotic Paternalism*, 127–30.

reflects, among other things, the absence of agreed mechanisms for settling political disputes and conflicts. For this reason, the interplay between the traditional legitimacy and the modern legitimacy is particularly salient when we compare their different views on the role that the law should play in moderating politics—or, in other words, in limiting the power of politicians, government officials (including uniformed officials), and judges.

If the modern legitimacy rather than the traditional legitimacy had the upper hand, the law would play a bigger role in the governance of Thailand. The purest version of the modern legitimacy would say that, guided and limited by <u>accepted</u> principles that are expressed in a <u>supreme</u> law (constitution), an <u>elected</u> Thai government would make laws. All citizens and all government authorities would be <u>equally</u> bound by this constitution and these laws, whose supremacy would be protected by an <u>independent</u> judiciary.

Some of the formal features of democracy are now accepted as norms, even if they are often more aspirational than real. These include a constitution, an elected parliament, an accountable executive and an independent judiciary. Yet, the emphasised words in the preceding paragraph help us to understand the task ahead for the modern legitimacy. Thai constitutions have not wanted for principles but, with the rare exception of the 1997 Constitution, the Thai public has not been consulted on these principles. Thai constitutions have not been considered the supreme law, even by judges. And the military, with the king's endorsement, has overturned constitutions with impunity. Fully elected Thai governments have been uncommon. Thai constitutions and laws have not applied equally to all citizens and all government agencies. The judiciary has not always acted independently.

These ideas and values of the modern legitimacy appeal to a growing number of Thais, but they are still transplants—they are not home-grown. The principles underpinning the rule of law are not as embedded in Thai social, cultural and ethical thought as the ideas and values of the traditional legitimacy. For adherents of the traditional legitimacy, the rule of law is a threat. It excludes them or disempowers them. So, naturally, they try to resist it or subvert it.

The ideas and values of the adherents of the traditional legitimacy, including ideas and values related to the role of the law, are linked to the moral and political constraints on the power of the government—or monarch—in pre-modern Siam. The moral constraint was *tham*, the cosmic law which is hard to reconcile with the thinking and values underpinning imported concepts of the rule of law. According to traditional thinking, the king was king because in previous lives he had accumulated the most *karma* or merit by observing *tham*. In his current life he was expected also to conduct himself according to *tham* and to help his subjects to follow *tham*. Proper observation of *tham* was essential to an hierarchical and harmonious society. Under the moral constraint of *tham*, if the king exercised his powers in ways that upset the cosmic order and flouted the teachings of the Buddha, his kingdom would enjoy neither peace nor prosperity and he would face retribution in his current life or in untold future lives.

The persistence of these ideas and values is evident in: claims by traditionalist critics of Thailand's electoral politics, including speakers at PAD and PDRC rallies, that elections would be unnecessary if everyone followed *tham;* their use of the term "dhamma-cracy" to try to capture the blend of traditional and democratic principles in Thai-style democracy; the emphasis in the 2017 Constitution on ethical standards rather than rights and the rule of law; and the durability in Thai thinking that the monarchy is more than a symbol, that the monarchy is not an anachronism.

The other broad constraint on the power of the monarch in pre-modern Thailand was a political constraint: competing sources of power. Domestically, the competing sources of power usually emerged within the king's family (other princes) and from the nobility. Externally, his power was limited by the relative power of neighbouring monarchies.

From the 1880s, Chulalongkorn and Vajiravudh fully protected themselves against competing domestic sources of power through administrative reforms; the creation of a standing army; the inculcation of a nationalist state ideology; and the new practice of designating an heir to the throne rather than allowing surviving princes to compete for the crown after the king died.

They could not protect themselves so easily from external powers—i.e., Western imperialists—who insisted that their subjects could not be subjects of Siamese laws until Siam reformed those laws and its courts. But the new external powers were not only a source of liabilities. They also offered Siam an opportunity to engage more deeply in international commerce, a tempting asset.

So Siam set about establishing Western-style legal institutions, such as courts, a ministry of justice and a law school and introducing criminal and civil codes based on Western models, thereby eventually discharging the main liability imposed by the imperial powers—extraterritoriality. Siam's new legal system also recognised property rights and said contracts were enforceable, providing Thais who were engaged in business, including the Thai monarchy and nobility, opportunities to expand their links with foreign traders and investors.

The critical point here is that Siam's leaders viewed these law-related reforms as instrumental. The adherents of the traditional legitimacy were prepared to adopt foreign ideas, practices and institutions to the extent that they helped Siam to shed extraterritoriality and to integrate into the world economy. Reforms to the law and the legal system were a means to an end, and the end wasn't the rule of law.

The adherents of the traditional legitimacy have continued to respond instrumentally as the moral and political constraints on modern Thai governments have broadened to include imported ideas like equality, individual rights and elections. They have accepted the need for a constitution as well as institutions like constitutional and administrative courts, anti-corruption agencies, electoral commissions and the like. They have also used the law instrumentally to increase their power: for example, by sponsoring strict *lèse majesté,* criminal defamation, sedition and computer crime laws. But the ideas of equality, individual rights and electoral democracy, and the idea of the rule of law itself, have not supplanted *tham,* which still provides their hierarchical world with an ideological justification. *Tham* may no longer be supreme, but nor is the law. They co-exist.

Central to the traditional legitimacy is an attachment to hierarchical order. In a hierarchy, disputes are mediated or settled by a person, not an impersonal and autonomous agency or institution outside the hierarchy. The more senior the disputants, or the bigger the dispute, the higher up the hierarchy it is resolved. Adherents of the traditional legitimacy ask: who should mediate? Who should adjudicate? Who should govern? They have not accepted the idea that the electorate has a moral right to choose who should govern and a moral right to have a say in how disputes should be mediated and adjudicated.

So the 2017 Constitution and its enabling legislation, mostly authored by adherents of the traditional legitimacy, especially in the military, give "good people" the best chance of maintaining control: through an appointed senate, the prospect of an appointed prime minister, a 20-year national strategy, and an even stronger and less independent judiciary. After the constitution was drafted and endorsed in a heavily managed referendum, the king, who of all the "good people" enjoys the highest status, rewrote parts of it to make sure that the monarch retained his authority.

Other provisions of the constitution, as well as new laws on political parties and elections, were written to try to determine who should not govern Thailand—i.e., Thaksin Shinawatra.

Many adherents of the modern legitimacy have reacted by focusing largely on who will be prime minister: either an elected MP or a military-endorsed appointee. Like the traditionalists, they have been preoccupied with <u>who</u> should govern Thailand, and rarely focused on <u>how</u> Thailand should be governed.

This is partly explained by the exclusion of adherents of the modern legitimacy from the bodies that drafted the new constitution and enabling laws. They haven't had a platform from which to advocate.

But, in part, it also reflects the continuing dominance of "who" in the broader society and culture, which still rest on traditional foundations. In their daily lives, Thais who are intellectually committed to the modern legitimacy are still likely, even obliged, to be more aware of their duties than their rights—in their families, educational institutions, workplaces, temples, clubs and associations, political movements and political parties. More often than not, those duties are defined by whether the people they are dealing with are senior or junior to them—superior or inferior, or to use the Thai terms, *phuu yai* (big person) or *phuu noi* (little person). To get ahead, or to live a relatively trouble-free life, or to get out of trouble, Thais need to know who can help them. When disputes arise, they are more likely to be resolved within the hierarchy of their family, educational institution, workplaces, etc., than by an autonomous agency or institution outside this hierarchy. At the risk of over-statement and over-generalization, in Thai society the reflex is to ask: "Who can solve my problem?" not "How can my problem be solved?"

This deeply entrenched person-centered conduct in day-to-day lives, as well as the person-centered traditional legitimacy's control of the political agenda, limits the space for sustained discussions about <u>how</u> Thailand might be governed more effectively, or even discussions about the value of discussions.

Co-Existing Legitimacies and Freedom of Expression

In addition to being constrained by person-centeredness, discussion about governance is constrained by the longing among adherents of the traditional legitimacy for a society that is harmonious and ordered. They are instinctively wary of differences of opinion and opposed to a political system, like democracy, that fosters debate. Within the hierarchical society of the traditional legitimacy, questioning or criticizing superiors is improper. Nor should superiors be subject to demands they might consider unreasonable; on the contrary, their seniority sometimes allows them to act with impunity. So adherents of the traditional legitimacy have used their ascendancy to try to muzzle questioning NGOs and public intellectuals, often casting doubt on their morality and Thai-ness. Because Siamese law was punitive and pedagogic, the traditional legitimacy is not troubled by Thai laws—like the *lèse majesté,* sedition and defamation laws—that turn critics into criminals, or by restrictive laws on "computer crimes", which can be as simple as a mildly irreverent social media post. In addition, adherents of the traditional legitimacy have sought to control the media and, where possible, own it.

The modern legitimacy favours discussion and debate, arguing that better policies would emerge from deliberations that were more open and inclusive. Its adherents would assert that Thailand has become a fairer society because, during periods of fleeting democracy, the previously unheard had a bigger, and overdue, say. On the monarchy, they claim that the punitive *lèse majesté* law should be administered less vigorously and amended because, in their view, its harshness damages the institution it is supposed to protect.

Yet purported supporters of a more democratic Thailand have not always supported freedom of expression. As early as 1933, Pridi Banomyong sponsored legislation that threatened to imprison anyone who spoke against the 1932 Constitution. In 1990, the elected government of Chatichai Choonhavan tried to close a newspaper that embarrassed it. In 2000, the elected prime minister Chuan Leekpai used force to disperse villagers protesting under the Assembly of the Poor banner against his government's policies, then bought a charge of criminal defamation against a newspaper that called him cruel. Thailand's highest-profile champion of elections, Thaksin Shinawatra, also suppressed protesters. In addition, he used his controlling interest in a TV station for political purposes, interfered in free-to-air stations owned by the government and military, intimidated the press (including by denying anti-Thaksin newspapers access to government advertising), and publicly abused NGOs and intellectuals. Under Thaksin, the US-based Freedom House downgraded Thailand's media from "free" to "partly free". Under Thaksin's staunchest opponents, who have been in power since the 2014 coup, Thailand has been rated as "not free".

The social media boom is helping to narrow the gap between the co-existing legitimacies. Social media has made it harder for the traditional legitimacy to control information, stifle debate and limit political participation. Social media is breaking down social and political barriers. As a result, more Thais are politically engaged and informed. If social media wasn't a threat to the traditional legitimacy, the military government would not have introduced such strict laws to try to control it.

At the same time, social media encourages political activists to play the man, not the ball, by providing avenues for anonymous but often misinformed and hateful attacks against political opponents. In other words, social media can make Thailand's already highly personalised and polarised politics even more so. It doesn't lower the political temperature or quieten politics; it makes politics hotter and louder. So social media makes it harder for Thais to have open discussions on governance, including on the critical question of how to settle the political disputes that are an essential element, even the lifeblood, of a democracy.

Co-Existing Legitimacies and Nationalism
The shadow of nationalism over Thai politics makes an already

unwelcoming environment for open discussions on governance more forbidding.

The differences between the co-existing traditional and modern legitimacies on the issue of nationalism are often only differences of degree. Because Thai elites never needed to deploy nationalism to oust a foreign power, the traditional governing elite as well as the aspirational modern elite defined and deployed nationalism to retain or seek power, and to legitimise their right to power. Both of them harnessed nationalism to their cause. On Thailand's narrow nationalism spectrum, the traditional legitimacy is ultranationalist and the modern legitimacy is highly nationalist.

The traditional legitimacy's view of nationalism is found in the chauvinistic ideas and policies of King Vajiravudh, the ultranationalism of Phibun, the despotic paternalism of Sarit, the paramilitary movements like Nawaphon, Red Gaurs and the Village Scouts in the 1970s, and today's "hyper-royalism"—a growing demand from the state and in popular culture for expressive loyalty to the monarchy, exaltation of the monarchy's achievements, and the wider application of the *lèse majesté* law.[4] It is also evident in the ethnocentric scorn of the urban elites for people from Isaan and others who do not conform to a Central Thai ideal, and in the government's largely unquestioned response to the insurgency in the southern border provinces.

Thai ultranationalism, like ultranationalism elsewhere, springs from insecurities. In Thailand, these insecurities have been deepened by waves of domestic pressure—and ripples of international pressure—for more democratic government. The firmest adherents of the traditional legitimacy see equality and the rule of law as a subversive, even contaminating, challenge. They respond by erecting a "we-know-best" world of their own. They expect fellow Thais to find both comfort and security by joining them. Those reluctant to join

---

4   Thongchai, "The Monarchy and Anti-Monarchy," 89–92.

or, worse still, critics of their world, are derided as immoral and un-Thai sponsors of disharmony, disorder and disunity. In this "Fortress Thailand", nationalism is a political weapon, not a political tool.

Adherents of the modern legitimacy mostly share the nationalist ardour of other Thais, but they usually feel less insecure about Thailand as a nation than adherents to the traditional legitimacy do. They tend to see nationalism as a tool. They are more sensitive to the interests of minorities at home and more willing to engage with the foreign community on issues like human rights and trade barriers. Rather than erect a fortress around nationalist sentiment, they try to promote a nationalism that is more inclusive. They are less strident in advocating Thailand's distinctiveness and achievements. They look for opportunities to argue that a more democratic political system, in which individual rights are protected and the rule of law is observed, would make Thailand even stronger and even more respected.

Very few adherents of the modern legitimacy are republican or anti-monarchy. Rather, they favour a fully-fledged constitutional monarchy, usually citing Japan and Britain as models. They believe an authentic constitutional monarchy offers better prospects for political stability than an extra-constitutional monarchy. They wince at the harm to Thailand's image that the ultranationalism of the traditional legitimacy can sometimes cause, for example through the dozens of *lèse majesté* cases following the 2014 coup, including the highly publicised case of a man who mocked King Bhumibol's dog and another case involving a prominent intellectual, Sulak Sivaraksa, who questioned whether King Naresuan, a 16th century king, had engaged in a famous elephant battle.

Yet, after generations of tutoring, most adherents to the modern legitimacy, like adherents to the traditional legitimacy, believe that their primary loyalty is to the Nation, Religion and King, and they also rely largely on the state to determine what sort of nation Thailand is and how Thais should express their loyalty.

Co-Existing Legitimacies and the Cycle of Coups

The risks associated with questioning orthodoxy in Thailand as well as the inherent tension between the two legitimacies have inhibited open and inclusive discussions about better governance. As a result, Thailand has not yet found a way to discuss differences and resolve disputes that is accepted by adherents of both the traditional legitimacy and the modern legitimacy. Because neither *tham* nor the law is supreme, Thai politics lacks a trusted referee. Put simply, adherents of the traditional legitimacy distrust the electorate and its representatives, and advocates of the modern legitimacy distrust the monarchy, military and judiciary. If we return to our branches-of-government analysis: the legislature has been kept weak and, in any event, legislators have displayed meager loyalty to the institution of the legislature; and the judiciary neither accepts that the law is supreme nor values its own independence. So the monarchy and military continue to hold sway.

Without the means to mediate and arbitrate disputes, Thailand has been politically unstable. What might have been discussions have become debates, debates have become disputes, disputes have tended to become crises, and crises have tended to become conflicts. In the absence of trusted dispute settlement mechanisms, coups—military and judicial—have therefore been frequent. Following each coup, the balance of power between the co-exiting traditional and modern legitimacies has changed, but eventually power has again become unbalanced, then so unbalanced that the debates-become-coups cycle has restarted.

Even if open discussions about governance were possible, this cycle of coups might not be broken. Imagine for a moment that the modern legitimacy had more platforms from which to advocate, and that credible and articulate champions of the modern legitimacy had emerged. The intellectual task would still be formidable: to explain that recently imported ideas like equality, individual rights and elections are superior to, or can be reconciled with, the idea of a moral hierarchy, which lies at the heart of the centuries-old traditional legitimacy. The idea that even "good people" should be governed by the law is a long way from the idea that "good people" should govern. Put another way, the idea that political power belongs to elected representatives of all the people is the antithesis of the idea that political power emanates from a king through a hierarchy that is endorsed by religion.

Notwithstanding this stark picture, since the late 1970s, the gap between the traditional legitimacy and the modern legitimacy has narrowed; they now co-exist more easily, though still uneasily. At present, the ascendant traditional legitimacy is not inclined to give ground to the modern legitimacy. That may change as the adherents of the traditional legitimacy—ever-focused on who should govern—adjust to the reign of a new king and, eventually, to the political demise of Thaksin, whenever that happens. For their part, the adherents of the modern legitimacy are still confident and resilient enough to challenge the thinking behind the 2014 coup and the 2017 Constitution, which were the most recent attempts by adherents of the traditional legitimacy to deny the modern legitimacy a bigger role in Thailand's governance.

An appreciation of Thai history and political culture suggests that the 2014 coup won't be Thailand's last coup and the 2017 Constitution won't be Thailand's last constitution.

Following political bloodshed on the streets of Bangkok in 1992, which left dozens of people dead and millions physically or emotionally scarred, and the trauma of the Asian financial crisis in 1997, which dislocated the national economy and disrupted the lives of millions, Thailand tried to break the cycle of coups. Minds were applied, collectively, to finding ways to end chronic political instability. The result was the 1997 Constitution, which sought to articulate how Thailand could be governed more effectively. Time has shown that it was an imperfect response. But it was not a wasted effort. Some of the ideas and institutions embedded in the 1997 Constitution survive. At the same time, the ideas and institutions of the traditional legitimacy have shown their durability.

Over two decades since 1997, the unanswered question is whether adherents of both the traditional legitimacy and the modern legitimacy can agree soon that recasting Thailand's governance is again urgent, or whether the urgency will become apparent only after more bloodshed and trauma.

APPENDICES

Historical Periods

Sukhothai	c. 1239–1438
Ayutthaya	1351–1767
Thonburi	1767–82
Bangkok (Rattanakosin)	1782–present

Chakri Kings (Bangkok Period)

Phra Phuttayotfa	Rama I	1782–1809
Phra Phuttaloetla	Rama II	1809–1824
Phra Nangklao	Rama III	1824–1851
Mongkut	Rama IV	1851–1868
Chulalongkorn	Rama V	1868–1910
Vajiravudh	Rama VI	1910–1925
Prajadhipok	Rama VII	1925–1935
Ananda	Rama VIII	1935–1946
Bhumibol	Rama IX	1946–2016
Vajiralongkorn	Rama X	2016–

Prime Ministers

Phraya Manopakon Nithithada	1932–1933
Phraya Phahon Phonphayuhasena	1933–1938
Phibun Songkhram	1938–1944
Khuang Aphaiwong	1944–1945
Thani Bunyaket	1945
Seni Pramoj	1945–1946
Khuang Aphaiwong	1946
Pridi Banomyong	1946
Thawan Thamrongnawasawat	1946–1947
Khuang Aphaiwong	1947–1948
Phibun Songkhram	1948–1957

Phote Sarasin	1957
Thanom Kittikachon	1958
Sarit Thanarat	1959–1963
Thanom Kittikachon	1963–1973
Sanya Dharmasakti	1973–1975
Seni Pramoj	1975
Kukrit Pramoj	1975–1976
Seni Pramoj	1976
Thanin Kraivichien	1976–1977
Kriangsak Chomanand	1977–1980
Prem Tinsulanond	1980–1988
Chatichai Choonhavan	1988–1991
Anand Panyarachun	1991–1992
Suchinda Kraprayun	1992
Anand Panyarachun	1992
Chuan Leekpai	1992–1995
Banharn Silpa-archa	1995–1996
Chavalit Yongchaiyudh	1996–1997
Chuan Leekpai	1997–2001
Thaksin Shinawatra	2001–2006
Surayud Chalanont	2006–2007
Samak Sundaravej	2007–2008
Somchai Wongsuwat	2008
Abhisit Vejjajiva	2008–2011
Yingluck Shinawatra	2011–2014
Prayuth Chan-ocha	2014–

Main Personalities

Abhisit Vejjajiva (1964–) A career politician who was elected to parliament at the age of 27. Mentored by Chuan Leekpai. Became prime minister in 2008 when the military persuaded the Bhumjaithai Party to defect from the Thaksin-sponsored government and form a coalition with Abhisit's Democrat Party. His government was distracted by large pro-Thaksin protests, which sought fresh elections. A military crackdown against protesters in April–May 2010, resulting in over 90 deaths, left him open to charges of complicity, which were thrown out in 2017 by the courts under the military government of Prayuth Chan-ocha (who was deputy army commander during the crackdown). Defeated in the 2011 election when the Yingluck Shinawatra-led Pheu Thai Party won 265 seats against the Democrat Party's 159 in the 500-seat parliament. More a parliamentarian than a firebrand or grass-roots politician, in 2013–14 Abhisit was overshadowed and outmanoeuvred by Suthep Thaugsuban, who exploited large anti-Pheu Thai rallies that led to the 2014 coup.

Anand Panyarachun (1932–) Appointed prime minister on the first occasion by coup leader Suchinda Kraprayun in 1991. Appointed prime minister again by King Bhumibol in 1992 when Suchinda's bid to become prime minister himself led to bloody demonstrations in Bangkok. Both his governments were efficient, clean and reformist. Earlier he had served in the foreign ministry, including as permanent secretary and ambassador to the United Nations and United States. After resigning from government service, he had a successful business career. Played a major role in drafting the 1997 Constitution. Governments have sought his advice on issues as diverse as the insurgency in the southern border provinces and political reconciliation.

Ananda, King Rama VIII (1925–1946) Selected by the Thai cabinet to succeed King Prajadhipok, who abdicated in 1935. As he was a minor, a regency council acted on his behalf. Mysteriously shot dead in 1946. Not formally crowned, but his crown was consecrated after his death.

Banharn Silpa-archa (1932–2016) The consummate provincial politician, as an MP, minister and ultimately prime minister, Banharn diverted government resources into his province of Supharnburi, which was nicknamed "Banharn-buri" (one of Banharn's nicknames was "Walking ATM"). His ability to satisfy his electorate's aspirations ensured him repeated electoral success. He said openly that his guiding political principle was to ensure his Chart Thai Party was part of the government coalition and therefore had access to resources. He headed an unstable seven-party coalition government in 1995–96.

Bhumibol Adulyadej, King Rama IX (1927–2016) Reigned from 1946 to 2016—the longest reign in Thailand's history. Initially, his youth and the anti-royalism of Phibun Songkhram limited his role. From the prime ministership of Sarit Thanarat, his profile and influence grew to the extent that he could intervene at times of political crisis. He remained a constitutional monarch on paper, but his longevity, personal conduct and charisma—buttressed by the traditional power of the monarchy, all-encompassing state-sponsored publicity and the strong backing of the military—gave him extra-constitutional authority.

Chamlong Srimuang (1935–) Chamlong held formal political positions as secretary to Prime Minister Prem (1980–81), founder of the Palang Dharma (Moral Force) Party and elected governor of Bangkok (1985–91). A leader of the anti-communist and anticapitalist "Young Turks" clique in the Thai army in the 1970s, he flirted with the ultranationalist Village Scouts. In 1992, the king publicly admonished him and Suchinda Kraprayun after he led public protests against Suchinda's bid to become prime minister. Triggered an election in 1995 when he withdrew his party from the Chuan government over alleged corruption by ministers, including Suthep Thaugsuban. Initially pro-Thaksin, from 2005 he was a leader of the anti-Thaksin People's Alliance for Democracy (PAD). In 2013–14 he supported Suthep's PDRC.

Chatichai Choonhavan (1922–98) After following his father, Phin, into the military (Phin led the 1947 coup against an elected government), Chatichai transferred to the foreign service. Co-founded the Chart Thai Party in 1974. Elected to parliament in 1975. His elected, six-party coalition government (1988–91) was best known for its "battlefields into marketplaces" policy towards Thailand's Indo-Chinese neighbours, its attempt to establish independence from the military and the bureaucracy, and its corruption. Ousted in a coup led by Suchinda Kraprayun in 1991, he lived temporarily in exile in the United Kingdom, and re-entered electoral politics after his return.

Chavalit Yongchaiyudh (1932–) After a military career during which he was mentored by Prem and played a major role in offering amnesties to surrendering communists, Chavalit established the New Aspiration Party (NAP) in 1990. His advocacy of an elected prime minister in the 1980s led to accusations of anti-monarchy sentiments. NAP won the most seats in the 1996 election and he led a five-party coalition government. His government's defence of the baht contributed to the Asian financial crisis in 1997, which in turn led to the collapse of his coalition. In 2002, he merged NAP with Thaksin's Thai Rak Thai Party.

Chuan Leekpai (1938–) After a career as a lawyer, he entered parliament as Democrat Party MP for Trang Province in 1969. Like many critics of military domination of politics, he was accused of communist sympathies in 1976. Leader of the Democrat Party from 1990. Prime minister of a five-party coalition government after the 1992 elections. Chuan's personal probity raised expectations of a cleaner government, but in 1995 his coalition collapsed over alleged corruption by ministers, including Suthep Thaugsuban, in land deals in Phuket. Became prime minister again in 1997 after the Chavalit government fell following the Asian financial crisis. His government's adoption of the IMF's post-crisis prescriptions improved Thailand's financial governance, but an inability to stimulate the economy and meet aspirations of the rural electorate led to defeat by the Thaksin-led Thai Rak Thai Party in the 2001 elections. In 2003, he resigned as head of the Democrat Party, but remains a respected elder of the party.

Chulalongkorn, King Rama V (1853–1910) Reigned from 1868 to 1910. Initially constrained by his youth and the power of the nobility. From the 1880s, Chulalongkorn applied modern, largely colonial, administrative methods to the governance of Siam, thereby increasing the authority of the monarchy. Rejected the idea of a constitution and parliamentary system of government, but intimated that his successor (Vajiravudh) should not.

Damrong Rajanuphap, Prince (1862–1943) Son of King Mongkut and younger brother of King Chulalongkorn. Initially as minister for education and then as minister for interior (for 23 years), he played a critical role in Chulalongkorn's administrative reforms. Also known as the "father of Thai history", he was a prolific scholar and one of the founders of the nationalist school of Thai history. Sidelined by King Vajiravudh, but consulted by King Prajadhipok. He advised

Prajadhipok against constitutionalism. In 1932 he went into exile in Penang, Malaya, until the year before his death.

Dhani Nivat, Prince (1885–1974) Served five kings from Chulalongkorn to Bhumibol, for whom he was both regent and a privy councillor. Well known for his contribution to the theory of Thai kingship and other scholarly works.

Khuang Aphaiwong (1902–68) A founding member of the People's Party. Succeeded Phibun as prime minister towards the end of World War II because he had the diplomatic skills to deal with the still-occupying Japanese as well as the soon-expected Allies. Co-founder and first leader of the Democrat Party in 1946. Two other brief stints as prime minister in 1946 and 1947–8.

Kukrit Pramoj (1905–1995) Probably better known now for his writing (as a journalist and novelist) and cultural pursuits than his politics, he was initially aligned with the Democrat Party. With his brother, Seni, he led a campaign against Pridi Banomyong, including unfounded accusations that Pridi was involved in the death of King Ananda. Founded the Social Action Party in 1974. Prime Minister 1975–76, during which period he oversaw the withdrawal of US troops from Thailand. His most famous literary work, *Sii Phaendin (Four Reigns)*, depicts court life under the four kings from Chulalongkorn to Ananda.

Mongkut, King Rama IV (1804–68) Reigned from 1851 to 1868. Served as a monk for 27 years before his reign, establishing the strict Thammayut sect of Buddhism. Attracted to Western science and fostered Western education for his many sons. Recognised the inevitability and potential benefits of greater Siamese diplomatic and commercial engagement with the West. Made the monarchy more accessible to the Siamese public.

Phahon Phonphayuhasena, Phraya (1887–1947) Army officer who was also one of the early members of the People's Party. Over time, his seniority brought him *de facto* leadership of the party. Became prime minister in 1933, after leading a coup. His government was preoccupied with royalist challenges, including the Boworadej rebellion in 1933. His government was damaged by a scandal over profiteering from the sale of crown property. Eclipsed by his defence minister, Phibun Songkhram. Forced to resign in 1938.

Phao Siyanon (1910–60) As police chief in the 1950s, he was one of the three most powerful men in Thailand, together with Phibun Songkhram and Sarit Thanarat. Funded by massive US aid, opium trading and protection rackets. Used emergency powers to suppress communists and non-communists alike, usually brutally. Phao gave the police the motto, "There is nothing under the sun that the Thai police cannot do." Fled to Switzerland after Sarit's coup against Phibun in 1957.

Phibun Songkhram (1897–1964) Born Plaek Khitasangkha, but normally referred to in English as Phibun or Phibun Songkhram, shortened forms of his official title Luang Phibunsongkhram. He was a founding member and head of the military faction of the People's Party. Played a critical role in quelling the royalist Bowodarej rebellion. Became prime minister in 1938, appointing himself army chief, defence minister, and (later) foreign minister, and promoted himself to field marshal—a position until then only held by the monarch. His anti-royalist and ultranationalist policies had a major impact in his lifetime; his ultranationalism still survives, but without its anti-Chinese aspect. He sided with Japan during World War II, sending Thai troops to fight British troops in Burma. This cost him the prime ministership in 1944, but he escaped conviction as a war criminal. Following a coup in 1947, he became prime minister again in 1948. In the 1950s, his authority was challenged by the army chief, Sarit Thanarat, and police chief, Phao Siyanon. Sarit ousted him in a coup in 1957. Went into exile in Japan. Thailand's longest-serving prime minister (17 years over two terms).

Prajadhipok, King Rama VII (1892–1941) Reigned from 1925 until he abdicated in 1935. Inherited a government that, owing partly to his brother Vajiravudh's excesses, was unsettled by civilian bureaucrats and military officers who resented princes and nobles limiting their career opportunities. They also believed absolute monarchy was an antiquated system of government. Prajadhipok seemed to half-listen and half-agree, but then accepted recommendations from brother-princes and foreign advisers that Siam was not ready for either a constitution or a parliament. Did not resist demands for an end to absolutism, but abdicated rather than accept additional curbs on royal prerogatives.

Prayuth Chan-ocha (1954–) After leading a military coup in 2014, he became prime minister, granting himself an amnesty for staging the coup, sweeping powers, and immunity from future prosecution. Army commander from 2010 to 2014. As deputy army commander, in 2009–10 he played a key operational role in the suppression of red-shirt protesters. Strongly pro-monarchy and disdainful of elected politicians, he has reacted impulsively to even mild criticism. The 2017 Constitution provided scope, but not certainty, for Prayuth (or his nominee) to retain the prime minister's position after an election.

Prem Tinsulanond (1920–) Distinguished military career, during which he developed a more effective political strategy for countering communists. Army commander 1978–82. Minister of defence 1979–86. Unelected prime minister 1980–88, heading various coalition governments that always included the Democrat Party. Thailand's third-longest serving prime minister (eight years). Survived coup attempts in 1981 and 1985, because King Bhumibol openly supported him. Privy councillor from 1988. President of the Privy Council from 1998. Became disaffected with Thaksin, who later accused him of masterminding the 2006 coup. On the death of Bhumibol, he became regent *ex officio* until Vajiralongkorn was proclaimed king. Vajiralongkorn re-appointed him as president of the Privy Council.

Pridi Banomyong (1900–83) A founding member and intellectual leader of the People's Party. Author of the 1932 handbill, which condemned absolute monarchy, and Thailand's first constitution. Drafted a radical economic plan in 1933, which led to accusations of communism and temporary exile. Founded Thammasat University. Energetic and modernizing minister for interior, foreign affairs and finance portfolios from 1934 to 1941. Opposed Phibun's pro-Japanese foreign policy, and organized anti-Japanese resistance movement, *Seri Thai*. Regent from 1941 to 1945. Major power-broker behind the scenes, and briefly prime minister in 1946. Opponents, especially Seni and Kukrit Pramoj, accused him of complicity in the unexplained death of King Ananda in 1946, after which he resigned. Involved in unsuccessful coup against Phibun in 1949. Went into exile, first in China, then France.

Samak Sundaravej (1935–2009) Started his political career in the Democrat Party. An instigator of anti-student violence in October 1976. As Minister of Interior in the repressive post-October military government he oversaw the arrest of alleged leftist sympathisers. Deputy prime minister in short-lived military government of Suchinda in 1992. Elected Governor of Bangkok 2000–04. Chosen by Thaksin to lead his People's Power Party in the 2007 election. Prime minister January–September 2008 before the Constitutional Court disqualified him on conflict-of-interest charges because he was paid for appearances on a TV cooking show.

Sarit Thanarat (1908–1963) After service in the Shan states during World War II, he played a leading role in the 1947 coup against the elected pro-Pridi government. As army commander from 1954, he vied for political power with Phibun (prime minister) and Phao (police chief). Ousted Phibun in 1957 coup. Assumed prime ministership in 1958. Used anti-communist campaign to attract substantial funds from the United States and to suppress political opponents, often brutally. Less influenced by the West than his predecessors, he promoted himself as a paternal ruler within a Thai tradition. Lifted the profile and political role of King Bhumibol. Fostered close ties between the military and civilian bureaucracies.

Seni Pramoj (1905–1997) Co–founder of the Democrat Party. Prime minister on three brief occasions (1945–46, 1975, 1976). In 1941, as ambassador to the United States, he refused to deliver Phibun's declaration of war. Co-organizer (with Pridi Banomyong) of *Seri Thai,* an underground resistance movement. Political and personal tensions with Pridi contributed to the end of his first prime ministership, and to Seni (with his brother Kukrit) leading an anti-Pridi campaign that saw Pridi accused of complicity in the death of King Ananda and self-exiled. In 1962, he represented Thailand unsuccessfully in International Court of Justice case on Preah Vihear. His 1975 and 1976 prime ministerships were rocked by the political turmoil and anti-student violence preceding the coup of 1976.

Sondhi Limthongkul (1947–) A media entrepreneur who initially supported Thaksin, from 2005 he led the anti-Thaksin PAD. Survived an assassination attempt in 2009. In 2016, he was convicted of falsifying documents to secure a loan in 1997 and sentenced to prison for 20 years.

Sonthi Boonyaratglin (1946–) Led the 2006 coup against the Thaksin government and installed Surayud Chulanont as prime minister. First Muslim army commander. Mentored by General Prem. Retired from the army in 2007 and became a deputy prime minister in Surayud's government.

Suchinda Kraprayun (1933–) As supreme commander of the armed forces, he led a coup against the Chatichai government in 1991. After the 1992 elections, he reneged on a promise not to accept the prime ministership, sparking mass demonstrations and massive casualties on Bangkok's streets. Publicly admonished (with protest leader, Chamlong) by King Bhumibol, who replaced him with Anand Panyarachun.

Surayud Chulanont (1943–) Although his father defected from the army to become a leader of the Communist Party of Thailand, Surayud had a successful army career, rising to army commander (1998) and supreme commander (2003). Mentored by General Prem. Appointed privy councillor by King Bhumibol in 2003. Appointed prime minister in 2006, following the coup against the Thaksin government. Relinquished the position after the 2008 election. In 2016, reappointed privy councillor by King Vajiralongkorn.

Suthep Thaugsuban (1949–) In 2013, Suthep took over the leadership of protests in Bangkok, under the auspices of the PDRC, which eventually led to the coup of May 2014. A Democrat Party MP since 1979, he was deputy prime minister under Abhisit and secretary-general of the party from 2005 until 2011. He had served in various ministerial roles in earlier coalition governments, including the first Chuan Leekpai government, which fell because of alleged corruption by Suthep and others. He resigned from the Democrat Party when he established PDRC. After the 2014 coup, which he welcomed warmly, he openly supported the Prayuth-led military government.

Thaksin Shinawatra (1949–) After attending the Armed Forces Academies Preparatory School and serving as a police officer, which included postgraduate study in criminology, Thaksin was a highly successful businessman, relying largely on government concessions. Entered formal politics in 1994 as a member of Chamlong's Phalang Tham Party. Served briefly in the first Chuan, Banharn and Chavalit governments. Formed Thai Rak Thai Party in 1998. Prime Minister 2001–06, following highly successful campaigns in the 2001 and 2005 elections. Won widespread support for stimulatory economic policies, a moratorium on rural debt, funds for village development, a universal health-care scheme, a war on drugs and a tough approach to the insurgency in the southern border provinces (although the latter two policies led to large-scale human rights abuses). Gradually lost support in important circles for his perceived disrespect for the monarchy, interference in military appointments—including through appointing a cousin as army commander—and abuse of power to benefit his family financially. Ousted by a military coup in 2006. Chose self-exile in 2008 after a tribunal established by the military government found him guilty of corruption. Continues to attract grass-roots support and to influence politics through the Pheu Thai Party and red-shirt movement.

Thanom Kittikhachon (1911–2004) Prime minister of military-led governments in 1958 and from 1963 to 1973. With his son, Narong, and Narong's father-in-law, General Praphas Charusathien, he was one of the "three tyrants" whose repressive rule led in 1973 to student-led demands for a constitution and elections. Three days of violence forced him to resign and flee abroad. His return from exile in October 1976 provoked further protests, the massacre of students at Thammasat University, and another military coup. Thailand's second-longest serving prime minister (12 years over two terms).

Vajiralongkorn, King Rama X (1952–) Reign commenced in 2016. Military trained and strong involvement in armed forces, especially as a pilot. Appointed crown prince in 1972. Through amendments to the constitution and administrative changes, he has indicated clearly that he wants to protect and enhance his influence as monarch.

Vajiravudh, King Rama VI (1881–1925) Reigned from 1910 to 1925. First Siamese king educated in the West (Oxford University and Sandhurst Military Academy in Great Britain). Alienated traditional allies of the monarchy by establishing a paramilitary force (Wild Tiger Corps), profligate spending, indifference to court life, and unconventional social life. Firmly rejected proposals for a constitution and parliamentary system of government. His ultranationalism was reflected in his policies and numerous essays, literary works and translations.

Wichit Wathakan (1898–1962) A major contributor to the design and dissemination of Thailand's official national identity under Phibun Songkhram and Sarit Thanarat. A strong advocate of the change of name from Siam to Thailand. Served as minister for foreign affairs, minister for finance, and as an ambassador, including to Japan during World War II. Prolific author of nationalistic plays, songs and radio programs.

Yingluck Shinawatra (1967–) Younger sister of Thaksin, who elevated her to the leadership of the Pheu Thai Party on the eve of the 2011 election, which the party won by a large majority. Thailand's first female prime minister, she had leadership roles in the family businesses before entering politics. Initially established harmonious relations with the monarchy and military, but her government was criticised for the high costs of its rice subsidy scheme. In 2013, attempts to amnesty Thaksin provoked public protests, which

Suthep Thaugsuban exploited. Yingluck tried to resolve the crisis through elections, but was thwarted by Suthep, the PDRC, Democrat Party, and Electoral Commission. Shortly before the 2014 coup the Constitutional Court removed Yingluck from office for abuse of power in 2011 when she had transferred a senior official, opening the way for Thaksin's former brother-in-law to become police chief. In September 2017, the Supreme Court found her guilty of dereliction of duty over the rice subsidy scheme, and sentenced her to five years in prison. Yingluck had chosen self-exile a month earlier.

FURTHER READING

This annotated list of books and articles is designed to help the newcomer to build a firmer understanding of Thai politics. Publication details are in the bibliography, which also contains a fuller list of the works consulted for this volume.

Chris Baker and Pasuk Phongpaichit, *A History of Thailand*.
An accessible and comprehensive introduction to the economic, social, cultural and political changes that have shaped modern Thailand. After outlining the main pressures and trends in the pre-1932 period, the book concentrates on the post-war period. The first port of call for anyone looking for basic information on, and clear analysis of, modern Thailand. If they need to look further, they should go to Pasuk and Baker's *Thailand: Economy and Politics* (Oxford, 2002, revised edition), for a more detailed account of Thailand's modern history.

B. J. Terwiel, *Thailand's Political History: From the 13th Century to Recent Times*.
Terwiel's book covers a broader period than *A History of Thailand* and focuses less on the economy. It deals mostly with the pre-modern period, while ending with chapters on post-war Thailand, including an assessment of the Thaksin phenomenon. The author's decades-long access to archival material in a range of languages, and his interest in anthropology as well as history and politics, emerges in a volume that is rich in insights and a persuasive counter-narrative to nationalist interpretations of Thai political history.

Thongchai Winichakul, *Siam Mapped: A History of the Geobody of a Nation*.
A ground-breaking analysis of how Siam adapted to Western

imperialism by adopting imperialist methods to overpower the lesser kingdoms and fiefdoms in the peripheral areas of what is now the territory of Thailand. Thongchai explains how a border-free kingdom became a territory-obsessed nation sustained by an ultranationalist ideology, while remaining a kingdom. A stimulating assessment of the history, nationalism and political geography of Thailand.

Scot Barmé, *Luang Wichit Wathakan and the Creation of a Thai Identity.*

Scot Barmé's book remains the only full-length study in English of a prolific and influential ideologue of Thailand's ultranationalism, Luang Wichit Wathakan, who has been called "Thailand's Dale Carnegie". With King Vajiravudh and Phibun Songkhram, he was a one of the main architects of Thailand's official national identity.

Thak Chaloemtiarana, *Thailand: The Politics of Despotic Paternalism.*

An assessment of the political philosophy and methods of Sarit Thanarat, prime minister from 1959 to 1963. Sarit had a profound impact on modern Thai politics, including through his cultivation of symbiotic relationships between the military and the monarchy and between the military and civilian bureaucracies—and his concomitant disdain for elected politicians. The priority Sarit attached to strong leadership and social orderliness still resonates in Thailand.

David Morell and Chai-anan Samudavanija, *Political Conflict in Thailand: Reform, Reaction, Revolution.*

Part I of this volume is a compelling introduction to traditional Thai political culture. Although focused on the way political culture influenced responses to the challenges facing the governing classes, their challengers, and the general society in the 1970s, its coverage of elements like hierarchy, family structure, monarchy, Buddhism, duty, charisma and the natural environment remains valuable for the student of current politics.

Katherine A. Bowie, *Rituals of National Loyalty: An Anthropology of the State and the Village Scout Movement in Thailand.*

In her analysis of the Village Scouts in the 1970s, Bowie explains how traditional political culture was exploited through initiation rituals to disseminate ultranationalism to villagers who were recruited to this paramilitary movement—as part of a two-pronged effort to counter communism and build unquestioning allegiance to a paternal state under a benevolent king.

Pavin Chachvalpongpun, "The Necessity of Enemies in Thailand's Troubled Politics."

Pavin's exploration on the role of enemies and otherness in Thai politics draws on the Thongchai's view that "the enemy must always be present" and considers in a different context the ultranationalism that was the focus of Bowie's study.

Paul M. Handley, *The King Never Smiles: A Biography of Thailand's Bhumibol Adulyadej.*

Handley's book introduces readers to the man who was king of Thailand for all but 14 years of its first 84 years of constitutional monarchy. He demythologises the monarch of nationalist historiography and humanises the portraits that hang in all corners of the country. In outlining the context in which King Bhumibol ruled, the book reveals the main trends in Thailand's modern political history, and shines a spotlight on the way in which the monarchy has assumed a central political role.

Duncan McCargo, "Network Monarchy and Legitimacy Crises in Thailand."
Terms like "network monarchy" and "legitimacy crises" encapsulated much that was true about politics in Thailand under King Bhumibol, although the network may not always have operated as conspiratorially as the term suggests and, in the minds of many Thais, the crises may have been less than critical.

Charles Keyes, *Finding Their Voice: Northeastern Villagers and the Thai State*.
Andrew Walker, *Thailand's Political Peasants*.
Naruemon Thabchumpon and Donald McCargo, "Urbanized Villagers in the 2010 Thai Redshirt Protests."
These two books and one article introduce the "cosmopolitan villagers" of northeastern Thailand (Keyes), "middle-income peasants" of northern Thailand (Walker) and "urbanised villagers" on the urban fringe of Bangkok (Naruemon and McCargo), who have emerged as a powerful electoral bloc behind the Thaksin-aligned political party, as well as the foot soldiers of the red-shirt movement.

Yoshinori Nishizaki, *Political Authority and Provincial Identity in Thailand: The Making of Banharn-buri*.
This book humanises the maligned (and sometimes justifiably maligned) Thai provincial politician who engages in "money politics" and the rural voters who support him (almost always a "him"). An illuminating study of how a clever and well-connected politician used state resources to meet the rational aspirations of his electorate.

Nidhi Eoseewong, "The Thai Cultural Constitution." See also his "Understanding the Cultural Constitution."
Nidhi's "cultural constitution" comprises the unwritten rules that have allow Thais to survive by counterbalancing authority (power

recognised by law or custom) with influence (power not recognised by law or custom). The unwritten rules change as the culture changes. Nidhi argues that the veracity of the unwritten cultural constitution explains why it has been easy to tear up so many written constitutions in Thailand.

Chang Noi (pseud), *Jungle Book: Thailand's Politics, Moral Panic, and Plunder, 1996–2008.*

A collection of 64 of the columns that appeared regularly in *The Nation* newspaper from the height of the economic boom, through the Asian financial crisis and 1997 Constitution, until mid–2008, when Thaksin went into self-exile. The columns capture the colour and flavour of developments, giving the reader a feel for Thai politics, not just the facts.

Nirmal Ghosh, *Unquiet Kingdom: Thailand in Transition.*

An account of recent Thai politics by a journalist who takes the reader to events that he saw, heard, smelt, tasted and touched. His descriptions are complemented with finely tuned assessments of trends and challenges he observed in Bangkok from 2003 to 2016.

BIBLIOGRAPHY[1]

Abuza, Zachary. "Military should focus on clear and present dangers." *Bangkok Post*. 14 July 2015.

Akin Rabibhadana. *The Organisation of Thai Society in the Early Bangkok Period 1782–1873*. Ithaca New York: Cornell University, 1969.

Albritton, Robert B. and Thawilwadee Bureekul. *Are Democracy and 'Good Governance' Always Compatible? Competing Values in the Thai Political Arena*. Working Paper No 47. Chile: Global Barometer and International Political Science Association, 2009.

Anderson, Benedict. "Studies of the Thai State: The State of Thai Studies," in *The Study of Thailand: Analyses of Knowledge, Approaches, and Prospects in Anthropology, Art History, Economics, History, and Political Science*, edited by Eliezer B. Ayal, 193–247. Athens, Ohio: Ohio University Center for International Studies, 1978.

———. *The Spectre of Comparisons: Nationalisms, Southeast Asia and the World*. London and New York: Verso, 1998.

Apirat Petchsiri. *Eastern Importation of Western Criminal Law: Thailand as a Case Study*. Littleton Colorado: Fred B. Rothman and Co, 1987.

Asia Foundation. *Constitutional Reform and Democracy in Thailand: A National Survey of the Thai People*. Bangkok: Asia Foundation, 2009.

———. *2010 National Survey of the Thai Electorate: Exploring National Consensus and Color Polarization*. Bangkok: Asia Foundation, 2011.

———. *Profile of the "Bangkok Shutdown" Protestors: A Survey of Anti-Government PDRC Demonstrators in Bangkok*. Bangkok: Asia Foundation, January 2014.

Baker, Chris and Pasuk Phongpaichit. *A History of Thailand*. Cambridge: Cambridge University Press, 2014 (third edition).

---

1 This bibliography follows the normal practice in books on Thailand of listing Thai authors alphabetically according to their first name, not surname. Non-Thai authors are listed alphabetically by their surnames.

———. "The Revolt of Khun Phaen: Contesting Power in Early Modern Siam." in Maurizio Peleggi (ed). *A Sarong for Clio: Essays on the Intellectual and Cultural History of Thailand.* Ithaca: Cornell University Press, 2015, 19–40.

———. tr and ed. *The Palace Law of Ayutthaya and the Thammasat: Law and Kingship in Siam.* Ithaca: Cornell University Press, 2016.

———. *A History of Ayutthaya: Siam in the Early Modern World.* Cambridge: Cambridge University Press, 2017.

Barmé, Scot. *Luang Wichit Wathakan and the Creation of a Thai Identity.* Singapore: Institute of South East Asian Studies, 1993.

Batson, Benjamin, ed. *Siam's Political Future: Documents from the End of the Absolute Monarchy.* New York: Cornell University Southeast Asia Program, 1974.

———. *The End of the Absolute Monarchy in Siam.* Singapore: Oxford University Press, 1984.

Battye, Noel A. "The Military, Government and Society in Siam, 1868–1910: Politics and Military Reform during the Reign of King Chulalongkorn," PhD diss., Cornell University, 1974.

Bingham, Tom. *The Rule of Law.* London: Penguin, 2010.

Blanchard, Wendell. *Thailand: Its People, Its Society, Its Culture.* New Haven: Hraf Press, 1970.

Blofield, John. *King Maha Mongkut of Siam.* Bangkok: Siam Society, 1987.

Bowie, Katherine A. *Rituals of National Loyalty: An Anthropology of the State and the Village Scout Movement in Thailand.* New York: Columbia University Press, 1997.

———. *Of Beggars and Buddhas: The Politics of Humor in the* Vessantara Jataka *in Thailand.* Madison: University of Wisconsin Press, 2017.

Brereton, Bonnie Pacala and Somroay Yencheuy. *Buddhist Murals of Northeast Thailand: Reflections of the Isan Heartland.* Chiang Mai: Mekong Press, 2010.

Callahan, William A. "Beyond Cosmopolitanism and Nationalism: Chinese and Neo-Nationalism in China and Thailand." *International Organization*, 56, (Summer 2003): 481–517.

Campbell, Charlie. "The Thai Junta's 'Happiness' Song Is a Hit! (But Who'd Dare Say Otherwise?)," *Time*, 10 June 2014.

Cassaniti, Julia. *Living Buddhism: Mind, Self, and Emotion in a Thai Community.* Ithaca and London: Cornell University Press, 2015.

Chambers, Paul. "Superfluous, Mischievous or Emancipating: Thailand's Evolving Senate Today." *Journal of Current Southeast Asian Affairs*, 28, 3, (2009), 3–38.

———. "A Short History of Military Influence in Thailand," in *Knights of the Realm: Thailand's Military and Police, Then and Now*, edited by Paul Chambers, 109–446. Bangkok: White Lotus, 2013.

Chang Noi (pseud). *Jungle Book: Thailand's Politics, Moral Panic, and Plunder. 1996–2008,* Chiang Mai: Silkworm Books, 2009.

Charnvit Kasetsiri. "The First Phibun Government and Its Involvement in World War II." In *Studies in Thai and Southeast Asian Histories,* edited by Charnvit Kasetsiri, 275–350. Bangkok: The Foundation for the Promotion of Social Science and Humanities Textbooks Project and Toyota Thailand Foundation, 2015.

Chatthip Nartsupha. *The Thai Village Economy in the Past.* Translated by Chris Baker and Pasuk Phongpaichit. Chiang Mai: Silkworm Books, 1999.

Cheesman, David. *Opposing the Rule of Law: How Myanmar's Courts Make Law and Order.* Cambridge: Cambridge University Press, 2015.

Chula Chakrabongse. *Lords of Life.* London: Alvin Redman, 1960.

Connors, Michael. "Framing the 'People's Constitution.'" In *Reforming Thai Politics,* edited by Duncan McCargo, 37–55. Copenhagen: Nordic Institute of Asian Studies, 2002.

———. *Democracy and National Identity in Thailand.* Copenhagen: Nordic Institute of Asian Studies Press, 2008.

Copeland, Matthew. "Contested Nationalism and the 1932 Overthrow of the Absolute Monarchy in Siam." PhD diss., Australian National University, Canberra, 1993.

Dhani Nivat, Prince. "The Old Siamese Conception of the Monarchy." *Journal of the Siam Society,* 36, 2 (1947): 91–106.

Dressel, Bjorn. "Thailand's Elusive Quest for a Workable Constitution, 1997–2007." *Contemporary Southeast Asia,* Vol 31, No 2 (2009): 296–325.

——. "Judicialization of Politics or Politicization of the Judiciary? Considerations from Recent Events in Thailand." *The Pacific Review,* 23, 5, (2010): 671–91.

——. "Thailand: Judicialization of Politics or Politicization of the Judiciary." In *The Judicialization of Politics in Asia,* edited by Bjorn Dressel, 79–97. London and New York: Routledge, 2012.

Engel, David M. *Law and Kingship in Thailand during the Reign of King Chulalongkorn.* Ann Arbor: Center for South and Southeast Asian Studies, University of Michigan, 1975.

——. *Code and Custom in a Thai Provincial Court: The Interaction of Formal and Informal Systems of Justice.* Tucson: University of Arizona Press, 1978.

Engel, David M. and Jaruwan S. Engel. *Tort, Custom, and Karma: Globalization and Legal Consciousness in Thailand.* Chiang Mai: Silkworm Books, 2010.

Englehart, Neil A. *Culture and Power in Traditional Siamese Government.* Ithaca: Cornell University Press, 2001.

Ferrara, Federico. *The Political Development of Modern Thailand.* Cambridge: Cambridge University Press, 2015.

Fuller, Thomas. "Taking On Thailand's Crisis With a Bit of Western Bite." *New York Times,* 8 February 2014.

Ghosh, Nirmal. *Unquiet Kingdom: Thailand in Transition.* Singapore: Straits Times Press, 2017.

Ginsburg, Tom. "Constitutional Afterlife: The Continuing Impact of Thailand's Postpolitical Constitution." *International Journal of Constitutional Law,* Vol 7: 83 (January 2009): 83–105.

Girling, John L. S. *Thailand: Society and Politics,* Ithaca: Cornell University Press, 1981.

Goldman, Minton F. "Franco-British Rivalry over Siam, 1896–1904." *Journal of Southeast Asian Studies,* Vol 3, No 2 (Sept, 1972): 210–228.

Griswold, A. B. *King Mongkut of Siam.* New York: Asia Society, 1961.

Haberkorn, Tyrell. *Revolution Interrupted: Farmers, Students, Law, and Violence in Northern Thailand.* Madison: University of Wisconsin Press, 2011.

Handley, Paul M. *The King Never Smiles: A Biography of Thailand's Bhumibol Adulyadej.* New Haven and London: Yale University Press, 2006.

Hanks, L. M. "The Thai Social Order as Entourage and Circle." In *Change and Persistence in Thai Society: Essays in Honor of Lauriston Sharp,* Edited by G. William Skinner and A. Thomas Kirsch, 197–218. Ithaca and London: Cornell University Press, 1975.

———. "Merit and Power in the Thai Social Order." *American Anthropologist,* New Series, Vol. 64, No. 6 (Dec, 1962): 1247–1261.

Harding, Andrew, and Peter Leyland. *The Constitutional System of Thailand: A Contextual Analysis.* Oxford and Portland, Oregon: Hart Publishing, 2011.

Harrison, Rachel V., and Peter A. Jackson, eds. *Ambiguous Allure of the West: Traces of the Colonial in Thailand.* Hong Kong: Hong Kong University Press, 2011.

Hewison, Kevin. "The Monarchy and Democratisation." In *Political Change in Thailand: Democracy and Participation,* edited by Kevin Hewison, 58–74. London and New York: Routledge, 1997.

Hong Lysa. *Thailand in the Nineteenth Century: Evolution of the Economy and Society.* Singapore: Institute of South East Asian Studies, 1984.

Hooker, M. B. *A Concise Legal History of South-East Asia.* Oxford: Clarendon Press, 1978.

Ingersoll, Jasper. "Merit and Identity in Village Thailand." In *Change and Persistence in Thai Society: Essays in Honor of Lauriston Sharp,* edited by G. William Skinner and A. Thomas Kirsch. 219–51. Ithaca and London: Cornell University Press, 1975.

James C. Ingram. *Economic Change in Thailand: 1850–1970.* Stanford: Stanford University Press, 1971.

Ivarsson, Soren, and Lotte Isager, ed. *Saying the Unsayable: Monarchy and Democracy in Thailand.* Copenhagen: Nordic Institute of Asian Studies Press, 2010.

Jory, Patrick. *Thailand's Theory of Monarchy: The Vessantara Jātaka and the Idea of the Perfect Man.* New York: SUNY Press, 2016.

Keyes, Charles F. *Thailand: Buddhist Kingdom as Modern Nation State.* Boulder and London: Westview Press, 1987.

———. *Finding Their Voice: Northeastern Villagers and the Thai State.* Chiang Mai: Silkworm Books, 2014.

———. *Democracy Thwarted: The Crisis of Political Authority in Thailand.* Singapore: Institute of South East Asian Studies, 2015.

Klausner, William J. "Reflections on the Independence of the Thai Judiciary: Past, Present and Future." in *Thai Institutions and National Security: Danger and Opportunity,* 53–79. ISIS Paper 3, Bangkok: Institute of Security and International Studies (ISIS), 1999.

———. *Transforming Thai Culture: From Temple Drums to Mobile Phones.* Bangkok: The Siam Society, 2004.

Klein, James R. *The Constitution of the Kingdom of Thailand, 1997: A Blueprint for Participatory Democracy.* Bangkok: Asia Foundation, 1998.

———. "The Battle for Rule of Law in Thailand: The Role of the Constitutional Court." in *The Constitutional Court of Thailand: The Provisions and Working of the Court,* edited by Amara Raksasataya and James R. Klein, 34–90. Bangkok: Constitution for the People Society and Asia Foundation, 2003.

Kobkua Suwannathat-Pian. *Thailand's Durable Premier: Phibun through Three Decades, 1932–1957*. Kuala Lumpur: Oxford University Press, 1995.

Kullada Kesboonchoo Mead. *The Rise and Decline of Thai Absolutism*. London: Routledge/Curzon, 2004.

La Loubère, Simon de. *The Kingdom of Siam*. Kuala Lumpur: Oxford University Press, 1969. Reprint of 1693 edition.

Larsson, Tomas. *Land and Loyalty: Security and the Development of Property Rights in Thailand*. Singapore: NUS Press, 2013.

Lingat, R. "Evolution of the Conception of Law in Burma and Siam." *Journal of the Siam Society*, 38 (1), (1950): 9–31.

———. *The Classical Law of India*. Berkeley: University of California Press, 1973.

Loos, Tamara. "Issaraphap: The Limits of Individual Liberty in Thai Jurisprudence." *Crossroads: An Interdisciplinary Journal of Southeast Asian Studies*, 12, No 1, (1998): 35–75.

———. *Subject Siam: Family, Law, and Colonial Modernity in Thailand*. Chiang Mai: Silkworm Books, 2002.

———. *Bones Around my Neck, The Life and Exile of a Prince Provocateur*. Ithaca and London: Cornell University Press, 2016.

McCargo, Duncan. "Network Monarchy and Legitimacy Crises in Thailand." *The Pacific Review*, 18, 4 (December 2005): 499–518.

———. "Thaksin and the Resurgence of Violence in the Thai South," in *Rethinking Thailand's Southern Violence*, edited by Duncan McCargo, 35–68. Singapore: NUS Press, 2007.

———. *Mapping National Anxieties: Thailand's Southern Conflict*. Copenhagen: Nordic Institute of Asian Studies Press, 2012.

———. "Competing Notions of Judicialization in Thailand." *Contemporary Southeast Asia*, Vol 36, No 3 (2014): 417–41.

McCargo, Duncan, and Ukrist Pathmanand. *The Thaksinization of Thailand*. Copenhagen: Nordic Institute of Asian Studies Press, 2005.

McCargo, Duncan, Saowanee T. Alexander and Petra Desatova. "Ordering Peace: Thailand's 2016 Constitutional Referendum." *Contemporary Southeast Asia,* Vol 39, No 1 (2017): 65–95.

Moffat, Abbot Low. *Mongkut, the King of Siam.* Ithaca: Cornell University Press, 1961.

Morell, David and Chai-anan Samudavanija. *Political Conflict in Thailand: Reform, Reaction, Revolution.* Cambridge (Mass): Oelgeschlager, Gunn and Hain, 1982.

Munger, Frank. "Culture, Power, and Law: Thinking About the Anthropology of Rights in Thailand in an Era of Globalization." *New York Law Review,* Vol 51 (2006–07): 817–38.

———. "Globalization, Investing in Law, and the Careers of Lawyers for Social Causes – Taking on Rights in Thailand." *New York Law School Law Review,* Vol 53 (2008–9): 745–802.

———. "Global Funder, Grassroots Litigator–Judicialization of the Environmental Movement in Thailand." (September 1, 2012). NYLS Legal Studies Research Paper No. 12/13 #38. Available at SSRN: https://ssrn.com/abstract=2145543

———. "Cause Lawyers and Other Signs of Progress: Three Thai Narratives." In *An Unfinished Project: Law and the Possibility of Justice,* edited by Scott Cummings, 243–273. Palo Alto, California: Stanford University Press, 2010.

———. "Revolution Imagined: Cause Advocacy Consumer Rights and the Evolving Role of NGOs in Thailand." (May 20, 2014). *Asian Journal of Comparative Law,* 2014, DOI: 10.1515/asjcl-2013-0054. Available at SSRN: https://ssrn.com/abstract=2439377

———. "Trafficking in Law: Cause Lawyer, Bureaucratic State and the Rights of Human Trafficking Victims in Thailand." *Asian Studies Review,* Vol 39, No 1 (2015): 69–87.

———. "Constitutional Reform, Legal Consciousness, and Citizen Participation in Thailand." *Cornell International Law Journal,* Vol 40, Issue, 2, (Spring 2007), 455–475.

Murashima, Eiji. "The Origin of Modern Official State Ideology in Thailand." *Journal of Southeast Asian Studies,* Vol 19, No 1 (March, 1988): 80–96.

Naruemon Thabchumpon and Donald McCargo. "Urbanized Villagers in the 2010 Thai Redshirt Protests." *Asian Survey,* Vol 51, Number 6, (November–December 2011): 993–1018.

Nelson, Michael H. "Thailand's House Elections of 6 January 2001: Thaksin's Landslide Victory and Subsequent Narrow Escape." In *Thailand's New Politics: KPI Yearbook 2001,* edited by Michael H. Nelson, 283–435. Bangkok: King Prajadhipok Institute and White Lotus Press, 2002.

Nidhi Eoseewong. "The Thai Cultural Constitution," *Kyoto Review of Southeast Asia,* Issue 3, March 2003 (translated by Chris Baker. Original published in Thai in 1991) https://kyotoreview.org/issue-3-nations-and-stories/the-thai-cultural-constitution/

———. "Understanding the Cultural Constitution." *Bangkok Post,* 13 August 2014.

Nishizaki, Yoshinori. *Political Authority and Provincial Identity in Thailand: The Making of Banharn-buri.* Ithaca: Cornell University Southeast Asia Studies Program Publications, 2011.

Ockey, James. "Broken Power: The Thai Military in the Aftermath of the 2006 Coup." In *"Good Coup" Gone Bad: Thailand's Political Developments Since Thaksin's Downfall,* edited by Pavin Chachavalpongpun, 49–78. Singapore: Institute of South East Asian Studies, 2014.

Paine, Thomas. "Common Sense." *Paine's Political Writings During the American and French Revolutions,* edited by Hypatia Bradlaugh Bonner, London: Watts and Co, 1909.

Pasuk Phongpaichit and Chris Baker. *Thailand: Economy and Politics.* Oxford: Oxford University Press, 2002 (revised edition).

———. *Thaksin.* Chiang Mai: Silkworm Books, 2009 (second expanded edition).

———. eds. *Unequal Thailand: Aspects of Income, Wealth and Power.* Singapore: NUS Press, 2016.

Pasuk Phongpaichit and Sungsidh Piriyarangsan. *Corruption and Democracy in Thailand.* Chiang Mai: Silkworm Books, 1996.

Pavin Chachvalpongpun. "The Necessity of Enemies in Thailand's Troubled Politics," *Asian Survey,* Vol 51, No 6, November/December 2011, 1019–41.

Peleggi, Maurizio. *Lord of Things: The Fashioning of the Siamese Monarchy's Modern Image.* Honolulu: University of Hawaii Press, 2002.

———. Thailand: *The Worldly Kingdom.* London: Reaktion Books, 2007.

Porphant Ouyyanont. *A Regional Economic History of Thailand.* Singapore: ISEAS Yusof Ishak Institute, 2017.

Pridi by Pridi: Selected Writing on Life, Politics, and Economy. Edited by Chris Baker and Pasuk Phongpaichit. Chiang Mai: Silkworm Books, 2000.

Puangthong R. Pawakapan. *The Central Role of Thailand's Internal Security Operations Command in the Post-Counter-Insurgency Period.* Singapore: ISEAS Yusof Ishak Institute, 2017.

Raymond, Gregory Vincent. *Thai Military Power: A Culture of Strategic Accommodation.* Copenhagen: Nordic Institute of Asian Studies, 2018.

Reeve, W.D. *Public Administration in Siam.* London and New York: Royal Institute of International Affairs, 1951.

Reynolds, Craig. *Seditious Histories: Contesting Thai and Southeast Asian Pasts.* Seattle and London: University of Washington Press, 2006.

———. "Buddhist Cosmography on Thai History, with Special Reference to the Nineteenth-Century Cultural Change." *Journal of Asian Studies,* Vol 35, No 2 (February 1976): 203–20.

———. "On the Gendering of Nationalist and Postnationalist Selves in Twentieth-Century Thailand." In *Genders and Sexualities in Modern Thailand,* edited by Peter A. Jackson and Nerida M. Cook, 261–74. Chiang Mai: Silkworm Books, 1999.

Reynolds, E. Bruce. *Thailand's Secret War: The Free Thai, OSS, and SOE during World War II*. Cambridge: Cambridge University Press, 2005.

Riggs, Fred W. *Thailand: The Modernization of a Bureaucratic Polity*. Honolulu: East–West Center, 1966.

Sarasin Viraphol. "Law in Traditional Siam and China: A Comparative Study." *Journal of the Siam Society*, 65 (1), (1977): 81–135.

Seni Pramoj and Kukrit Pramoj., tr. and ed. *A King of Siam Speaks*. Bangkok: Siam Society, 1987.

Skinner, G. William. *Chinese Society in Thailand: An Analytical History*. Ithaca: Cornell University Press, 1957.

Sng, Jeffrey, and Pimpraphai Bisalaputra. *A History of the Thai-Chinese*. Singapore and Bangkok: Editions Didier Millet, 2015.

Sombat Chantornvong. "To Address the Dust of the Dust Under the Soles of the Royal Feet: A Reflection on the Political Dimension of Thai Court Language." *Asian Review*, 6 (1992): 145–63.

Sophorntavy Vorng. *A Meeting of Masks: Status, Power and Hierarchy in Bangkok*. Copenhagen: Nordic Institute of Asian Studies: 2017.

Stowe, Judith. *Siam Becomes Thailand: A Story of Intrigue*. Honolulu: University of Hawaii Press, 1991.

Strate, Shane. *The Lost Territories: Thailand's History of National Humiliation*. Honolulu: University of Hawaii Press, 2015.

Streckfuss, David. *Truth on Trial in Thailand: Defamation, Treason and Lèse Majesté*. New York and London: Routledge, 2011.

———. "Freedom and Silencing under the Neo-Absolutist Monarchy Regime in Thailand, 2006–2011." In *"Good Coup Gone Bad:" Thailand's Political Developments since Thaksin's Downfall*, edited by Pavin Chachavalpongpun, 109–38. Singapore: Institute of South East Asian Studies, 2014.

Tagore, Rabindranath. *Nationalism*. London: Macmillan and Co, 1917.

Tamanaha, Brian Z. *On the Rule of Law: History, Politics, Theory*. Cambridge: Cambridge University Press, 2004.

Tej Bunnag. *The Provincial Administration of Siam, 1892–1915: The Ministry of Interior under Prince Damrong Rajanubhab.* Oxford: Oxford University Press, 1977.

Terwiel, B.J. *The Ram Khamhaeng Inscription: the fake that did not come true.* Gossenberg, Ostasien Verlag, 2010.

———. *Thailand's Political History: From the 13th Century to Recent Times.* Bangkok: River Books, 2011 (revised edition).

Thak Chaloemtiarana, ed. *Thai Politics: Extracts and Documents.* Bangkok: The Social Science Association of Thailand, 1978.

———. *Thailand: The Politics of Despotic Paternalism.* Chiang Mai: Silkworm Books, 2007 (originally published in 1979).

———. "Distinctions with a Difference: The Despotic Paternalism of Sarit Thanarat and the Demagogic Authoritarianism of Thaksin Shinawatra." *Crossroads: An Interdisciplinary Journal of Southeast Asian Studies,* Vol. 19, No. 1 (2007): 50–94.

Thanapol Limapichart. "The emergence of the Siamese public sphere: colonial modernity, print culture and the practice of criticism." *South East Asia Research,* Vol 17, No 3 (2009): 361–99.

Thanet Aphornsuvan. "The West and Siam's quest for modernity: Siamese responses to nineteenth century American missionaries." *South East Asia Research,* Vol 17, No 3 (2009): 401–31.

Thawatt Mokarapong. *History of the Thai Revolution: A Study in Political Behaviour.* Bangkok: Chalermnit, 1972.

Thitinan Pongsudhirak. "The Tragedy of the 1997 Constitution." in *Divided Over Thaksin: Thailand's Coup and Problematic Transition,* edited by John Funston, 27–37. Singapore: Institute of South East Asian Studies, 2009.

Thongchai Winichakul. *Siam Mapped: A History of the Geobody of a Nation.* Honolulu: University of Hawaii Press, 1994.

———. "Toppling Democracy." *Journal of Contemporary Asia,* Vol 38, No 1, (February 2008): 11–37.

———. "Coming to Terms with the West: Intellectual Strategies of Bifurcation and Post-Westernism in Siam." In *Ambiguous Allure of the West: Traces of the Colonial in Thailand,* edited by Harrison, Rachel V., and Peter A. Jackson, 135–151. Hong Kong: Hong Kong University Press, 2011.

———. "The Monarchy and Anti-Monarchy: Two Elephants in the Room of Thai Politics and the State of Denial." In *"Good Coup Gone Bad:" Thailand's Political Developments since Thaksin's Downfall,* edited by Pavin Chachavalpongpun, 79–108. Singapore: Institute of South East Asian Studies, 2014.

Tips, Walter E.J. *Siam's Struggle for Survival: The Gunboat Incident at Paknam and the Franco-Siamese Treaty of October 1893.* Bangkok: White Lotus, 1996.

Van Roy, Edward. *Siamese Melting Pot: Ethnic Minorities in the Making of Bangkok.* Chiang Mai and Singapore: Silkworm Books and ISEAS Yusof Ishak Institute, 2017.

Vella, Walter F. *Chaiyo: King Vajiravudh and the Development of Thai Nationalism.* Honolulu: University of Hawaii Press, 1978.

Wales, H.G. Quaritch. *Years of Blindness.* New York: Cromwell, 1943.

Walker, Andrew. *Thailand's Political Peasants.* Madison: University of Wisconsin Press, 2012.

Warr, Peter G. and Bhanupong Nidhiprabha. *Thailand's Macroeconomic Miracle: Stable Adjustment and Sustained Growth.* Washington DC: World Bank, 1996.

Warren, James A. *Gambling, the State and Society in Thailand, c. 1800–1945.* London and New York: Routledge, 2015.

Wenk, Klaus. *The Restoration of Thailand under Rama I, 1782–1809.* Tucson: University of Arizona Press, 1968.

Wilson, David A. *Politics in Thailand.* New York: Cornell University Press, 1962.

Wright, Joseph. *The Balancing Act: A History of Modern Thailand.* Bangkok: Asia Books, 1991.

Wyatt, David K. *The Politics of Reform in Thailand.* New Haven: Yale University Press, 1969

———. *Thailand: A Short History.* Chiang Mai: Silkworm Books, 2003 (second edition).

———. *Studies in Thai History: Collected Articles.* Chiang Mai: Silkworm Books, 1994.

INDEX[1]

1932 xx, 13-22, 113, 116, 124, 131, 149, 164, 168, 187, 188

Abhisit Vejjajiva 82-3, 90, 141, 145, 218, 252, 253, 262

academia 141

Act for the Protection of the Constitution (1933) 208

administrative courts/law 61, 66-7, 75, 78, 211, 213-4, 227, 242

ammat (aristocrats) 181

amnesty bill 87, 89, 91, 141, 264

Anand Panyarachun 57, 58, 76, 93 fn 33, 94, 141, 252, 253, 262

Ananda, King Rama VIII 17, 27, 41, 45, 251, 254, 257, 260, 261

Anupong Paochinda 81

Arabia 179

army, establishment of 8-9, 122, 142, 156, 168, 241

Arsa Sarasin 93 fn 33

Asian financial crisis 59, 60, 67, 103, 180, 249, 255, 256, 270

Assembly of the Poor 244

Assets Scrutiny Committee 77, 81, 138

astrology 197, 223

Auditor General 98

Austria-Hungary 7 fn 10

autonomous/independent agency, absence of xix-xx, 7, 125-7, 204-5, 217-8, 242, 243

Ayutthaya vi, 113 fn1, 115, 123, 167, 170, 175, 184, 185, 201, 251

Baker, Chris 123, 266

Bang Chan 129

Bangkok Post 69

Banharn Silpa-acha 58, 252, 254, 263, 269

Barmé, Scot 267

Batson, Benjamin 18

Battambang vi, 153

Belgium 7 fn 10

Bhumibol Adulyadej, King Rama IX 35, 38-9, 40, 41, 44, 45, 46, 47-8, 49-50, 57-8, 60, 73, 74-5, 88, 96, 124, 130, 169, 180, 183, 189, 236, 247, 251, 253, 254, 257, 260, 261, 262, 268, 269

    and judiciary 35, 74-5

    and military 46, 47-8, 51

    and nationalism 183, 189

    and Thai-style democracy 189

    and unity 183

Bingham, Tom 192-3

bodhisatta 44-45

Boonjuti Klubprasert 215

Boonlert Kaewprasit 84

Bowie, Katherine A. 268

Boworadej Rebellion 16, 23, 258

Bowring Treaty 7, 150

Boy Scouts 159, 165

branches of government xiv, 2-4, 10, 27, 29, 61-2, 85, 88-93, 194, 210-2, 219, 248

Britain/British xvi, 5, 6, 7, 8, 9, 24-5, 27, 102, 117, 73, 131, 149-50, 151, 152, 153, 155, 159, 171, 175, 183, 184, 185, 203, 206, 247, 258, 264

Buddhism xi, 17 fn 12, 24 fn 29, 38, 39, 40, 42, 42 fn 71, 44-5, 50, 73 fn 20, 96, 102, 115, 116, 118, 121 fn 13, 155, 156, 159, 171, 179, 198-9, 206-7, 223, 224-5, 228, 229, 240, 257, 267

Bunnag family 151

bureaucracy 5-6, 7, 18, 31, 34, 48, 54, 64-5, 89, 101-3, 110, 129, 134, 137, 142, 144-6, 157, 160, 162, 168, 169, 174, 209, 229, 255, 259, 261

Burma (Myanmar)/Burmese vi, 25, 34, 44 fn 80, 80, 107, 108, 162, 167, 171, 184, 185, 201, 203, 258

---

1   This index follows the normal practice in books on Thailand of listing Thais alphabetically according to their first name, not surname. Non-Thais are listed alphabetically by their surnames.

ABOUT THE AUTHOR

JAMES WISE was Australia's Ambassador to Thailand from 2010 to 2014. He also worked in Thailand from 1995 to 1998, when he was Deputy Head of Mission at the Australian Embassy. He is now an independent consultant providing assessments and presentations on trends in the political economy of Thailand.

James was an Australian diplomat for over 30 years. In addition to two postings to Thailand, he was High Commissioner to Malaysia (2003–2007) and had earlier postings to the Soviet Union (1987–1991) and Papua New Guinea (1983–1985).

James graduated from the University of Tasmania with a First Class Honours Bachelor of Arts degree in History.